THE SCOTS KIRK IN LONDON

THE SCOTS KIRK
IN LONDON

by

George G. Cameron

Becket Publications
Oxford

© *G.G. Cameron 1979*
First published by Becket
Publications, Saint Thomas
House, Becket Street,
Oxford OX1 1SJ

ISBN 0 7289 0009 2

Typeset by Oxford Publishing Services
Oxford and Printed in Great Britain by
Billings of Worcester

CONTENTS

FOREWORD

This is a fascinating account of a little known story of considerable historic significance: the life, activity and influence of Scottish congregations and churches in London since the union of the Crowns under James VI and I. It is a fluctuating story, for many congregations of Scots arose and disappeared across the centuries, and others kept on springing up in their place. The records have inevitably been fragmentary, but Dr Cameron has done a magnificent job in uncovering all that seems to be extant and in extracting telling evidence from many different sources. Moreover, he has worked it all so beautifully into a continuous narrative, that he has given us a very readable and illuminating book. The whole story is set against the backcloth of the Scottish People and its Kirk, but it is also told in the context of changing events and shifts in culture in the great Metropolis, and of the world-wide impact of the British People in which Scots have played so notable a part. Here too we have captured the authentic spirit of the Scots Kirk in London as an overspill of the Church of Scotland on English soil, remarkably reflected both in the continuing life and work of Scots congregations and in some of their robust and colourful personalities who were also great national figures.

Only two congregations with close Church of Scotland ties now remain in London, Crown Court Church in Covent Garden, and St Columba's Church in Pont Street. Although rebuilt more than once Crown Court Church, 'the Kirk of the Crown of Scotland', still bears the Royal Arms which are a relic of its historic connections, and maintains a close link with The Houses of Parliament through its Kirking Service for Scottish Parliamentarians at the beginning of each new Parliament.

St Columba's was destroyed by bombing during the last war and is now entirely rebuilt, one of the loveliest and most imposing of modern London Churches, exercising an extensive influence throughout greater London. To both these Churches the General Assembly of the Church of Scotland sends its Moderator each year when he visits Parliament and Whitehall during St Andrew's

Tide, for together they constitute the extension of the Church of the Scottish Nation in London through which the Church of Scotland maintains continuing contact with the State, and with her sister Church of England. As such Crown Court Church and St Columba's Church have a unique place in the visitation of the Moderator accorded to no other Church in Scotland itself, and it is as such that they take their share in the Christian life and work of the South.

Half a million Scots are still found living and working in London. Many of them link up with local parishes and congregations, and many retain jealously connections with their home Churches in Scotland, but not a few seem to lose contact with the Church altogether. It is to be hoped that this superb book will help all Scots in London to rediscover the Scots Kirk in their midst, and continue through it to maintain and extend the great tradition of the past.

THOMAS F. TORRANCE

OF LONDON

"It is the folly of too many to mistake the echo of a London coffee-house for the voice of the kingdom". Jonathan Swift (1711) — an Irishman.

"That monstrous tuberosity of civilised life, the capital of England".

Thomas Carlyle (1834) — a London Scot.

"O thou, resort and mart of the the earth,
Chequered with all complexions of mankind
And spotted with all crimes; in which I see
Much that I love and more that I admire,
And all that I abhor".

William Cowper (1783) — an Englishman.

OF THE SCOTS
as understood by the Angles

The only people who are stupid enough to disagree with the whole world are these Scots and their obstinate adherents the Picts and Britons, who inhabit only a portion of these islands in the remote ocean.

Abbot Wilfrid of Ripon (664) — an Anglo-Saxon.

OF THE KIRK
as understood by the Scots reformers

As we believe in one God, Father, Sonne, and haly Ghaist; so do we maist constantly believe, that from the beginning there hes bene, and now is, and to the end of the warld sall be, ane Kirk, that is to say, ane company and multitude of men chosen of

ix

God, who richtly worship and imbrace him be trew faith in *Christ Jesus,* quha is the only head of the same Kirk, quhilk alswa is the bodie and spouse of *Christ Jesus;* quhilke Kirk is catholike, that is, universal, because it conteins the Elect of all ages, of all realmes, nations and tongues, be they of the Jewes or be they of the Gentiles, quha have communion and societie with God the Father and with his son *Christ Jesus,* throw the sanctificatioun of his haly Spirit: and therefore it is called the communion, not of prophane persones, bot of Saincts, quha as citizenis of the heavenly *Jerusalem* have the fruitioun of the maist inestimable benefites, to wit, of ane God, ane Lord *Jesus,* ane faith, and ane baptism. . . This Kirk is invisible, knawen onelie to God . . . and comprehends as weill the Elect that be departed, commonlie called the *Kirk Triumphant,* and they that zit live and fecht against sinne and Sathan as sall live hereafter.

Article XVI of *The Scots Confession* (1560)
— the Scots Reformers.

PREFACE

Scotland's two languages are interestingly different as regards the derivation of their terms for the community of Christ's people.

Gaelic, the ancient Celtic tongue preserved in the Highlands, speaks of *an Eaglais*. This comes from the Greek *ekklesia* — literally 'the called-out' — which is the New Testament word for the assembly of the faithful, the new people of God, called forth from the old Israel. It would be the task of an etymologist to determine whether *Eaglais* (or the French *église*) came directly from the Eastern Church or was adopted from Rome when Jerome at the end of the 4th century transliterated the Greek *ekklesia* as the Latin *ecclesia* in his Vulgate version.

Lowland Scots, on the other hand, speaks of *The Kirk*, and there is no doubt as to the direct eastern derivation of this word. It is the Greek *kuriakos,* the possessive form of *kurios,* 'the Lord'. *Kuriakos* occurs only twice in the New Testament, referring to 'the Lord's Table' (I Cor. xi:20), and to 'the Lord's day' (Rev. i:10). By natural extension it came to be used also of 'the Lord's people' and of 'the Lord's house'; and when missionaries from Constantinople brought the Goths of the lower Danube to the knowledge of Christ *kuriakos* became part of their new Christian vocabulary, and through them of the vocabularies of other tribes of Teutonic stock, and so into Anglo-Saxon.* Anglo-Saxon usage later corrupted *Kirk* to *Church,* but the earlier pronunciation survives in Germany, Holland, Scandinavia, and most plainly in Scotland where it retains its primary meaning of 'the Lord's people', with the secondary implication of 'the Lord's house', where His people meet in worship and fellowship and for inspiration in service.

Such is The Kirk, as defined in Article XVI of the Scots Confession of 1560.

---

* See Archbishop Trench, *On the Study of Words,* p. 122; and E.G. Atkinson, PHSEJ, I. 98f.

Other words, traditions and practices survive also in original form as distinctive features of Scottish religious life. Some are wholly admirable; others have served their day but linger needlessly on like some spiritual vermiform appendix. When the national Kirk of the northern part of the United Kingdom turns up in the capital of the southern, both sorts are liable to mark its distinctive contribution to Christian witness and ministry, for the Scottish religious genes are not on the whole recessive. The account of the Kirk in London which follows in these pages will undoubtedly reflect this conservational insistence; but it will also, the author hopes, reveal that the Scot is ready to prove all things as well as to hold fast to that which is good. And if the Scots Kirk may appear at times to have been too narrowly literal in its insistence that 'the word of God as contained in the scriptures of the Old and New Testaments is the supreme rule of faith and life,' there is nevertheless ample evidence that, like Pastor John Robinson of Amsterdam in 1620, she 'is persuaded that the Lord has more truth yet to break forth out of His holy Word', and that for every generation as for every individual soul there must be a unique rediscovery of the truth as it is in Jesus Christ.

The story which claims this title is by no means a complete account of the Kirk in London, for many records have been lost and some traditions cannot now be verified or disproved. Thus, for example, it remains uncertain whether Dr Patrick Colquhoun, Glasgow's Lord Provost, became a member of Founders' Hall Scots Kirk when he removed to London in 1790, there to develop his interest in sociology, to organise soup-kitchens for London's hunger- and poverty-stricken thousands, to produce a pioneering treatise on the causes of crime, and to form along with Jeremy Bentham the first official police organisation, the Marine Police Force, now the Thames Division of the Metropolitan Police. Similarly it cannot be verified that Crown Court Scottish Church included in its membership in the 1780s the Scots saddler David Pollock, three of whose sons, Sir David, Sir Jonathan, and Sir George, rendered such conspicuous service as legal and military leaders in the nineteenth century, as some of their descendants have done in this century in jurisprudence, literature and education. Gaps also appear in the archives of the Presbytery of London, which meanwhile lack the Minute-books covering the periods 1843-61, 1861-78 and 1887-1909, although the whereabouts of these may yet be discovered. It has seemed good, therefore, to collect, now, such information as can still be found and to preserve it in as connected a form as can be contrived. This has been the author's endeavour, and where the facts might be suceptible of differing interpretations he has been content to seek out and record all the available facts and leave interpretation to the reader.

Such an aim would have been impossible of achievement without the willing and able help of many people. The officials of the National Library of Scotland in Edinburgh, Dr Barbara L.H. Horn of the Scottish Record Office, Mrs Weinstein of the Museum of London, Miss Coburn, Head Archivist, and her assistant Mrs Kenealy, of the Greater London Record Office, Mr D.H.G. Bourke of the British Library, Mrs J. Barnes of Dr Williams' Library, and Miss Hines and Miss Gellatly of the Guildhall Library have all gone out of their way to suggest sources and pursue clues relating to my search. In particular I am indebted to Mr A.G. Esslemont, secretary and librarian of the United Reformed Church History Society, who, with his colleague Dr Keay, has unearthed documents and provided copies of MSS of whose existence I could never have guessed, and without whose help the blank areas in the story would have been even more extensive than they are.

The most fruitful source of information concerning the last century of the story has been such records as survive of the Presbytery of London and of the Kirk Sessions of Crown Court and St Columba's congregations. For access to these and to the bound volumes of their congregational magazines I am indebted to the Presbytery Clerk and to the ministers and session clerks of both congregations; and if in this connection special mention is made of the Rev. Dr J. Fraser McLuskey of St Columba's it is because without his constant encouragement and practical help there might have been an early abandonment of the whole project. The Revs. Charles Meachin and Sandy Cairns and Mr Bill Waddell have contributed three of the plates, and the inclusion of illustrations in the text has been made possible by the generosity of the Friends of St Columba's.

Professor James McEwen of Aberdeen has been kind enough to read the typescript, and his suggestions have indicated several necessary corrections and clarifications to this story, which still bears the marks of an amateur historian's authorship.

In conclusion I wish to record my deep gratitude to the Very Rev. Professor Torrance, who made time in a very busy life to read the final draft, and has so kindly enhanced the book by contributing the Introduction.

Note: Any profits from this publication will be devoted to the work of the Royal Scottish Corporation for young Scots in London at St Columba's Hostel, to the work of St Columba's Church for retired Scots at Lyle Park, Putney, and to the Royal Caledonian Schools.

CHAPTER 1

Scotland's most lasting invasion of England dates from the seventeenth century, and the story of the Scots Kirk in London begins only thereafter. There had, however, been several earlier unwarlike incursions into England from the north, and some understanding of that background may help to give perspective to the story. This chapter attempts only to sketch its more prominent features, on the assumption that the reader will make allowance for the necessary omission of much detail.

The earliest encounter of the southern inhabitants of these islands with Christian emissaries from the north took place in 635, by the invitation of Oswald, king of Northumbria. The Church had been in what is now called Scotland since about 400 A.D., when Ninian's settlement at Whithorn on the Solway became the power-house of evangelism amongst the Britons of Galloway and Strathclyde and amongst the Picts of the eastern coasts and the islands of the north. Columba, a century later, arriving to work amongst his fellow-Scots from Ireland who had established their colony of Dalriada on the west coast, made the little island of Iona his centre, and from there began the task of drawing together the three Celtic races of Scot, Briton and Pict. The fourth race — the invading Angles from across the North Sea — greatly hindered the spread of the Gospel south of the Forth, and their stronghold in Northumbria was only briefly touched by Christianity through Paulinus' visit from the young Roman mission at Canterbury, for six years later their king, Edwin, was defeated and slain by the pagan king of Mercia. It was Oswald, son of Edwin's predecessor, who regained the throne in 634. Immediately he sent to Iona, where he had found refuge when his father was slain and where he had become a Christian, asking for someone from that holy isle in the west to come and teach the Christian faith to his people. When Aidan and his companion monks arrived he gave them Lindisfarne to be a new Holy Isle in the east; and it was from that centre, and through the Celtic Church, that the Angles came to hear and respond to the message of Christ. Before the Augustinian mission had effectively reached beyond Kent, or that of Birinius beyond Wessex, the Lindisfarne monks had succeeded in evangelising the whole Anglian territory, from the shores of the Forth to the banks of the Thames. As James Bulloch has written, "It is tolerably accurate to say that all England north of the Thames was indebted to the Celtic mission for its conversion"[1], and Bishop Lightfoot names the Holy Isle of Lindisfarne as "the true cradle of English Christianity"[2].

The Synod of Whitby in 664 brought the Celtic Church in England under the rule of Rome. In Scotland, through the influence of Queen Margaret, it came under the same control in the 11th century. The two nations, however, were not thereby brought nearer in understanding. On one occasion, in fact, we find the Scots nobles appealing to the Pope for support in their resistance to English claims for feudal superiority and in their defence of "that liberty which no true man relinquishes but with his life"[3] — a sentiment to be borne in mind in relation to later phases in the story of the Scots Kirk.

The reformation of the Church of Scotland took a course different from that of England's politico-ecclesiastical breach with Rome, but there were reciprocal counsellings and encouragements between the leaders in both countries. In Edward VI's reign John Knox was in England, and as one of the young king's royal chaplains he played a part with his fellow-chaplain, Edmund Grindall, in the compilation of the English prayer book and the revision of the Forty-three (later Thirty-nine) Articles of the Church of England. He is credited with securing, as a rubric to the Order for the Administration of the Lord's Supper, the statement in the Prayer Book regarding the meaning of the kneeling posture to be adopted by the communicant. Archbishop Cranmer and John Knox, although differing in some matters, had much in common; and a church polity acceptable both in Scotland and in England might well have been worked out between them. But with the accession of Mary Tudor such hopes ended. Soon Cranmer, Ridley, Latimer, Hooper and many others were on their way to the stake. There, also, perished the Scots minister, John Rough, who had been

The Communion.

¶ And if any of the Bread and Wine remain unconsecrated, the Curate shall have it to his own use: but if any remain of that which was consecrated, it shall not be carried out of the Church, but the Priest and such other of the Communicants as he shall then call unto him, shall immediately after the Blessing, reverently eat and drink the same.

¶ The Bread and Wine for the Communion shall be provided by the Curate and the Church-wardens, at the charges of the Parish.

¶ And note, that every Parishioner shall communicate at the least three times in the year, of which Easter to be one. And yearly at Easter every Parishioner shall reckon with the Parson, Vicar, or Curate, or his or their Deputy or Deputies, and pay to them or him all Ecclesiastical duties, accustomably due, then and at that time to be paid.

¶ After the Divine Service ended, the money given at the Offertory, shall be disposed of to such pious and charitable uses, as the Minister and Church-wardens shall think fit. Wherein if they disagree, it shall be disposed of as the Ordinary shall appoint.

Whereas it is ordained in this Office for the Administration of the Lords Supper, that the Communicants should receive the same Kneeling; (which Order is well meant, for a signification of our humble and grateful acknowledgment of the benefits of Christ therein given to all worthy Receivers, and for the avoiding of such profanation, and disorder in the holy Communion, as might otherwise ensue) Yet, lest the same Kneeling should by any Persons, either out of ignorance and infirmity, or out of malice and obstinacy, be misconstrued and depraved; It is here declared, that thereby no Adoration is intended, or ought to be done, either unto the Sacramental Bread and Wine there bodily received, or unto any corporal presence of Christs natural Flesh and Blood. For the Sacramental Bread and Wine remain still in their very natural Substances, and therefore may not be adored, (for that were Idolatry to be abhorred of all faithful Christians) And the natural Body and Blood of our Saviour Christ are in Heaven, and not here; it being against the truth of Christs natural Body, to be at one time in more places than one.

O   The

The Black Rubric — so-called because it was originally printed in Black Letter type, as in this seventeenth century Prayer Book — was appended to the *Order for the Administration of the Lord's Supper, or Holy Communion* in the English Book of Common Prayer, probably at the suggestion of John Knox.

the means of persuading Knox to accept the call to minister to the reformed congregation of St Andrews in 1547. He had been arrested for preaching to a secret society of Protestants in London in 1557. Knox himself escaped and spent the next few years in Dieppe, Frankfurt and Geneva, before returning to Scotland. He played no further part in the English Church story, but some of his descendants, as we shall see, had much to do with that of the Scots Kirk in London.

Elizabeth's succession brought some relief to the reformed cause in England, but her claim to ecclesiastical and spiritual supremacy arrested the development of English reformation and made the Church captive to the Crown. When Archbishop Grindall dared to explain to her that as a bishop he was subject to a higher power than hers, and added "I choose rather to offend your earthly majesty than to offend the heavenly majesty of God", she suspended him and took over the archiepiscopal powers herself, and made sure, when he died in 1583, that the chair of Canterbury went to Whitgift. With that, once more, a chance to fashion a Church which would be representative of the whole gamut of reformed Christian thinking was lost. The *Whitgift Articles,* backed by the *Test* which they imposed and *The New High Commission* which was set up to enforce their sanctions, set seal to the doctrine of the Royal Supremacy. The "Puritans", whose aim was to complete the reformation of the English Church and purify her from the last vestiges of papal superstition, were therefore particularly marked out as the enemies of the erastian[4] establishment of the Church of England.

Returned exiles from Frankfurt and Geneva accounted for much of the vigour and conviction which marked the puritan cause. They knew the reformed Church of the continent, and many of them were convinced that the Geneva Church was the most faithful model of the New Testament community of Christians. The presbyterian principle, therefore was strongly represented in puritan thinking, not as an import from Scotland but as a native English preference. At that time, in fact, there were too few Scots in England to exert any influence. During Elizabeth's reign no more than forty were known to be resident in London[5], apart from a brief period shortly to be noted. Elsewhere there may have been isolated colonies of Scots, such as those who were responsible for the name "Little Scotland" still attached to a group of cottages in the Wiltshire village of Horningsham. They were employed by Sir John Thynne in the building of Longleat House — where the lions are now *couchant* rather than *rampant* —, and to meet their needs in face of what the local record calls "the persecuting spirit which in those days prevailed" he built for them in 1566 a beautiful little thatched "Meeting House" where they might be able "to worship God according to their own tenets. ... These pious men were followers of and had imbibed the doctrines of the famous John Knox and John Calvin", and they used the Scots Psalter of 1564. Their church is still in regular use, as a Congregational place of worship — "The Oldest Free Church Building in England"[6].

There may have been other such "Little Scotlands", but they played no part in the rise of English Presbyterianism, which was an indigenous movement. Its leaders were English churchmen — John Field, Walter Travers, Thomas Cartwright and others, who set up the first English Presbytery, with eleven elders, at Wandsworth "near London" in 1572. It began as no more than a parochial presbytery — that is, what in Scotland would be called a Kirk Session. Its discipline was confined to those who would accept it. It interfered with none of the ecclesiastical jurisdictions or powers, and so long as Grindall remained Archbishop of Canterbury it was free from interference. It became, in fact, "the herald and model of hundreds of others that spread through the parishes of England". Although the Scottish Church had played no part in its origin its progress was watched with interest from north of the border. Thomas Cartwright and Andrew Melville had worked together in Geneva. Grindall and Knox had been fellow-chaplains in Edward's time. Mutual recognition of clerical orders signified an open door of understanding — for example John Morison was granted license to celebrate the Divine Office and minister the Sacraments in the Church of England, having been "called to the ministry by the imposition of hands according to the laudable form and rite of the Church of Scotland"[7]. But all these threads of possibility for unity within the Church and between the Churches were cut by Whitgift, who set himself in 1583 to crush the Wandsworth movement of "Presbytery within Episcopacy".

5

Perhaps it was his action which encouraged James VI to similar action in Scotland. When Whitgift's policy became known there, the General Assembly appointed three ministers to ask the king to convey to the queen of England a motion "to disburden their brethren of England of the yoke of ceremonies, ... and especially that sincere men may have liberty to preach without deposing by tyrany of bishops". James promised to do so, but broke his word[8]. He was in fact about to make his own claim to the royal supremacy in matters spiritual, and the "Black Acts" passed by the Scottish Parliament in 1584 rendered him head of the Church as of the State. No assemblies were to be held without his sanction; bishops were to be appointed, by himself; and any minister expressing his opinion on public affairs would be answerable to the charge of treason. Almost all the leading ministers had to flee the country, while the congregations expressed their views by ignoring the episcopally-appointed substitutes. This was what led to the brief period mentioned above when the Scottish population in London rose above a handful.

Berwick had at first received most of the exiled Scots ministers and their families, but in time a number of them turned up in London, where "they took part in a critical stage of evolution of that 'discipline within a discipline, Presbytery in Episcopacy'", of which Wandsworth was the pioneer. For a year or two at least the London Scottish community "was so numerous ... that it was suggested it should have its own church, as the French, Italian and Dutch did[9], ... but the council decided against and refused the Scots a 'peculiar church'". The Lieutenant of the Tower, however, friendly to the ministers, "allowed some of them to preach and form a congregation in his own church, which was exempt from episcopal jurisdiction, and Andrew Melville's lectures there were much frequented"[10]. The Chapel of the Tower of London may thus be said to have housed the first Scots Kirk in London[11], but as almost all of the 20 or so exiled ministers had returned to Scotland by 1588 it can have had but the briefest of existences. In any event, despite Whitgift's efforts, English Presbyterianism within the Church of England survived. Although 200 clergymen were suspended, deprived, or imprisoned for refusing to subscribe the Test Articles, it is reckoned that in 1590 no less than five hundred were quietly following the Wandsworth pattern in their own parishes. The few Scots residing in England would find with them the form of worship and order they sought.

Change came with the arrival of James VI as James I of England, and there was a sudden enlargement of the Scottish colony in London, especially in the area between London and Westminster. James Howel remarked on this in 1657: "The Union with Scotland did not a little conduce to make union 'twixt London and Westminster; for the Scots, multiplying here mightily, neasted themselves about the Court, so that the Strand, from mud walls and thatched houses, came to that perfection of buildings as now we see"[12]. Many of those Scots were either the king's courtiers or men who had come to seek place and favour. These would not be likely to withstand his growing hostility to presbytery and his increasing insistence on the Divine Right of Kings. And if the sorely-harried Presbyterians and other puritan upholders of Christ's Headship of His Church were pinning their hopes on the encouraging facts that James had signed the Scots Confession of 1560, that he had protested with all solemnity before both Parliament and General Assembly that "theirs was to his mind the truest Kirk in the world, and he would maintain its principles as long as he lived"; that at Andrew Melville's suggestion he had offered professorial chairs at St Andrews to both Cartwright and Travers; and that he had brought with him as one of his chaplains the noted Presbyterian minister, Patrick Galloway, they must have been soon disillusioned. The Hampton Court Conference extinguished such expectations. The only puritan hope which it fulfilled was the authorisation of a new version of the Bible, for which James had heard a plea at the 1601 General Assembly of the Church of Scotland in Burntisland[13]. He completely misunderstood the puritans' moderate commendation of a system of episcopacy in presbytery, and the four puritan spokesmen left the Conference to the parting words of "the wisest fool in Christendom": "If this is what your party have to say, I will make them conform, or I will harry them out of the land, or worse!" Hampton Court revealed "the king's grave underestimation of the strength and potentiality of English puritanism, and this error on his side was to have damaging consequences for the whole Church and nation"[14].

The damaging consequences were to be aggravated when Charles I succeeded him in 1625 and when William Laud became Archbishop of Canterbury in 1633. Laud's notoriety in Scotland sprang from the attempt in 1637 to force upon the Church the liturgy which bore his name. In England he had provoked dangerous tensions even before he became archbishop. As Dean of Gloucester he had introduced the innovation of having the Communion Table fixed altarwise against the east wall and insisted upon the practice of bowing to it, although by the Canons of 1603 it was to be taken from its place at the east end when needed for Communion and placed where the communicants could best see and hear the minister[15]. One Scots minister in particular became the victim of this strange man of intellect, mysticism and narrow-minded bigotry, whose policy in making the English Church the wolf's-paw of Rome John Milton so unsparingly condemned in 1637[16]. That Scotsman was Alexander Leighton, native of Edinburgh, presbyterially ordained, and a Doctor of Medicine, who in 1624 wrote a book highly critical of the prelatic use of power in Church and State. While he was in London in 1628 he was arrested under warrant from the High Commission, signed by Laud; and in June 1630, by judgement of the Star Chamber, 'committed to the prison of Fleet, there to remain during his life, be degraded of his ministry, pay a fine of £10,000, be brought into the pillory, whipped, have one of his ears cut off, his nose slit, and be branded in the face with a double S for Sower of Sedition'. Ten years later, blind, deaf, and unable so much as to crawl, he was liberated under Cromwell, and made Keeper of Lambeth Palace and Library in compensation for 'his great damage and suffering sustained by the illegal sentence in the Star Chamber', as the Commons resolution phrased it[17]. Laud's over-ruling of canon law, his return to the pre-reformation symbolic separation of priest from people, and his savage treatment of those who opposed totalitarian episcopacy, alienated the puritans to a degree which provoked the almost as extreme measures of the reaction which followed under Cromwell.

Charles himself had taken his share in sowing the seeds of that revolt, but although he had thereby lost some of England's best leadership in church and state to the New World there remained enough to set a new course when under the threat of Scots rebellion he was forced to summon what became known as the Long Parliament. Presbyterianism was now a formidable force amongst the English middle classes, and heed had also to be paid to the views of Scotland's Parliament and General Assembly. The English Parliament therefore nominated 121 ministers and 30 laymen from its own number to consult and advise for the reformation of the Church of England ... in a manner 'most agreeable to God's most holy word and most apt to procure and preserve the peace of the Church at home, and nearer agreement with the Church of Scotland and other reformed churches abroad'. This advisory body, *The Westminster Assembly,* met first in July 1643, and in response to its invitation the Church of Scotland in August sent eleven members who, although without voting powers, could advise it in its discussions. In September the *Solemn League and Covenant* was accepted by both Parliaments, the English, equally with the Scots, pledging themselves amongst other things 'to bring the Churches of God in the three Kingdoms to the nearest conjunction and uniformity in religion, confession of faith, form of Church government, direction of worship and catechising, according to the Word of God and the example of the best Reformed Churches'. Towards that end the Westminster Assembly was already working, but when its tasks were completed the English Parliament showed little desire to act upon them. The doctrinal documents expressed a Calvinism more rigid by far than Calvin's; the laymen in the Commons disliked the notion of Church discipline being exercised other than within the structure of civil law; the execution of the king had set Cromwell and and the Presbyterians at odds[18]; and the Independents saw no scriptural warrant for a national church. In the end this particular and purely advisory visit of the Scots Kirk to London left little mark on English Church life; whereas in Scotland, where the documents of that English Assembly were somewhat reluctantly adopted by the General Assembly in the interests of a hoped-for uniformity, they have remained the official standards of the Church of Scotland and her daughters throughout the English-speaking world, although now with considerable freedom in their interpretation and use[19]. Cromwell became increasingly impatient with the Presbyterians, and the Independents were growing in strength and in influence on the affairs of the state[20]. Nevertheless the years of the Long Parliament, the Commonwealth and the Protectorate gave recognition to Presbyterianism. From 1646 there were twelve Presbyteries, probably of the parochial sort, in London, with a Synod meeting twice a year until 1655. The Scot in London would still have had little difficulty in finding a place of worship congenial to his convictions.

Then came the restoration of Stewart rule. Charles II, who had been crowned at Scone as king of Scotland in 1651, having signed the Covenant the year before, assured the Scottish presbyteries in a royal letter after his arrival in England in May 1660 that he would 'protect and preserve the government of the Church of Scotland as it is settled by law, without violation'; but Scotland was soon to learn how little his royal word was worth. In England his Declaration of Breda had promised 'that no man shall be quieted or called in question for differences of opinion in matters of religion which do not disturb the peace of the kingdom'; but England, also, was to find that their new king was no more to be trusted than his father had been. If Charles had been a man of his word the 1660's might even yet have ushered in a new era in the religious life of the two countries. There was, as Macaulay has written, a new willingness to find common ground. 'It did not seem impossible to effect an accommodation between the moderate Episcopalians of the school of Usher and the moderate Presbyterians of the school of Baxter. The [one] would admit that a bishop might lawfully be assisted by a council. The [other] would not deny that each provincial council might lawfully have a permanent president and that this president might lawfully be called a bishop. There might be a revised liturgy which should not exclude extemporaneous prayer; a Baptismal Service in which the sign of the Cross might be used or omitted at discretion; a Communion Table at which the faithful might sit if conscience forbade them to kneel. But to no such plan would the great body of Cavaliers listen with patience'[21]. Charles, in fact, had quite other plans. He had pubicly promised a conference for consultation and agreement, but when at his summons the twelve bishops and twelve Presbyterian divines met in the Savoy Palace the latter found themselves treated as petitioners whose amendments the bishops were entitled to reject without appeal. The outcome was inevitably 'a defeat of the charitable design which the Conference had ostensibly been convened to promote'[22].

There followed a series of Acts of his 'Pension Parliament', restoring bishops to the Lords, and requiring all ministers to be re-ordained if their ordination had not been episcopal. *The Corporation Act* barred from public office, university or other teaching posts, or offices under the Crown, any who did not attend the parish church or receive the Lord's Supper in a parish church according to the rites of the Church of England. Most savage of all, *The Act of Uniformity,* timed to come into effect on 24th August, 1662, enforced the use of the Prayer Book and the Prayer Book only in all public worship, demanded from every minister an unfeigned consent and assent to all its contents, and — for the first time since the Reformation — rendered legally invalid all orders save those conferred by the hands of bishops. On that Sunday — the 100th anniversary of France's St Bartholomew's Day massacre of the Huguenots — one-fifth of the entire clergy of the Church of England, two thousand in number, 'voluntarily forsook their churches, parsonages and livings, casting themselves with their destitute families on the providence of heaven'. Dr McCrie goes on to remark in the same passage upon the quietness and dignity with which this sacrificial protest was made, and Samuel Pepys makes a similar comment on the farewell sermons of Dr Bates and Mr Herring in St Dunstan's[23]. The refinement of cruelty in the Act, which made no allowance out of their livings for the ejected clergy, lay in the date of its operation. St Bartholomew's Day came at the end of a quarter. The incoming clergy would receive the revenues for that quarter, while the ejected, who had done the work, departed unpaid.

With this the stage is set for the appearance of the first Scots Kirk in London of which records remain. Presbyterianism had been cast out of the Church of England. Its continuance in England was to be encouraged by the emergence of congregations of those Scots who could no longer find a spiritual home in any Church of England place of worship and who banded themselves together to follow what had been the forms of their own national Church.

NOTES

1. Bulloch, *The Life of the Celtic Church,* p. 72.
2. Lightfoot, *Leaders in the Northern Church,* p. 14. After the Synod of Whitby, he adds, 'Devout and upright men, ... writing when the memory of those Celtic days was fresh, looked back with longing eyes on the departed glory. It was the golden age of saintliness, such as England would never see again'.
3. *The Arbroath Declaration* of 1320.
4. Erastian — an adjective derived from the teaching of Thomas Erastus of Heidelberg in the sixteenth century, that the State is supreme in ecclesiastical causes.
5. Rosalind Mitchison, *History of Scotland,* p. 12.
6. Church Minute Book of Horningsham Meeting House, quoted in *Horningsham Chapel — The Story of England's Oldest Free Church,* p. 10. See also the *Journal of the Presbyterian Historical Society of England,* vol I, no. 3, pp. 73—87.
7. J. Strype, *History .. of Edmund Grindal,* ii, appendix xvii.
8. Patrick Collinson, *The Elizabethan Puritan Movement,* p. 235. Also R.M. Gillon, *John Davidson of Prestonpans,* pp. 262—3.
9. The earliest of all such 'peculiar churches' was *The Church of the Strangers',* for which Edward VI granted a charter to John a'Lasco in 1550. This was a Dutch-German congregation organised in Presbyterian form, which still worships in Austin Friars. A painting, dating from the 17th century and thought to have been prompted by Laud's attempt to crush The Church of the Strangers in 1633, depicts King Edward delivering the Charter to a'Lasco, with Cranmer, Ridley, Northumberland and Knox as witnesses. It hangs in the rooms of the United Reformed Church History Society in Tavistock Place, London.
10. Gordon Donaldson, *The Scottish Presbyterian Exiles in England,* art. in the *Scottish Church History Society Records,* XIV, pp. 67ff. Also Collinson, *op. cit.,* p. 277. Andrew Melville was to know the Tower of London under harsher circumstances, when James had him imprisoned there in 1607, releasing him four years later only after repeated pleas from the continent that Scotland's finest scholar should be freed to teach at the University of Sedan.
11. The first, that is, if we except any congregation which may have worshipped in the chapel of the Scots Ambassadors in Scotland Yard. 'Then there is a large plot of ground, inclosed with brick, called Scotland Yard, where the Kings of Scotland were wont to be lodged, and

Margaret Queen Dowager of Scotland, eldest sister to Henry the 8, kept her court there after the king her husband had been killed in Flodden Field' — James Howel, *Londinopolis* (1657), p. 350. The site, later absorbed in Whitehall Palace, left its name in Great Scotland Yard, and when the first Metropolitan Police headquarters removed thence in the 1890s its new buildings, further south, were renamed New Scotland Yard.

12. *Ibid*, p. 346.

13. This, the *Authorised Version* — or in the U.S.A. *The King James Version* — took over 30 years to replace in popular favour the *Genevan* (or Breeches) *Bible*, which was a careful revision by exiles in Geneva of Tyndale's and others' translations, was published by Barker in London in 1560, was largely financed by John Bodley whose son founded the Bodleian Library in Oxford, and went through over two hundred editions. It was printed, except for one edition, in the clearer Roman instead of the old Black-letter style, had numbered verses for easy reference, and contained an appendix of metrical Psalms. James disliked it because of the democratic tendentiousness of its marginal notes. Its name derives from its translation of Genesis iii, 7 — 'they made themselves breeches'.

14. Collinson, *op. cit.*, p. 462.

15. Drysdale, *History of the Presbyterians in England*, p. 7; and Bogue & Bennett, *History of Dissenters*, i, 63.

16. Milton, *Lycidas*, lines 125—129.

17. Leighton's son, Robert, born in London, educated in Edinburgh, exiled in Douai, and ordained at Newbattle in 1641, eventually accepted the bishopric of Dunblane in 1662, reluctantly but in the sincere hope that he might thus help to reconcile Presbytery and Episcopacy. He failed, but his saintly influence undoubtedly mediated grace to both sides, and his name is one of the most honoured in Scottish church history. See Walter C. Smith's poem *The Bishop's Walk.*

18. Cromwell complained that 'he and his council of officers could not go on with their designs against the king's life because of the opposition of the Presbyterian ministers' (Neale's *Puritans*, p. 216, quoted by Bogue & Bennett, *op. cit.*, p. 67). The Westminster Assembly 'declared unanimously for the release of the king', and 'many ministers drew up a serious and faithful representation of their judgement' (*Minutes of the Westminster Assembly*, and *Life of Robert Blair*, p. 215).

19. Burleigh, *A Church History of Scotland*, pp. 226f.

20. Cromwell's impatience was aggravated when some Presbyterians, such as Thomas Watson of St Stephen's Walbrook, Christopher Love of St Laurence Jewry, and Thomas Langham a parliamentarian, opened

correspondence with the Scots for the purpose of inviting their exiled King Charles to return. Cromwell had eight of them imprisoned in the Tower, and Love was executed. Finally, like Milton, he was repelled by the intolerance of the extremist Presbyterians. Milton had earlier been a whole-hearted Presbyterian, quick to defend his old Scots tutor, Thomas Young, the Presbyterian vicar of Stowmarket and later Master of Jesus College, Cambridge. His *Sonnet VI* reveals his later revulsion from the intolerant Presbyterianism that would 'force our consciences that Christ set free'; and in the sonnet *To the Lord General Cromwell, May 1652* he transfers his image of the wolf's paw, applying it to what elsewhere he calls 'New Presbyter is but old Priest writ large'.

21. Macaulay, *History of England*, i, 159. See also the Preface to Baxter's *Penitent Confessions*, and his *Life and Times*, ii, 259,264.
22. Canon Molesworth,*History of the Church of England from 1660*, p. 45.
23. Thomas McCrie, *Annals of English Presbytery*, pp. 235ff., and Samuel Pepys, *Diary*, Everyman edition, i, 275.

CHAPTER 2

'Whatever sort of Nonconformists or Recusants'

Founders' Hall Scotch Church 1665–1944

Uniformity of religion had been the English Parliament's aim when it appointed the Westminster Assembly in 1643. Had they had their way the extreme Presbyterians would have enforced that uniformity with all the rigour of the law. Now in 1662 just such a legally enforced uniformity was enacted, but of such a kind that the Puritans perforce became the noncomformists and outlaws. It is reckoned that altogether 60,000 of them suffered for their principles, 5,000 of them dying in prison and 15,000 families being financially ruined[1].

How did their cause survive? The answer must be 'like leaven', the vitality of truth working silently and unseen within the sad lump of Restoration sensualism. Richard Green sums up the process in a memorable passage: 'Puritanism. . . . ceased from the long attempt to build up a kingdom of God by force and violence, and fell back on its true work of building up a kingdom of righteousness in the hearts and consciences of men. . . As soon as the wild orgy of the Restoration was over, men began to see that nothing that was really worthy in the work of Puritanism had been undone. The revels of Whitehall, the scepticism and debauchery of courtiers, the corruption of statesmen, left the mass of Englishmen what puritanism had made them, serious, earnest, sober in life and conduct. Slowly but surely it introduced its own seriousness and purity into English society, literature, politics. The whole history of English progress since the Restoration, on its moral and spiritual side, has been the history of Puritanism'[2].

But there was a price to be paid, and the fact that the 2,000 ejected clergymen and their congregations — of whom two thirds were Presbyterian — survived the next quarter-century of persecution is evidence of the vitality of their faith and of the courage it gave them, for the *Corporation Act* and the *Act of Uniformity* were almost immediately followed by the *Conventicle* and the *Five Mile Acts,* which sent nonconformity underground[3]. Consequently the beginnings of most of its congregations are obscure.

Some, certainly, were helped by influential favour, and the Crosby Hall congregation is an example. When Thomas Watson was ejected from the living of St Stephen's, Walbrook, he found a friend in Sir Thomas Langham who like himself had been in the Tower as a Presbyterian opponent of Cromwell's execution of the king and because of his correspondence with Charles' son. Langham, who had been knighted as a member of the deputation which in 1660 invited Charles II to return to England, was a man of some influence, sheriff of London, member of Parliament, and in favour with Charles. He was still, also, a strong Presbyterian; and being the lessee of Crosby Place or Palace in Bishopsgate[4] he came to Watson's rescue with the offer of the upper floor of its Great Hall as a place of worship for his flock. With this kind of influential protection the Crosby Hall congregation, and some others which enjoyed similar favour, must have found a continuing existence less hazardous than most. Nevertheless, in a *Guide for Constables and Informers,*[5] published in 1683 when the Rye House Plot furnished a pretext for a new outburst of persecution, we find, amongst the list of 'The Conventicles and Unlawful Meetings within the City of London', that 'Crosby Hall, Presbyterian' is mentioned, along with such others as 'At a Ship Chandler's near the Hermitage, Presbyterian', 'Swallow Street, St Martin's in the Fields, Presbyterian', and two identified as 'Blackfreyars, near the King's Printing House' and 'Another, near Scotch Hall', both being labelled 'Scotch Presbyterian'.

We shall come across Scotch Hall in the next chapter, but of the two Scotch Presbyterian congregations nearby nothing further is known. There may in fact have been others, as short-lived as these seem to have been. There certainly were Scots ministers serving English Presbyterian conventicles in London and Westminster. One of them merits passing mention. Alexander Shields, an Edinburgh graduate, had become amanuensis to John Owen about 1661, and was eventually licensed 'by Scots

A LIST
OF THE
Conventicles or Unlawful Meetings
Within the City of LONDON and Bills of Mortality;
With the Places where they are to be found; As also, The Names of divers of the PREACHERS, and the several FACTIONS They profess.

To the Right Honourable the Lord Mayor of the City of London ; and to the Right Worshipful the Recorder, and Aldermen of the same City. And to the Worshipful the Justices of the Peace, inhabiting in the City of Westmin. and the Counties of Middlesex and Surrey, within the weekly Bills of Mortality ; And to all High-Constables, Pety-Constables, Church-Wardens, Overseers of the Poor, and all other Officers and Ministers of the Peace ; the perusal of the following List of Unlawful Conventicles, is humbly presented.

City and Liberties of London, as they are Ranged.	(S.W. Prichard) (Lord Major.)	

Leaden-hall-street, near Creed-church.	Independ.	Dr. Owen.
Bishops-gate-street within, Crosby-House.	Presbyt.	
Bishops-gate-street without, Devonshire-Buildings.	Independ,	
A Quakers Meeting at the same House		
Meeting-house-Alley, near Bishops-Gate-Church.	Anabap.	Griffis.
A Meeting-house in Petit-France.	Independ.	
Pin-makers-Hall near Broad-street.	Presbyt.	
Near All-hallows the Wall.	Independ.	
Whites Alley in Little Moor-fields.	Presbyt.	
Another in the same Ally.	Independ.	
Ropemakers-alley, near Whites-alley.	Presbyter.	
Lorimers-Hall near the Postern, between Moor-gate & Cripple-gate	Presbyt.	
Between White-cross & Red-cross-street, near the Peacock Brew-House	Independ.	Cockin.
Pauls Ally in Red-cross-street, at the Old Play-house.	Anabap.	Plant.
Beech-lane at Glovers-Hall.	Presbyt.	
In the same Lane near it.	Independ.	
Jewin-street.	Presbyt.	Jenkins.
Westmorland-house in Aldersgate-str.	Independ.	
Bartholomew-close.	Presbyt.	
St. Martins le Grand, Bull & Mouth.	Quakers.	
Embroyderers-Hall in Gutter-lane near Cheapside.	Presbyt.	S. Lamb
Near Criplegate.	Presbyter.	Presbit.
Staining-lane near Haberdashers-Hall.	Presbyter.	Jacomb.
High-Hall near St. Sepulchers.	Presbyter.	
Cow-lane in a School-house.	Independ.	
Stone-cutter-street near Fleet-ditch.	Presbyter.	
Wine Office-court in Fleet-street.	Independ.	
Goldsmiths-court in Fetter-lane.	Presbyter.	Turner.
Black-Fryers near the Kings Printing-House.	Scotch Presbyter.	
Another near Scotch-Hall.		
Broken Wharfe George-yard.	Anabap.	Knowles.
Three Cranes in Thames-street near Dowgate, over Stables.	Presbyter.	
Joyners-Hall on Dowgate.	Independ.	
Chequer-yard on Dowgate-Hill.	Anabap.	
Bell-Inn in Walbrook.	Presbyter.	Leigh.
Exchange-Alley at a Coffee house.	Independ.	
Bartholomew-lane by the Exchange.	Presbyter.	
Freemans-yard near the Exchange.	Presbyter.	Cruzo.
Grace-Church-street near Lombard-street.	Quakers.	

Grace-Church-street Talbot-Court.	Independ.	
St. Martins-Hill near crooked-lane.		
For the out-parts of Middlesex and Westminster within the Bill of Mortality.		Anabap.
Lower end of Limehouse next the Fields.	Presbyter.	
Near Stepney Church.	Independ.	Mead.
School-house-lane near Ratcliff-Cross.	Presbyter.	
A Quakers in the same place.		
Near Shadwel-Church.	Anabap.	
Meeting-house Alley between Shadwel and Wapping.	Presbyter.	Dollings.
In a Carpenters yard near the Hermitage.	Anabap.	
At a Ship-Chandlers near it.	Presbyter.	
Looking-Glass-Alley in West-smithfield.	Anabap.	
In Bell-lane near Spittle-fields.	Presbyter.	
Quakers-street in Spittle-fields.	Quakers.	
Windford-street.	Anabap.	
Near the Spittle.	Presbyter.	Dr. Ansloe
At Hackney near 3 or 4, but at present are all Suppressed.		
Near Hog-lane in Shoreditch, Old-street.	Presbyter.	
St. Johns-lane near Hicks's-Hall the Feel.	Presbyter. Quakers.	Partrige.
Greys-Inn-lane in Red-Lyon-yard.	Presbyter.	
Near Mountague-house in Blomsbu.	Presbyter.	Read.
Swallow-street St. Martins in the fields.	Presbyter.	Lobb's.
Near Tothil-street Westminster.	Presbyter.	Alsops.
In the same place.	Quakers.	
Near the Church.	Quakers,	
Clare-market at the Old Play-house	Presbyter.	Farindon.
In Southwark and County of Surrey within the Bill of Mortality.		
Farthing-Alley.	Presbyter.	Vincent.
Little Maze Pond.	Anabap.	
Horse-ly-down Fare-street.	Quakers.	
Horse-ly-down Free-School-street.	Anabap.	
Horse-ly-down.	Milliner.	Wheelers.
New Shad Thames.	Anabap.	Claytons.
Near Horse-ly-down New-street.	Presbyter	Flavels.
Unicorn-yard near Stony-lane.	Presbyter.	Cables.
Globe-Alley near the Bear-garden.	Pres. Ind.	
In street in Winchester-Park.	Quakers.	
Winchester-Park near Lownands Pond.	Anabap.	
IX : x³⁵ num.		

LONDON: Printed by Nat. Thompson Anno Domini, 1683.

Presbyterian divines' to minister to an English Presbyterian
meeting in Embroiderers' Hall, Cheapside. In 1685 he was
arrested while preaching in a private house in Gutter Lane on
Genesis 49:21 — 'Naphtali is a hind let loose'. He was imprisoned
in Newgate, later transferred to Scotland, and immured on the
Bass Rock, where he was offered his liberty on conditions he
refused to accept. Eventually he escaped in female clothing and
joined John Renwick and the Cameronians. When Renwick was
captured and executed he escaped to Holland, where he wrote
his account of the Covenanting cause under the title *Naphtali,
or The Hind let Loose*. After the Revolution he returned to
Scotland, and was one of the three Cameronian ministers[6] who
accepted the Revolution Settlement and joined the Church of
Scotland. He became chaplain to the Scots Brigade in Holland,
then minister of the second charge in St Andrews, and in 1699
was appointed senior chaplain to the second of the ill-fated
Darien Expeditions, taking part in the disastrous venture with
no less loss but with more credit than many of the fortune-
seekers who had embarked upon it. He died in Jamaica on his
way home[7].

Embroiderers' Hall, in which Shields' congregation worshipped, was one of the London Companies' Halls which the
Presbyterian sympathies of the City made available for nonconformists. Who the 'Scots Presbyterian divines' who licensed
Shields may have been, or to what kind of companies they ministered, we do not know, but one of them may well have been
the minister of a congregation whose meeting-place was another
of those Halls, Founders' Hall in Lothbury. Some time in the
middle of the 1660s there appeared in Lothbury a congregation
consisting of the members of St Antholin's, Watling Street,
whose minister, Elias Pledger, had been ejected in 1662. If its
meeting-place was Founders' Hall it can only have been three
years later that its membership consisted so largely of Scots that
it was known as the Scotch Church. It can be dated by the careful statement of a later minister, who wrote 'that the said congregation hath subsisted ever since there were a sufficient number
of people from Scotland to form a public religious society. And,
if tradition may be depended upon, Founders' Hall was originally
the place of worship or chapel where the Scots ambassadors

attended divine service; but not to lay stress on this unauthenticated circumstance it is certain that the Scots congregation at Founders' Hall ... was in being before Charles II created by his royal charter the Scottish Hospital or charitable corporation'[8]. As that charter was granted in 1665 this statement, if it is accepted, sets the beginnings of Founders' Hall Scotch Church near to the time of the Ejection, whether or not the congregation had originally been that which was led by the ejected minister of St Antholin's.

Meanwhile in Scotland a young man called Alexander Carmichael, having graduated M.A. at St Andrews in 1660, was licensed in June 1664 and ordained by the Presbytery of Lanark as minister of Pettinain in August of that year. In 1667 he was deposed, probably in the comb-out of suspect ministers which followed the Covenanters' Pentland Rising and the Battle of Rullion Green. Five years later he was arrested on a charge of 'keeping conventicles', and imprisoned. Under Lauderdale's temporary policy of clemency his sentence was reduced to one of banishment, which brought him by sea to London just at the moment when Founders' Hall not only needed a minister but was about to seize the offered opportunity of a legally-recognised existence.

This was the opportunity offered by Charles' *Declaration of Indulgence*. The king found himself under the necessity of pleasing those in his Council who wanted toleration for nonconformists, needing their support for his plans to join France in a war against the Dutch; so he relaxed the punitive sanctions of the *Act of Uniformity* by issuing, in 1672, his *Declaration of Indulgence,* ordering that 'all manner of penal laws on matters ecclesiasticall against whatever sort of Nonconformists or Recusants should from that day be suspended'. The suspension was in fact brief, for Parliament found good reason to question his motives in granting it. Roman Catholics were excluded from the amnesty, but events at Court, and further rumours about Charles' secret treaty with Louis of France in which he committed himself to conversion to Rome, raised strong suspicion that the Indulgence was designed to pave the way for the establishment of Roman Catholicism. So strong was this suspicion that Parliament took the first opportunity of resolving 'that penal statutes in matters ecclesiastical cannot be suspended but by consent of

Parliament', and refused supplies until the Declaration was recalled.

Its encouragement, however, had lasted long enough to bring back from banishment a considerable number of ministers. The gaols had been emptied of dissenting prisoners, and thousands of Presbyterians, Independents and others had taken out licenses under the Declaration and begun to worship openly in such places as Pinners' Hall, Salters' Hall, Plaisterers' Hall, Dyers' Hall — and Founders' Hall, where Carmichael became the first registered minister. Although the Declaration was soon repealed, this brief remission gave encouragement to nonconformist congregations, and for some of them, at least in the City where Presbyterian sentiment was strong and Presbyterians more than once became Lords Mayor, the advantage gained in 1672 was not wholly lost. But whatever protection may have sheltered this First Scotch Church in Lothbury it did not extend to saving Alexander Carmichael from a term of imprisonment in Newgate, or his immediate successor, Jeremiah Marsden, from death in the same prison. The congregation survived, nonetheless. continuing into the present century, although not without drastic change.

The Glorious Revolution of 1688 greatly bettered the situation in which Presbyterian and other nonconformist churches stood, and Founders' Hall Scots Kirk shared that improvement. It soon found itself, inded, in an unusually favoured position, with a minister who had the ear of the king although he took no personal advantage of that privilege.

Amongst the many ministers and members of the Church of Scotland who had found refuge in Holland in 1663 or during the Killing Times — men such as the Earl of Argyle, Richard Cameron, Sir Patrick Hume of Polwarth, George Baillie of Jerviswood and William Carstares — there was a group in Rotterdam, ministered to by Robert Fleming and constituting the Scots Kirk in that city. The minister's son, Robert Fleming the Younger, succeeded his father, and then in 1668, was called by the Founders' Hall congregation to succeed Nicholas Blaikie, who had followed Marsden in the charge. He accepted the call, 'that he might have the better opportunity of uniting his endeavours with those of his excellent friend, William Carstares, for the prosperity of the Church of Scotland as well as for the general good'. These motives received additional force from the sentiments of King William, who knew his worth and signified his desire to have him near his person'[9].

One of William's problems was the reluctance of the Presbyterian leaders in Scotland to purge their memories of the bitter sufferings and persecutions they had undergone for so long at the hands of the Episcopal party. They were quick, also, to suspect any appearance of royal interference with the affairs of the Church, and they regarded as such the king's recommendation of moderation and 'calm and peaceable procedure which', as he declared in a royal letter to the General Assembly of 1690, 'will be no less pleasing to us than it becometh you'. Episcopal clergymen were petitioning for admission to the Church, promising to take the oath of allegiance, to concur with Presbyterian government, and to subscribe the Westminster Confession, having been encouraged by the king's demand that the General Assembly should accept them on those terms. But the Assembly resented what appeared to be the king's interference in spiritual matters, and did nothing. Then the Privy Council appointed Commissions to purge the five Universities, and when complaints from those ejected aroused sympathy in England William ordered the purges to cease. He was finding difficulty in discovering a middle course between controlling Scottish authorities along peaceful lines on the one hand, and discouraging dangerous Jacobite episcopal intrigues on the other. Wisely he turned to trusted Scottish friends, such as Carstares, whose advice on one dramatic occasion averted a breach in the relations between Kirk and Crown and did much to win the General Assembly's compliance with William's desires. We do not know on what matters the king sent for Robert Fleming, or the outcome of whatever counsel he offered, but on William's side the confidence he reposed in his friend was maintained to the end, and on Fleming's 'with such prudence and modesty that he desired, whenever he was called to the Court that it might be done with the greatest privacy'[10].

Was William Paterson, one wonders, a member of Founders' Hall Scottish Church? He certainly had connections with Lothbury. A farmer's son from Dumfriesshire, he had left Scotland to escape the religious persecutions which followed the Restoration. With the traditional Scots pedlar's pack on his back he had made his way south, and after an interval in America during which he served as a lay preacher he returned to England with ambitious plans, two of which were crowned with success and the third with disaster. The latter was the ill-fated Darien Scheme of his *Company Trading to Africa and the Indies*. Boldly conceived as a means of breaking the trading monopolies established by the East India and Africa Companies which were strangling Scottish overseas trade, the Company was launched in 1695. But the English subscribers of half the necessary capital suddenly withdrew under pressure from the East India Company, subscriptions from the continent were by English influence withheld, and the Darien Scheme to which the Company was thereby restricted was mismanaged by enthusiastic but ill-informed directors. The expedition failed, with the loss of two thousand lives and the dissipation of a large proportion of Scotland's financial resources. It was a disaster which darkly shadowed the arguments both for and against union between Scotland and England, and left in the former a sense of resentment which the award of 'The Equivalent' in the Treaty of Union did little to assuage[11].

Paterson had more success with his English ventures. One of these had to do with a new water supply for north London. The other was the creation of the Bank of England, which he suggested in 1691 and helped to found in 1694, although in less than a year he disagreed with his fellow-directors and withdrew from the management. The Bank's business found its permanent home in Lothbury, where the First Scotch Church, until it moved to a new building in London Wall, worshipped in the shadow of Paterson's Bank, 'the old lady of Threadneedle Street'[12].

Robert Fleming published several important theological works and carried out a regular series of lectures. This illustrates a particular feature of nonconformist ministry. Despite the Revolution the *Tests* remained in force, and England's two Universities, Oxford and Cambridge, were closed to all but those who conformed. To supply this want of learning the nonconformist 'meeting houses' became teaching centres as well as places of worship, and for those intending to enter the ministry the great 'Dissenting Academies' were set up, under such renowned teachers as Dr Doolittle at Islington, Charles Morton in Newington Green, and Messrs Oldfield, Shadman and Lorimer in Hoxton

Square. So high a standard of education was attained in these academies that they began to be patronised by the sons of Anglicans as well as by Dissenters, and 'the dissenters blazed the trail towards a more modern system of higher education'[13]. Fleming's six-volume *Christology,* and others of his 14 publications, were contributions to the theological studies encouraged in the academies.

Fleming was held in high esteem, not only by fellow-nonconformists but by 'many learned and moderate Episcopalians'. He took a prominent part in the Salters' Hall Lectures, and was spokesman for the Three Denominations in congratulating Queen Anne on the successful Union of the Parliaments in 1707[14]. At about that time he was offered the Principalship of Glasgow University, but declined, preferring to remain with his London flock. For a year or two he was assisted by William Robertson, later to be minister of Old Greyfriars in Edinburgh and author of nos. 25, 42 and 43 of *The Scottish Paraphrases.* Robertson's son, William, (whom we shall meet in Chapter six and Appendix C), followed him in that pulpit and became Professor of History and eventually Principal of Edinburgh University.

It was during Fleming's ministry that Founders' Hall was rebuilt[15]. In the U.R.C. Library there is preserved the Bill of Charges, dated 1700–01, showing the total cost as £690:12:10, and revealing also the connection of a famous Scot with this First Scotch Church in London. Under 'Sums Received' appears an item: 'Wm Carstairs for yᵉ Dyall, £15.', and there may have been more than one William Carstairs in London at that time; but under 'Charges' his identity is confirmed by the item reading: 'Paid Mr Claget for yᵉ Clock being gift of yᵉ Reverd Mr William Carstairs, £15:0:0.' It is highly likely, also that the Thomas Coutts whose name appears as the donor of £25 was the Montrose-born grandfather of the banker of the same name whom we shall meet in Chapter six.

Fleming died in 1716, remembered not only as a scholar but as a faithful pastor and a trustworthy friend, whose understanding of those with views different from his own endeared him even to his opponents. As a student in Holland he had not been content to take his teachers' opinions as the last word, but

Acco of the sundry Soumes Received towards the building and Repairing of founders hall meeting house for the Reverend Mr Robert Fleming Congregation

1702 Received of Mr William Broun — £ 50: — : —

do of Mr Hugh Fraser . . . — — — 25 — —
of Mr Walter Stewart . . — — — 25 — —
of Mr Thos Coutts — — — — 25 — —
of Mr James Hackley — . . — — — 25 — —
of Mr Stephen Mitchall . — — 25 —
of Mr Wm Murray — — 25 — —
of Mr John Rayning — 25 — —
of Mr Daniell King . — — 25 — —
of Mr Andrew Bell — — — — 25 — —
of Mr George Louing . . — — 12. 10 —
of Mr William Fraser . . — — 12. 10 —
of Mr Robert Blackmore . . — 12. 10 —
of Mr James Campbell . — — 12. 10 —
of Mr James Crichly — — 12. 10 —
of Mr John Ferguson — — — 12. 10 —
of his Grace the Duke of Queensberry — — 50 —
of the Right hon the Earle of Hindsford — — 25 —
of Mr Robert Tead — — — — 5 —
of Wm Bowden — — — — 6 —
of Mr Wm Carstairs for the Dyall Clock — 15 —
of Mr John Broun — — — 4 . 6
of Esqr Alexr Hammelton — — 12. 10
of Mr James Hunter — — — 10 —
of Madam Marshall — — — 5 —
of Mr Fair — 9 —
of Mr Clyat & brother — — — 8
of the founders comp for the Windows allowed — 10 — —
of Severally for Seatts as p particular acct hereunto] 105: 15 —
Annexed — —
+ of Mr Pilly allowed for the penny p agreement — 20 : — : —
+ of do allowed for the Green Seats — — 24 14 — —
                                              660 : —

'made it my business also to procure.. the most famous writings of those of the contrary persuasion', thus discovering frequently that 'their arguments appeared quite another thing than as they were proposed under the name of objections by our authors'. Thus, 'if other students exceeded me in knowledge and learning, I seemed to exceed any I conversed with in charity to those of different sentiments and profession'[16].

John Cumming succeeded Fleming and maintained Founders' Hall's witness through the prominent part he took in the Salters' Hall Synod[17] and by his vigorous support of the 'subscriptionist' position in the ensuing controversy. Dr Cumming was followed by William Wishart, who stayed ten years and then became, after his distinguished father, Principal of Edinburgh University. One of his first actions there was to raise a fund to establish and endow the University Library. After him John Partington served in Founders' Hall for ten years, and in 1751 William Steele came in his place but died after only a few months. The next ministry, which lasted for twenty years, was that of Robert Lawson, author of the summary of the congregation's beginnings already quoted. In his time the congregation removed to a new building in London Wall, and seven years after that removal this 'earnest and faithful minister' died at the age of 50 and was succeeded in 1771 by a Scottish parish minister of unusual literary as well as philosophical gifts.

This was the distinguished Dr Henry Hunter, soon marked out as one of the most distinguished writers and ablest preachers in London[18]. During the thirty years of his London Wall ministry he was notably effective in 'maintaining the honour and extending the evangelistic influence of Presbyterianism in London'. That tribute by Walter Wilson has reference to the upholding of the trinitarian doctrine and to the establishment of the Scots Presbytery of London[19] at a time when English Presbyterianism was becoming Unitarian and its theological separation from the Scots Presbyterians threatened to leave the latter in a position of isolation. He himself became clerk to the Presbytery. Two of his sermons — *On the Trial, Conduct and Execution of Louis XVI*, and *The Universal and Everlasting Dominion of God* — reveal a mind fully familiar with the significance of contemporary events as seen *sub specie aeternitatis*, and alert to the pronouncements of 'The Enlightment' as they related to the Gospel. In the latter sermon, on Ps. 87, vv. 1 & 2, he speaks of this planet's relation to the sun and he pictures the possibility of other planets circling around other suns and playing their part, also, in God's purpose.

Under his successor, Dr Robert Young, the congregation of London Wall developed one of the early Sunday Schools in London, and in 1813 Thomas Chalmers, then in Kilmany, was invited to succeed him. He declined, but frequently preached in London Wall (when 'all London flocked to hear him') on his visits to London to meet his brother or to canvass Parliamentary support for the non-intrusionist cause. It is not surprising that when the Disruption occurred in 1843[20], London Wall 'came out' of its Church of Scotland connection and became part of the newly organised Presbyterian Church in England.

In 1856 the congregation moved from London Wall to a new building in Southgate Road and became known as Trinity Presbyterian Church, Canonbury. In 1935 it united with Highbury Presbyterian Church of England, and dissolved in 1944, the building having been destroyed by enemy action.[21]

NOTES

1. Drysdale, *History of the Presbyterians in England*, p. 406n.
2. Green, *A Short History of the English People*, p. 586.
3. *The Conventicle Act* of 1664 punished by fine or imprisonment or transportation all who took part in meetings of more than five persons for religious worship other than that of the Book of Common Prayer. *The Five Mile Act* of the following year forbade any ejected minister who refused to swear that he would not at any time 'endeavour any alteration of government in Church or State' to go within five miles of any borough or of any place where he had been wont to minister.
4. Crosby House had been built in 1470 by Sir John Crosby. In 1483 it was occupied by Richard, Duke of Gloucester; and Shakespeare (*Richard Third*, Act I, ii & iv, & III, i) has Richard name Crosby Place for his rendezvous with Anne, Catesby and the Murderers. After the Crosby Hall congregation became extinct in 1769 the Hall, which with its magnificent decorated oak ceiling had survived the fire that destroyed the Place, came sadly down in the world; but a great act of conservation in 1910 transported it from Bishopsgate and re-erected it on the site of the garden of Thomas More, one of its earlier owners, in Cheyne Walk, where its splendid 14th century ceiling may still be seen, 'a marvellous monument transplanted', as Henry James wrote.

5. 'A crowd of informers grew up who made a trade of detecting the meetings the ministers held at midnight'. (Green, *op. cit.*, p. 612). This *Guide*, a copy of which may be seen in Dr Williams' Library, was prepared to help them in that self-appointed task. (Williams, MS 208.33; British Library, 515.l.18 (22)).

6. The Cameronians, named for the Covenanter Richard Cameron, were the extreme upholders of the Covenants who refused to accept the Revolution Settlement of 1699 because, although it legally recognised the Church of Scotland as Presbyterian, it failed to renew the Covenants. Shields and his two fellow-ministers had been the only ordained men amongst them, and the Cameronians continued to exist as Societies until two ordained men joined them in 1743 and they became the Reformed Presbyterian Church, most of which united with the Free Church in 1876.

7. Walter Wilson, *History and Antiques of Dissenting Churches and Meeting Houses in London, Westminster and Southwark*, iii, 126. Hector Macpherson, *The Cameronian Philosopher, passim*.

8. See chapter three for an account of the Scottish Hospital. *A Tabular View of the Scottish Presbytery of London*, dated 1834, in the column headed 'When and where the congregation was originally constituted', states, against 'London Wall', 'About the year 1665 in Founders' Hall, as appears from the Royal Charter of the Scottish Corporation of the foundation of Charles II'.

9. Wilson, *op. cit.*, ii, 476.

10. *ibid*.

11. 'The Equivalent' was a sum of £398,000 to be paid to Scotland under the Treaty of Union, partly in return for taking over a share of the English National Debt and partly as compensation to the subscribers to the Darien Scheme. See David Daiches, *Scotland and the Union*, pp. 130, 179.

12. In 1764 the congregation moved to London Wall. The Bank of England is still in its windowless stronghold between Lothbury and Threadneedle Street.

13. Dorothy Marshall, *English People in the Eighteenth Century*, pp. 122–3.

14. For *The Three Denominations* see Appendix B.

15. The general preface to Fleming's *Christology* includes a description of the old Hall 'at the top of Founders' Court, with access by means of a flight of stairs, with a tavern below', oblong and having four galleries. Rebuilt, it had three, and seated 1,000 people.

16. *Ibid*.

17. See Appendix B.

18. Not only in London. In a famous case in the General Assembly his

name was invoked as an authority on the theological orthodoxy of the views held by the candidate for a professorial chair. This, the Leslie Case, is described by Ian D.L. Clark in the Scottish Church History Records, vol. 14, pp. 179ff. For an amusing account of the confusion relating to the quotation from Hunter's translation of Euler's Letters, see Lord Cockburn's *Memorials of his Times*, pp. 191f. The case marked the beginning of the end of Moderate domination of the Assembly.

19. See Appendix D.
20. See Appendix C.
21. The *Journal of the Presbyterian Historical Society of England*, Vol. I, no. 3, contains a picture of Robert Fleming, Yr. and another of the 1694 Communion Vessels which are now in the Museum of London.

CHAPTER 3

The Scots Box

The well-being of both Church and State in England suffered
severely from the measures encouraged by the restored Charles
II —

> that 'great and mighty king,
> Whose promise none relies on.
> He never said a foolish thing,
> Nor ever did a wise one'.

But even a stopped clock is right twice a day, and we can give
Charles credit for some actions which were both wise and
right. One of these gave encouragement to a body, already
mentioned in the preceding chapter, whose activities continue to this day and which has for the three and a half centuries of its existence been in close partnership with the Scots
Kirk in London.

We have already noticed how the Scots who came south
with the Stewarts colonised the area to the east of Westminster. Jacobean London quickly became used to the sight
— than which, as a Scot of this century observed, few are
more impressive — of 'the Scotsman on the make'. And the
records show that London and Westminster, no less than the
Scot himself, reaped the benefit of his enterprising, independent spirit.

Not every Scot, however, broke through into success. For this
there were many reasons. The most constant was the crippling
handicap of religious discrmination against those who refused to
change coats to avoid it. Other difficulties were of the sort
which still confront many Scottish arrivals in London, and it
was those which prompted the new Scots colony in the Westminster of James VI and I to devise some means of coping with
them. They saw some of their compatriots, far from home as
they were, falling by the way — victims of accident, disease,

religious discrimination, ill-chance, or plain inadequacy. They knew also that they themselves were not invulnerable; so they clubbed together and every time they met they gave or received that spare coin which could make all the difference between mere difficulty and dire disaster.

By 1613, with a meeting-place in Lamb's Conduit, the group owned a strong brassbound 'kist' or chest, which became known as *The Scots Box*. Into this kist regular contributions were placed by those able to do so, and from it distribution was made to those in need, on the principle set forth in Acts 4:34,35. It still exists, bearing on its brass-inlaid lid an inscription telling of its origin, together with a verse from the 133rd Psalm in the metrical version of the *First Scottish Psalter* of 1564 —

> Behold How Good A Thing It Is
> And How Becoming Well
> Together Such As Brethren Are
> In Unitie To Dwell.

Half a century later the status of the Society of the Scots Box underwent a dramatic change. 'In the year 1664 a worthy Member of the Society, being visited with a long fit of Sickness and in danger of Death, resolved to communicate to the Poor of his Country (whom he had found to be numerous and in great Streights), part of the Fruits of those his Labours which the Lord had been pleased to bless with Success'. He was advised 'to settle a perpetual Stock, and to obtain Letters Patent from His Majesty as the surest Expedient for that. This counsel was immediately imparted by the Sick Person to the most discreet and substantial Men of our Country who then had the direction of that voluntary contribution which by the Name of Box-money was collected for the Use of the Poor', and on September 3rd, 1665, a Royal Charter was granted and Mr James Kinneir, an eminent Merchant, was chosen first Master[1]. It is not clear whether or not he was himself the 'Sick Person', nor is it more than guesswork that he was a son of Kinneir of that Ilk, of Kilmany, Fife.

The time had undoubtedly been propitious for the Society's application. Two years earlier Charles had granted a Royal Charter to a group of scientists, thus inaugurating *The Royal Society*[2]. Some time later he was to accept Sir Stephen Fox's suggestion for a Soldiers' Home and eventually to grant the

Charter which established *The Royal Hospital at Chelsey*. 'The Scottish Hospital of the Foundation of King Charles the Second' is a further surviving token that the royal favour was sometimes extended towards constructive causes. And if, as tradition says, along with the Charter he also granted the disposal of three Nova Scotia baronetcies, by the sale of which the Scottish Hospital might enlarge its capital funds for the building of its 'Hospital', the gift was most timely. In that very year the Great Plague visited London, and the society's resources were immediately exposed to the severest strain. The 'eight able, honest and discreet men, natives of Scotland and inhabitants of London, Westminster or the Liberties thereof', whom the charter authorised as Governors thereof, must have been hard put to it to cope with their responsibilities. We read that 'more than three hundred Scots people were buried at the charge of the Corporation[3] with as much decency as the Publick Calamity would permit, and many of the Infected were maintained and taken care of until recovered and by God's Blessing the Contagion ceased, without putting the several Parishes where they lived to one Farthing of Expences'[4]. Do we detect a modest note of proud Scottish independence in the last clause?

The Great Fire of the following year brought further difficulties, and the Governors 'almost despaired of bringing the Design to any Maturity'. But they persisted, with such effect that in 1670 they were able to begin building their Hospital. They bought 'a piece of waste ground in Black Fryers' on which stood a large house. The owner, a widow, had been unwilling to part with it, but on learning the use to which it was to be put she generously made a lease to the Corporation for 1000 years. Beside that house they built four others, 'fronting the street in Black Fryers that leads to the River, with an inscription declaring they were for the use of the Poor of their Country; then a Hall with the Emblem of Charity cut in stone over the side of the Hall, facing Fleet Ditch, and afterwards another House for the Beadle', all being completed by 1672. The site can thus be exactly located, with the Fleet river in front just running into the Thames where Blackfriars Bridge now stands, and Water Lane giving access to the rear, past the King's Printing House. A map in Ogilby and Morton's survey, dated 1676, clearly shows The Scotch Hall; and a painting in the Guildhall Art Gallery jefty on that Subject, a Patent in ample Form; which took place the Third of *September* 1 6 6 5. and Mr. *James Kinnier* was chofen fift. Mafter.

So good a Work was almoft ftifled in the Birth; for the Contagious Plague which then difpeopled *London*, and thofe fatal Flames (which the Year following by the deplorable ruine of the City purified it from Infection to the very foundation;) if not wholly crufhed, yet fufpended for fome time the execution of our good Intentions. Thefe difmal Times, however, put not a ftop to the main Wheel of Charity, for during the Sicknefs Year, when our Beginnings were but fmall, there were Three hundred *Scots*, and of *Scotifh* Extraction, who dyed of the Plague in and about *London*, buried at the Charge of the Company, with as much decency as the Calamity of the Time would permit; and many who were Infected maintained, and taken care of, until they recovered, and by God's blefling the Contagion ceafed, without putting the feveral Parifhes where they had lived to one Farthing of Expences.

Whil'ft the City lay buried under its own Rubbifh, though many of our Members who had been fcattered by thefe two heavy Vifitations, were again returned, and as earneft in their defires as formerly to promote that Work of Charity; yet the lownefs of our Stock, which was hardly fufficient to fupply the Neceffities of the Poor that then lay upon us, made us almoft defpair of bringing our defigns to any accomplifhment. We wanted a Hall for our Meetings, Ground to build upon, and Money to purchafe and effectuate both. Neverthelefs in the Year 1 6 7 o, the City having to admiration recovered, or rather outdone much of its ancient fplendor, we refolved with revived hopes vigoroufly to fet upon the performance of our long intended refolutions. To that effect having feveral times affembled the Body of our Company, to confult about the meafures we were to take, we at length had notice given us of a piece of wafte Ground in *Black-Fryers,* where formerly had ftood a large dwelling Houfe belonging to a Lady: having after a view found the Ground for our purpofe, we made application to the Lady for the Purchafe. She was unwilling to fell the Ground right of her Inheritance, but being informed of the Pious and Charitable ufe that it was defigned for, fhe frankly granted us a Leafe of it for a Thoufand Years. Having laid this foundation, we again in

A 1677 account of the way in which the newly chartered 'Scottish Corporation and Hospital' in London survived the twofold crises of Plague and Fire and then set up its first Hall and hostel. *National Library of Scotland*

The Scots Box

depicts the buildings overlooking the Fleet.

Robert Kirk[5] describes the close-knit Scots community in London at the time of the Revolution. 'There is a club of Scotish Presbyterian Schoolmasters that meet at [   ] every Saturday about [   ] a'clock and any Scotish scholar that resorts to town and makes address to them, they contribute money to his charge till they find out a fit place for him and then he restores the money to their public box reserved for the like uses'. 'In the city there are about 30 hospital corporations acquired by the bounty of pious persons for the use of poor scholars and sick persons . . . Amongst others in Blackfryers is the Scotish Hall to which of Scotish men within and about London about 250 give a penny a week for the porter and increase of the stock for maintaineing any poor Scotishmen recommended by the minister and churchwardens of the parish he lives in, that he be troublesome to no Englishman in disparagement of his own nation. This House has a Master and two Wardens. The principal benefactor is Mr James Kinnyer a Scottishman (a weaver and after a Merchant) who bestowed 250 sterl. besides what he did in his own time . . . Almost all Scotishmen that frequent London are benefactors . . This Mr Kennyer appointed that still on St James Day the whole congregation should take a bowl of wine and drink in remembrance of the Scotish man and Welch woman who was Mr K Wife, which they yearly and cheerfully perform'.

The Scotch Hall remained the headquarters for the next hundred years; but before long the 'six tenements' were probably let or sold, for an interesting reason. It had been intended to use them, as the Charter authorised, 'for the maintenance of old or decaying artificers of the Scottish nation, and for training up their children in manual occupations', and to run them, as a later report says, 'in the manner of work-houses or alms-houses'. But 'experience having soon convinced them of the impropriety of separating married persons from their families', and Scottish self-respect taking unkindly to such institutionalised living-conditions, the Governors adopted the then novel practice of helping their needy clients to maintain themselves in their own homes.

'Discreet men' those Govenors indeed were, for they could judge where even that might not be the best form of help. John

33

Macky, whose three-volume record of his journeys throughout North and South Britain sheds much light on the life and customs of 1723, refers to 'the Scottish Nation having a Hall in Black-fryars, for relieving their indigent Countrymen, and providing them with necessary sums for carrying them into their own Country'[6]. Over the centuries the Royal Scottish Corporation must have relieved nearly a million London Scots, either in their own homes or by paying their passages back to Scotland.

The Corporation moved from its decaying Blackfriars building in 1782, selling the property to the City of London and with the proceeds purchasing 'certain Freehold Premises at the north end of Crane Court, Fleet Street, well-known by the name of The Apartments of the Royal Society'. The Royal Society had just moved to its new home in Somerset House, leaving, as the name of its principal hall, that of its principal founder, Isaac Newton. Newton Hall will appear again in this story of the Kirk in London. In Crane Court Dr Johnson was a near neighbour. One wonders whether the Great Lexicographer, in the last two years of his life, commonly passed the time of the day with his new neighbours; and if so whether the contact might have per-suaded him to withdraw, or to emphasise, his chaffing remark to Boswell: 'Sir, it is not so much to be lamented that Old Eng-land is lost, as that the Scotch have found it!'

There was in fact an undertone of seriousness behind that complaint. The Scot in London had to face a strong element of suspicion, couple with resentment, on the part of the Lon-doner of those days. The Union of the Parliaments had brought an increasing flood of Scots to the metropolis; three Jacobite rebellions had not sweetened the relationships between the two peoples; and English traders and merchants were less than pleased to find themselves faced by the lively competition, on equal terms, of their Scottish counterparts. As late as 1771 Boswell recorded the hostile reception accorded to two High-land officers when they took their place in a Covent Garden theatre. 'No Scots!', roared the mob in the gallery; 'Out with them!', and pelted them with apples[7]. It was a function of the Royal Scottish Corporation, as of the Scottish National Churches in London, not only to help those who suffered material loss through that hostility but also to promote a better understanding on both sides. That prevention is better than cure has always been the practice as well as the precept of the Corporation.

The Crane Court building was destroyed by fire in 1880, and in its place arose a fine new building, whose characteristically Scottish crow-stepped gable, with a noble lion-rampant crowning its peak, made it the easily-recognisable centre of Scottish charity during the next hundred years. Now, these premises having been found unnecessarily large for the changed conditions in which the work is administered, they have been sold for a good price, giving the increased capital resources for modern development. The new headquarters, in King Street, Covent Garden, were opened by the Queen Mother in 1975. There, in a fine hall, the Corporation's able-bodied pensioners gather every month for a short service, a substantial lunch, the distribution of pensions, and many an exchange of memories about the hills of home, the wynds or closes, the lands or platties, and the scenes and friendships which belong to the homeland. The 'dour Scot' has a strong element of sentiment, however concealed, in his make up, and the desire to hear the couthy tongue of his native land may become a longing as strong as David's for a draught of 'the water from the well of Bethlehem that is by the gate'. Alexander Gray has spoken for many a London Scottish exile: —

> Wae's me to think on't, but your weary feet
> May wander up and doon a hail year through,
> And never in the towmond will you meet
> A chield that's sib to ane that's sib to you.[8]

But in London's two Church of Scotland congregations, and in The Royal Scottish Corporation, you almost certainly will.

Two interesting relics of the older buildings have been incorporated into the present one — the inscribed stone from the wall of the Blackfriars Hall, and the Caroline royal coat of arms from Crane Court, with the heraldic emblazonment of the 1665 Charter.

For three centuries the work of the Corporation has centred mainly on helping people in their own homes. It has about 250 pensioners, receiving modest but helpful pensions, and about 150 others at any one time getting occasional help to tide them over difficulties of various kinds. All this is backed up by visits from six welfare workers, whose knock at the door is the welcome herald of that personal contact which adds the assurance of human interest and concern to the necessary formalities of material help. Even in the discussion of problems brought to the office by Scots in casual difficulty, where shrewd judgement of the story of woe and a comprehensive grasp of all the aids which social security provides are necessary if the Corporation's funds are to be responsibly used, this element of personal interest in maintained. 'The value of any charity', said the Queen Mother in opening the new premises 'is not only the degree to which it meets the demands of those in need, but rather the quality of love engendered in meeting that need'.

Now, in this latter half of the twentieth century, an old problem has emerged in a new form. A fresh Scots invasion has created it. The high incidence of unemployment, discord at home, social maladjustment, the attractions of the glamorous metropolis, the liberties of anonymity in a far country, or the hopes of a well-paid job — these pressures and attractions have brought many young people to London. One third of these, as a recent survey has shown, are from Scotland. Arriving with very little money, no firm arrangement about work, and small understanding of the difficulty of finding somewhere to stay, too many of them are quickly involved in the webs of petty crime, prostitution, and the drug scene. Concerned about this problem, six voluntary agencies closely involved in trying to help young drug addicts, alcoholics and 'west-end regulars' set up an organisation named Centrepoint[9], with the aim of helping young arrivals to evade such traps. This was preventive social medicine of the most fundamental kind, but necessarily limited by the length of time, three nights, during which these newcomers could be accommodated.

The Scottish Corporation, well aware that it takes little time for a homeless, penniless, workless young man or woman to drift into the hands of the drug and vice trafficers, and sensitive also to the comments of London magistrates on the number of young Scots who appear before them, was equally active. Now with its recently expanded capital resources its Governors have found themselves able to go further, in application of the principle that prevention is better than cure. They have taken over premises which St Columba's Church of Scotland maintained for over half a century as a hostel for young Scots business and professional women in London. Retaining the name of St Columba's House, and engaging a staff consisting of warden and two trained social workers, they are able to accept for a period of up to three months as many as 37 young Scots who need only this longer-term help to find their feet and establish themselves in London. Those who are unlikely to be able to do so will already have been identified and — if they are willing — 'provided with necessary sums for carrying them into their own country', or for transferring them to some other area where they will be less at risk.

At the other end of the age-range another new development has been made possible. The proportion of old folk in the community has much increased during the last two decades, and despite the provisions of the welfare state there is much need for the kind of care which the Corporation knows how to offer. Premises in north London have recently been secured and modified to house some fifty older people in sheltered conditions and with qualified care.

Three and a half centuries after The Scots Box was fashioned those generous givers whose regular contributions keep the working funds of the Royal Scottish Corporation in order are worthily maintaining the tradition to which it is committed by its seal. That seal bears around its margin the words of the Beatitude in Matthew 5:7 — BEATI MISERICORDES QUONIAM IPSIS MISERICORDIA TRIBUETUR — *Blessed are the merciful, because mercy shall be shown to them.*[10]

NOTES

1. *An Answer to Letters written by Scottish Gentlemen in His Majesties Dominions beyond the Seas, to the Master and Governors of the Scottish Corporation and Hospital in London, giving a true Account of the Erection of the said Company and its Progress from the Year 1663 to 1677, for the Satisfaction of such as desire that Information,* p. 2.
2. At least five ministers of the Scots Kirk in London have been Fellows of the Royal Society.
3. The Scottish Hospital of the Foundation of Charles the Second is otherwise variously known as The Scotch Hall, The Scottish Hospital, and The Royal Scottish Corporation.

The Scots Kirk in London

4. *An Answer, &c*, p. 3 — whence also the quotations following.
5. Robert Kirk, *Sermons, Conferences, Mens Opinions of the later transactions Ann 1689 written when the Irish Bible was printed in a final Roman letters there by Mr Ro Kirke minr of Aberfoyle in Menteith who then attended the press.* (Edinburgh University Library, MS, Shelfmark La III 545). Kirk had already put the Psalms into Gaelic in metrical form. His 1690 Gaelic Bible, the printing of which occasioned his London visit, being an edition of Bedell and O'Donell's Irish translation, was superseded by another of Scottish and Presbyterian origin a century later. His London visit, recorded in neat clear writing in this little commonplace book, brought him into interesting contact with such well-known figures as Baxter and Lob the Independents, Vincent Alsop the Presbyterian, Dr Tennison of St Martin's, Dr Tillotson of St Paul's, and Dr Stillingfleete of Lincoln's Inn Chapel ('I did sit that day in his pue; he also gave me 10 Guineas to assist the printing of the Bible in Irish'). His comments on their sermons and his conversations with them are extensive and illuminating.
6. John Macky, *Familiar Letters from a Gentleman to his Friend Abroad*, i, 287.
7. James Boswell, *London Journal, 1762-3*, pp. 71-2. The play was *Love in a Village,* and was sufficiently popular to be still playing in Covent Garden Theatre in April 1779 when a notorious murder took place as the audience left for their carriages. The victim was Margaret (or Martha) Keay, daughter of a Covent Garden staymaker who was probably a member of the Scots Kirk in Crown Court. Her murderer, a jealous suitor, who failed to kill himself with his second pistol, was the Rev. James Hackman. He was committed to Newgate by Sir John Fielding, step-brother of Henry Fielding the novelist and creator of the Bow Street Runners, tried before Mr Justice Blackstone, author of the famous *Commentaries on the Laws of England*, and hanged at Tyburn on 19th April, 1779. *(Gentleman's Magazine*, vol. 49, 7th & 14th April, 1779, and R. Angus Downie, *Murder in London*, p. 20f.)
8. Alexander Gray, *Babylon in Retrospect*, last verse. ('Towmond' = Twelvemonth).
9. See Chapter twenty, note 11.
10. The Latin is that not of the Vulgate but of Theodore Beza's translation, which was largely used for the 'Breeches Bible', the English version mentioned in Chapter one, note 13.

38

CHAPTER 4

The Eighteenth Century Scottish Church Connection in London

Between 1660 and 1800 Founders' Hall was joined by at least eleven other London congregations with a Scottish connection. Some of these had originally been English Presbyterian but later came to be represented on the Scots Presbytery of London and should therefore be noticed here.

1. One source of information is the 'Tabular View of the Scottish Presbytery of London' referred to in chapter two. The second congregation listed there is 'St Andrews', which is shown as having been 'Formed in Broad Street, St George in East, about 1660 by English Presbyterians'. It was known first as 'Mr Muir's Meeting House', later, by its location, as 'Broad Street, Wapping', or 'Broad Street, St George's, Middlesex', and afterwards as 'Shakespeare's Walk, Shadwell'. While still in Broad Street, it 'became a Scotch congregation in 1741 — removed afterwards to Shakespeare's Walk under Revd. Dr Rutledge'. It moved in 1823 from that location to a site 'near the Commercial Road', which was 'leased from the London Hospital for 99 years'. There it remained until the congregation dissolved in 1890, known variously as **St Andrew Scottish National Church, Stepney'**, 'St Andrew's, Whitechapel', 'St Andrews near the London Hospital', or simply 'St Andrew's, Stepney'. Its best-known minister was Dr Rutledge, who became one of the most prominent Scottish ministers in London and was an influential figure in the Presbytery. The backbone of the congregation seems to have the community of Scottish seamen and their families, who were numerous in the Wapping-Shadwell-Stepney area until steam supplanted sail. John Crombie succeeded Dr Rutledge in 1819. Under Alex McGlashan, who followed him in 1842, St Andrew's remained in the Church of Scotland connection at the Disrup-

39

tion the year after, although not without the loss of many of its members and elders. Six ministers followed in the next 34 years, and during the ministry of the seventh, Dr Souttar, the congregation dissolved in 1890. The remnant then joined John Knox Presbyterian Church of England which had been formed by a large group of St Andrew's members after the Disruption in 1843. We shall encounter St Andrew's in its closing years in chapter eleven.

2.   Another early English Presbyterian congregation which was later connected with the London Scots Presbytery was **Silver Street**. It had been gathered by the famous Dr John Howe and licensed under the Indulgence of 1672. Howe was a conspicuous figure amongst the nonconformists of his day. He had been ordained in strongly-Presbyterian Lancashire at the hands of the Rector of Winwich and his parochial co-adjutors. 'There are few ministers', Howe used to say, 'whose ordination has been so truly primitive as mine, having been devoted to the sacred office by a primitive bishop and his officiating presbytery'. While in Exeter soon after being ejected in 1662 he learned that there was a process against him and found himself brought before the Bishop of Exeter. The bishop was disposed to be friendly, and tried to persuade him to 'regularise' his status. 'What hurt is there in being re-ordained?', he asked. 'Hurt?', said Howe; 'it is shocking; it hurts my understanding. for nothing can have two beginnings . . . I can't begin again to be a minister. I *am* a minister of Christ!'

    Howe and his congregation somehow survived the last sixteen years of Stewart rule, and earned even the respect of the conformists, for in James VII and IIs time members of the Church of England acknowledged that when the king's orders ran counter to the law of the land, as when he offered some relief to dissenters in 1687, that relief was refused because James had dissolved Parliament in order to be able to offer it. 'At this conjucture', says Macaulay, 'the Protestant Dissenters of London earned for themselves a title to the lasting gratitude of their country. With noble spirit they arrayed themselves side by side with the members of the Church [of England] in defence of the fundamental laws of the realm. Baxter, Bates and Howe distinguished themselves by their efforts to bring about this coalition'[1] .

40

The Eighteenth Century Scottish Church in London

When the Glorious Revolution brought William and Mary to the British thrones a deputation of about ninety members of The Three Denominations waited upon them to present an address of congratulation, having chosen Dr John Howe to be their spokesman. He found himself spokesman for two other parties during the next few years.

In 1690, taught by twenty-eight years of common suffering, the Presbyterian and Independent bodies in London came together in what was known as *The Happy Union*. Unfortunately this alliance lasted only four years, owing to a theological dispute which polarised along denominational lines[2]. The Independents withdrew from the Fund which the Presbyterians had originated in 1689 'for the training of ministers, the aid of weak churches, and the extension of the Gospel', and barred Dr Williams from taking his turn at the Merchants' Weekly Lectures which together the two denominations had inaugurated in Pinners Hall. 'The Happy Union' in London broke up, and the Presbyterians took sole responsibility for the Fund, and established their own Merchants' Lectures in Salters' Hall. Howe's part in this unhappy affair was that of a reconciler, and although the *Pacificatory Paper* of which he was a co-author failed to heal the breach it took some of the heat out of the dispute. The consequences, however, were grievous for both sides, making more extreme the divergent views on the relationship of the Law and the Gospel, and tending towards the even more divisive 'Subscriptionist' controversy of 25 years later[3].

Dr Howe was involved in another controversy, of which a member of his Silver Street congregation was the centre. This was Sir Thomas Abney, who was Lord Mayor in 1710, as two other Presbyterians had been before him. Like them, on official occasions he attended the Church of England as an occasional conformist, although remaining a staunch Presbyterian. In Daniel Defoe's view this was an unacceptable compromise, and he re-issued his *Enquiry into Occasional Conformity,* with a preface addressed to John Howe.[4]

Sir Thomas Abney's name deserves further mention. In 1712 he and Lady Abney took the great hymn-writer, Dr Isaac Watts, who had had to retire from Mark Lane Meeting-house because of ill-health, into their home. There he continued to be their guest until his death in 1748, and there he wrote many of the hymns which are still so deservedly popular. From their first appearance these hymns 'did much to sweeten relations between Anglicans and Dissenters'. To this 'father of English hymnody' Scotland also owes a number of *Scottish Paraphrases,* including No. 54, 61, 63 and 66. Abney Park cemetery now occupies what was Sir Thomas's estate in Stoke Newington.

Silver Street's Scottish connection began when its minister, William Smith, in 1772 or earlier, became a member of the Scottish Presbytery in London. At least two meetings of the Presbytery were held in Silver Street, and Smith himself was Moderator in 1778 and again in 1785.

3.   By the latter date William Smith had moved to **Camberwell** where, next to his own house which he ran as a flourishing academy, he built a meeting-house. There he was assisted, and later succeeded, by a remarkable man, David Bogue. Bogue was a Berwickshire man, and one of a pioneering quartet of Scottish ministers whose full story must wait until chapter seven; but he has a claim to individual mention, for with James Bennett he wrote, between 1802 and 1812, an invaluable *History of Dissenters.* He was closely associated with Robert Haldane of Airthrey, who sold his family estate to provide funds for Bogue to go to India as a missionary. The East India Company managed to defeat that intention, and Bogue accepted an invitation to become minister of an Independent congregation in Gosport.

The Camberwell Meeting-house continued under two following ministries, until 1824. We may note, although it is not strictly within the limits of the Church of Scotland story, that the Haldanes' followers had constituted a congregation in Cateaton Street, of which in 1806 William Ballantine, who had studied under Bogue in Camberwell, was minister. His successor in the following year, James Mitchell, felt called to a wider evangelistic ministry, and, according to Walter Wilson[5] in 1808, was then 'itinerating through England under sanction of Mr Haldane'.

4.   A congregation, which later moved to Hanover Street, Long Acre, once worshipped in a meeting-house in **Drury Lane**. There, in 1687, it called Albert Hume to be its mini-

ster. Hume, a Scotsman, had been chaplain to the Duke of Lauderdale. In 1643, he was a lay commissioner to the Westminster Assembly, and in 1647 was ordained by members of the English Presbyterian Fourth London Presbytery. In 1653 he became minister of Whittingham, was ejected in 1662, formed a Presbyterian Meeting in Bishopsgate Street Without, and was separated from that by the passing of the Five Mile Act. Next we find him in Drury Lane where he ministered until his death in 1707, when his funeral sermon was preached by Robert Fleming of Founders' Hall. His immediate successor was Jabez Earle, and he preached the funeral sermon at Founder's Hall in 1729 for John Cumming, who had followed Fleming as minister there. We shall meet Jabez Earle in the next chapter. A later minister, after the congregation had moved to Hanover Street, was John Lee, who was 'ordained in 1804 by the Presbytery of Edinburgh to Hanover Street Presbyterian Church, Long Acre'[6], and was afterwards Principal of the University of Edinburgh.

5. One Scottish National Church, 'date of original formation unknown but existed in Glasshouse Street same parish previous to 1709 when it removed to the Old Church in **Swallow Street** which was taken down and rebuilt in 1799'[7], continued to flourish until the end of the nineteenth century. It was gathered by James Anderson, consisting 'of such persons of his own nation as resided at the west end of the town', and when they moved to the former French church in Swallow Street in 1710 they were joined by another Swallow Street Presbyterian congregation, of which Richard Baxter had been minister after his eviction from Oxendon Street.

James Anderson was a man of forceful character, and was soon acknowledged as a leader of the Presbyterian cause in London, becoming known as 'Bishop Anderson' amongst his fellow-Scotsmen. We shall meet him again in the next chapter. In 1734 he disagreed with his elders and took a number of his flock to form a new congregation in **Lisle Street**, where it continued with fair success, later removing to **Peter Street**, Soho, where it dissolved in 1814. From a sermon he preached in 1712 on Jeremiah 8:15 — *We looked for peace, but no good came; and for a time of health, and behold trouble!* — we may judge both the trials of the times and the quality of the preacher. God, he declared, is no idle spectator, like a clock-maker or architect. He is involved in His creation. He is not only goodness and mercy; He is holy and just. This is to be remembered in our provocation, when we look for peace after a long time of political disorder. There are those who long to return to the house of bondage; those who retreat into the shelters of scepticism or deism; those who indulge in vice and immorality to the extent that we must now have Societies for the Reformation of Manners; and even amongst protestants there are those who would go back to the authoritative absolut-ism of priests and the requirements of auricular confession and are prepared to do evil that good may come. Against such weak-nesses, in a time of disappointment, said Dr Anderson, we must summon the strength which comes from remembering the God who is holy and just, good and merciful, and present with man His creature. We must repent of the sin and guilt of our land; we must set ourselves towards personal reformation; and we must draw near to the throne of grace, for mercy and for help in time of need.

After Dr Anderson's departure another Aberdonian, William Crookshank, was called to Swallow Street. He left under a cloud 33 years later, but his ministry was distinguished. In 1749 he published a useful abridgement in two volumes of Robert Wodrow's 'voluminous work relating to the oppression of the Scotch nation under the unprincipled government of the Stuarts'. He was made a Doctor of Divinity shortly thereafter. Tobias Smollett was a friend of his, and 'A Funeral Sermon on the Death of Miss Jane Crookshank, a Pleasant and Hopeful Child, who died June 20, 1745, aged 3 years, preached by William Crookshank, A.M., at Swallow Street, St James, West-minster, 23rd June, on 2 Kings iv:26', and printed that year, is prefaced by *A Poem,* by Mr Smollett. A footnote to Crook-shank's ministry was added in 1826 when the election of William Woodrow to Swallow Street was questioned in a case which eventually went to court to settle whether or not the congregation should be disbanded. Woodrow had been elected by the subscribers, and not by the members. Crookshank, it was claimed, had been irregularly ordained 90 years before, 'not by Presbytery'. Such irregularities were contrary to Church of

Scotland procedure. But Woodrow was in the end duly ordained and the congregation's existence sustained. As for Crookshank's ordination in 1735 it is on record that the Rev. James Gordon preached on I Timothy iv:6, the Rev. James Galloway of Southwark preached the Sermon, and the Rev. Samuel Say, the notable minister of Long Ditch (later renamed Princes Street) English Presbyterian congregation in Westminster, gave the charge. James Gordon, minister of Alford, Aberdeenshire, was that year the Moderator of the General Assembly — and in fact a frequent visitor to London and an assiduous encourager of the Scottish National Churches in England. Presumably the presence of the Moderator would have been accepted as legitimising the ordinance in those days when strict Presbyterian procedure still had to be relaxed in the interest of interdenominational encouragement.

Crookshank's successor, Dr Trotter, remained for forty years. In 1796 William Nicol became his assistant, continuing as sole minister after Trotter's death in 1808 until his own in 1821. Dr Nicol, as he became, is linked with the life of the Kirk in London today by an interesting incident which occurred in 1812.

In that year a well-known, not to say notorious, lady of the Scottish nobility was living round the corner in the Pulteney Hotel, Piccadilly. Her Grace the Duchess of Gordon was a somewhat flamboyant soul, of inexhaustible energy. Her genial husband had become impatient with her appetite for social diversions and had departed, leaving her with little money for her accustomed gaieties. In 1808 her son Edward died. Soon afterwards she was returning to London from another deathbed when her coach passed a foot-traveller going in the same direction. She bade her coachman stop and have the traveller sit beside him in the dickey. The coachman soon tired of his 'sombre conversation', and found some excuse at the next stop to have him transferred to the coach with the Duchess. She was profoundly moved by the similarity of the views he expressed to those of her dead son. Her passenger was in fact one of Robert Haldane's missionaries[8]. Was his name, one wonders, James Mitchell? The message of the Haldanes was eagerly heard in those areas of Scotland where the cauldrife 'Moderate' preaching had left unsatisfied the people's needs for the Good News of God. No doubt the Duchess found something in her passenger's message which similarly filled an empty place in her own heart. When she fell ill in 1812 she sent a message to the little Scots Kirk around the corner in Swallow Street, and on Dr Nicol's arrival 'she earnestly desired the Communion of the Lord's Supper. He hesitated, but being satisfied of the sincerity of her repentance he assembled a few friends, and after a faithful admonition, addressed more especially to her, gave the Holy Supper to them all'. Before her death shortly afterwards she 'bequeathed a service of Communion Plate to his church', and the inscription on the two flagons now in use in St Columba's, Pont Street, records this gracious act[9].

During the next half century there were eight ministries in Swallow Street, and latterly a swift decline in its membership, which brought its contribution to the work of the Kirk in London to a close in the early '80s.

6.   In the church of St Giles, Cripplegate, the ministry of the Rev. Dr Samuel Annesley came to an end when he was ejected under the Act of Uniformity in 1662. The Indulgence of 1672 enabled him to take out licenses for himself and his Presbyterian Meeting-house in **Little St Helen's, Bishopsgate.** There, amongst his people, he numbered Daniel Defoe's father. He was a man of means, and although his goods were distrained for keeping a conventicle, enough remained to enable him to continue helping those in need. He died a man poor in worldly goods, but rich in his offspring. Before his death in 1696 the twenty-fifth and last of these, Susannah, had already been married for some time to the Rev. Samuel Wesley, Vicar of Epworth. It was in 1703 that their fifteenth child was born, a boy, whom they named John; and there are those who trace some of the distinctive features of Methodism to the influence on John and Charles of their redoubtable presbyterian mother, Susannah. Little St Helen's was originally an English Presbyterian congregation, but established a connection with the Scots Kirk some time before 1772, when its Aberdeen-born minister, George Stephen, was a member, and in 1776 Moderator, of the Scots Presbytery of London. Little St Helen's dissolved in 1790.

7. The Rev. James Galloway, whom we shall meet in the next chapter, was in 1698 minister of a church in **Parish Street, Horsleydown.** He baptised Patrick Russell's first child and preached the sermon at the ordination of William Crookshank of Swallow Street in 1735[10]. After his death in 1727 he was succeeded by Samuel Baker, who was followed in 1748 by John Henry[11]. When Henry returned to Scotland in 1749 he was assisted by a grant of £1 1s. from the Scotch Church in Crown Court.[12]

8. A Scottish congregation in **Hammersmith** appears in the Presbytery minutes in 1772, and its ministers seem to have taken an active part in Presbytery affairs, George Turnbull, for example, being Moderator in 1781. It has not been possible to discover anything about its origins, history, or the occasion of its dissolution, other than that it had disappeared before 1834.

9. Similarly it is known that there was a Scots congregation in Spitalfields, located on **Crispin Street** at Artillery Lane — or at least that its minister from 1788 to 1789 was a member of the Scots Presbytery and that the Presbytery met there on some occasions. That minister was John Love, whom we shall meet in chapter seven. It is recorded that when he departed for Glasgow he left his shoes in the pulpit for a testimony against those who would not hear him. (Luke ix:5)

10. Another member of the Scots Presbytery, from 1760 to 1796, was James Fordyce. He was minister of the English Presbyterian congregation in **Monkwell Street, Cripplegate,** where the Presbytery held at least two of its meetings during his ministry. The Monkwell Meeting-house had been built by the Rev. Thomas Doolittle, ejected Rector of St Alphage, and it was the first such place of worship erected after the Act of Uniformity. Naturally, being illegal, it was the scene of many dramatic incidents. On one occasion a company of soldiers threatened to shoot Mr Doolittle if he persisted in the service, but were abashed by his calm and courageous bearing. He was also the first to open an academy for training young ministers,

and his original college at Islington, opened in 1672, had twenty-eight students in residence when it was closed by force in 1685[13].

11. William Rutherford was minister of a Scots congregation in **Uxbridge** from 1773 to 1795, and was Moderator of Presbytery in 1779. His attendance at Presbytery is not recorded after 1787, and nothing further is known about the congregation.

12. A 1689 Presbyterian congregation in **Woolwich** became part of the Scots Presbytery in 1792 when Daniel Turner, who had been its minister in New Road, Woolwich since 1775, petitioned to be admitted. He was followed by John Bryce in 1796, after whom came Alexander J. Scott in 1831. Scott's career is of particular interest. Son of Dr Scott of the Middle Church, Greenock, he preached his first sermon in Rhu, 'to the peculiar delight' of the minister there. That minister was J. Macleod Campbell, one of Scotland's great theologians, whose book, *The Nature of the Atonement*, was an outstanding contribution to the subject, and whose spiritual discernment was acknowledged even by his bitterest theological adversaries. In 1828 Scott was again in Rhu, where his sermons on I Corinthians 12, concerning spiritual gifts, led to manifestations of 'tongues' which played a part in the development of Edward Irving's pentecostal convictions[14], although Scott himself was doubtful of the spiritual value of the Rhu phenomena. He was for a time Irving's assistant in Regent Square Scotch Church. He was called to Woolwich in 1831, but was refused ordination because he could not sign the Westminster Confession of Faith[15]. The Presbytery of Paisley, which had licensed him, charged him with heresy and deprived him of his license to preach, but his people supported him and he continued in Woolwich, with a large following, until in 1838 he was appointed Professor of English Language and Literature in University College, London. In 1850 he became Professor of Hebrew, and the first Principal, of Owen's College, Manchester. Thomas Erskine of Linlathen characterised him as the noblest man he knew. F.D. Maurice inscribed his *Mediaeval Philosophy* to him. George Macdonald, who spoke of his perfect command of English, dedicated his first novel, *Robert Falconer,* to him and included two poems in his honour in his *Poetical Works*.

Scott was succeeded at New Road by W.M. Thomson, who

for a number of years was also Secretary of the London Board of the Society for Propagating Christian Knowledge in the Highlands and Islands of Scotland. It was in the Woolwich Scotch Church that the Presbytery held its fateful meeeting on 13th June, 1843, when six congregations left the Church of Scotland connection. Thomson's was one of these, and thereafter it was the New Road Church of the Presbyterian Church in England.

It is already obvious that denominational barriers were low and that the 18th century Scots Presbytery of London embraced congregations of Secession and English Presbyterian heritage, requiring only assurance as to the regularity of their ministers' ordination. A 1792 *List of Churches and Chapels of Ease, &c* shows, under 'Scots Churches', **Bow Lane, Cheapside**, and **Wells Street, Oxford Street**. Both of these were Secession congregations[16], and their ministers, George Jerment and Alex Waugh (whom we shall meet again in chapter seven) appear in the Scots Presbytery minutes and as signatories to an important Declaration issued by the Presbytery to make its theological and ecclesiastical position clear in 1793[17]. Other non-Scottish-National-Church ministers who signed were Robert Crawford, minister of the Presbyterian Meeting in **Deal, Kent**, and Alex Easton, another Secession minister whose congregation was then worshipping in **Red Crosse Street, Cripplegate**. Crawford was in fact a member of the Special Committee which drew up the Declaration, although on the sederunt of Presbytery meetings he is recorded as a visitor except on one occasion where he appears amongst the members. Easton's congregation was formed from members of Dr Waugh's who found Oxford Street too far from their homes and to whom Waugh had ministered as a second congregation until he secured Easton's help. Easton was ordained on September 17th, 1792, by the Scots Presbytery, Drs Rutledge and Hunter and the Rev Messrs Steven, Love and Waugh officiating. His congregation moved three years later to a former Independent meeting house in **Miles Lane**, a name preserved in British hymnology by the tune which William Shrubsole wrote for his friend Edward Perronet's hymn, 'All hail the power of Jesus' Name'.

Two other Scots Churches appear in the list mentioned above — **Little Carter Lane, Old Change**, and **Gaelic, Lewisham**

West. Neither is mentioned in the Minute Book of the Scots Presbytery, and they must remain no more than names. Doubtless there were others which came into being during the eighteenth century and disappeared after a comparatively brief existence — perhaps to begin with because of the pressures of the law, and later because the little Scots colonies within which they had arisen began to move, in a second generation, to other areas. This certainly happened in the nineteenth century as a later chapter will briefly show. In all there have been more than twenty-four Scottish congregations in connection with the Church of Scotland in and around London during the last three hundred years, beside at least one Reformed Presbyterian congregation meeting in the Strand, and some fifteen or so associated with the Secession and later with the United Presbyterian Church. These last, uniting in 1873 with the Presbyterian Church in England, became the Presbyterian Church of England, which is now, since union with the Congregational Church, the United Reformed Church in England and Wales. Five of the others re-united with their parent congregations; seventeen have dissolved, six of the Scottish National churches went out at the Disruption, and the fate of the remainder is not known, apart from the three whose story, beginning in the next chapter, will occupy most of the rest of this narrative.[18]

NOTES

1. Macaulay, *op. cit.*, iii, 347. It was of Howe that a later writer advised: 'A young minister who wishes to attain eminence in his profession, if he has not the works of John Howe and can procure them in no other way, should sell his coat and buy them; and if that will not suffice, let him sell his bed and lie on the floor, and if he spend his days reading them he will not complain that he lies hard at night'. Quoted in *Under the Dome*, iv, 151 (1900).
2. See Appendix B.
3. See Appendix B.
4. An *Occasional Conformity Act* was eventually passed in 1711, inflicting severe penalties on any who received the Sacrament in the parish church but thereafter attended any conventicle. However, along with the *Schism Act* of 1713, which was aimed at depriving nonconformists of all their schools by allowing only a conformist to be a

tutor or teacher at any school, it was suspended, despite the strenuous opposition of both archbishops, immediately after Anne's death, and both were repealed in 1719.

5. Wilson, *op. cit.*, ii, 522.

6. *Fasti Ecclesiae Scoticanae*, vii, 497. Lee was added to the Roll of the London Presbytery in October, 1807. 'Jupiter' Carlyle, to whom Lee acted as amanuensis before going to London, referred to him in one of his last letters as 'a trusty friend and an able physician, an uncommonly good divine and an eminent preacher, all in the person of one young man whom I have taken to live with me'. (*Autobiography*, p. 602). On his death in 1805 Carlyle entrusted the MS. of his Autobiography to Lee. (*Dict. of Nat. Biography*, xi, 802f.; *Fasti*, i, 73).

7. *Tabular View of the Scottish Presbytery of London, 1834*. See Appendix D.

8. Robert and James Haldane of Airthrey (where the University of Stirling now stands), concerned by the neglect of Gospel-preaching by parish ministers in certain parts of Scotland, set up a *Society for the Propagation of the Gospel at Home,* and a College for evangelists. They were disowned by the Church; the General Assembly acted to exclude from the Church's pulpits any unqualified person, and enjoined Presbyteries to supervise all schools and forbid all 'vagrant teachers and Sunday Schools'. But the Haldaneites, whose successes lay in the parishes of the 'moderates', performed a real service in encouraging the growth of a lively evangelical concern within the Church's own ministry.

9. Alex Moody-Stuart, *Life and Letters of Elizabeth, last Duchess of Gordon*, pp. 50–52. Dr Moody-Stuart gives a sympathetic explanation for the previous Duchess of Gordon's feverish search for excitements and gaiety as dating from a day on her honeymoon when a letter from her previous fiance, who had been reported killed on the field of battle, reached her, informing her that he was on his way home to marry her. The Communion Plate referred to is described in J.M. Napier's *St Columba's — The New Building and the Old*, p. 27. Dr Moody-Stuart, a later generation of whose family is still represented on the Kirk Session and the membership of St Columba's, Pont Street, began his own ministry as Church of Scotland missionary on Holy Isle, Lindisfarne (see chapter one). The Gordon Highlanders were founded by the Duchess for her husband and son.

10. *Fasti*, iv, 292.

11. Wilson, *op. cit.*, iv, 278.

12. *Crown Court Session Minutes*, 1 Jan., 1748/49.

13. Drysdale, *op. cit.*, pp. 479ff. Dr Doolittle's license (MS 12.19 in Dr Williams' Library) for his meeting house in Monkwell (or Mugwell)

Street was taken out under the Indulgence. It reads, in part: 'In pursuance of our Declaration of the eleventh of March 1671—2 we . . . do allow of a certain room adjoining to the dwelling house of Thomas Doolittle in Mugwell Street to be a place for the use of such as do not conform to the Church of England, who are in the persuasion commonly called Presbyterian to meet and assemble in order to their public worship and devotion. . . All and singular are strictly charged and required to hinder any tumult or disturbing and to protect them in their said meeting and assembly. 2nd April, 24th year of our reign, 1672.'

14. See Chapter eight.
15. The acceptance of some of the articles of the 17th century Westminster Confession of Faith in their literal meaning presented many candidates for the ministry of the Church of Scotland in the 19th century with a dilemma of conscience. The United Presbyterian Church in 1879, and the Free Church in 1892, passed Declaratory Acts recognising 'diversity of opinion on such points of doctrine as do not enter into the substance of the Faith', in both cases reserving to the Church the right to determine what points fall within that description and thus to guard against injury from the abuse of that liberty. In the case of the Free Church the Act itself resulted in other injury, two ministers and 4,000 members in the Highlands seceding to form the Free Presbyterian Church in protest against that relaxation. The Church of Scotland, however, as then established, required Parliamentary sanction for any such action. This was at last granted by a clause appended to a Bill drafted for another purpose in 1905 (see Chapter thirteen); and in 1910 the phrase 'and that I believe the fundamental doctrines of the Christian Faith contained therein' was added to the formula in which ministers and elders subscribed the Confession of Faith. Today the re-united Church 'holds as its subordinate standard the Westminster Confession of Faith, recognising liberty of opinion on such points of doctrine as do not enter into the substance of the Faith, and claiming the right, in dependence on the promised guidance of the Holy Spirit, to formulate, interpret or modify its subordinate standards, always in agreement with the Word of God and the fundamental doctrines of the Christian Faith contained in the said Confession — of which agreement the Church itself shall be sole judge'. *The Book of Common Order* — Preamble to Services for Ordination of Ministers and Elders.
16. See Appendix C regarding the Secession Church.
17. See Appendix D.
18. Three congregations, with slight Scottish connections, have not been included because neither they nor their ministers appear in the Minutes

The Eighteenth Century Scottish Church in London

of the Scots Presbytery of London. The *Fasti*, vii, 497f, mentions the distinguished Aberdonian, Dr Alex. Crombie, LL.D., F.R.S., as having officiated at a Presbyterian Meeting-house in **Southwood Lane, Highgate**, from 1791–98 while running his well-known Academy there. *Fasti*, vii, 498, also shows J. Sutherland as the minister of a Presbyterian congregation in **Staines** from 1741–45. And an undated press-cutting pasted in a collection relating to Crown Court and other London Scottish churches, in the library of the United Reformed Church History Society, refers to a congregation in **Paddington**.

CHAPTER 5

'The Noblest Prospect which a Scotsman ever Sees'

The arrival of James VI in London had brought many Scots to the capital of England in 1603. The Union of 1707 brought very many more along 'the high road to England' and into what was now to be the Capital of Britain.

This Scottish invasion was greeted there with no enthusiasm. English traders resented the new Scottish competition permitted by the Union. Jacobite uprisings added suspicion to resentment. Contempt for the Scottish manner and accent added a third ingredient to the common attitude of latent hostility.

Not surprisingly, then, the Scot in London tended to present himself in what today would be called a low profile, although that in no way inhibited his get-ahead propensities. In some cases the first was contrived and the latter assisted by his taking on a protective colouration. Over fifty years after the Union James Boswell was taking tea in Mr Davies' bookshop in Russell Street when the great Dr Johnson entered. 'Don't tell him where I come from!', whispered Boswell; but 'He comes from Scotland', said Davies roguishly as he led him forward to be introduced. 'Mr Johnson, I do indeed come from Scotland', confessed Boswell, 'but I cannot help it' — to which Johnson returned the mordant comment: 'That, Sir, I find is what a great many of your countrymen cannot help!'[1] The English air of unassuming superiority in matters of accent, manners and ecclesiastical conformity has continued to persuade the Boswells of later years of the advantages of obsequious imitation. In 1827 the Scots Presbytery of London, in a pastoral letter, referred sadly to the fact that 'many of the great and noble members of our land have been drawn aside, not from conviction but from compliance, to the practices of the Church established in these parts (though we consider the Church of England a true sister and give her all honour in the Lord), which leads to diversity of feeling engendered between the upper and lower ranks in our land', and went on to lament the growth of such class-distinctions amongst people who in their own land had sat in equality around the Table and in the Courts of the Kirk[2]. And in 1833 the General Assembly in Edinburgh heard with sorrow of 'the great number of Scots, nobles and others, [who] stayed aloof from the Church of their fathers in England, not wanting to be thought dissenters'

Despite such temptations, however, there were Scots in London in 1707, noblemen, gentlemen and commoners, who at once looked for some place of worship where their religious principles were practised and the accents of their homeland could be heard. It would not have been difficult to find such a place, although its members might be labelled 'pantilers'[3] and its building have to be called a meeting-house and be inconspicuously sited in some side-street. There were the well-established Scotch churches in Founders' Hall and Glasshouse Street, beside those English Presbyterian congregations with Scottish ministers, and — if they had survived the last five years of Stewart rule — the 'Scotch Presbyterian Conventicle near the King's Printing House' and that other 'near the Scotch Hall'. There was also another, of obscure origin but convenient location to the main Scots colony along the Strand, which was just beginning to find its place in the religious life of London and which maintains that place purposefully and effectively to this day. Its first recorded home was in St Peter's Court, St Martin's Lane.

The obscurity of its beginnings arises from lack of early records and profusion of later traditions. One of these traditions, which seems to have originated no earlier than this century, ascribes the congregation's ancestry to the former Scottish Embassy chapel in Scotland Yard and claims for it the title 'The Kirk of the Crown of Scotland' on that account[4]. Kenneth Black, writing in 1910, quotes the 1838 *Report of the Commissioners appointed to Inquire into the State, Custody and Authenticity of Registers, etc.*, as giving 1700 for the Date of Foundation of the Congregation, and himself adds 'There is a persistent tradition that on the site [of the *later* building] there once stood a chapel, where, prior to the Union of the Crowns, the Scots Ambassadors to the English Court worshipped in accordance with their own form of Church service and Discipline'[5]. Walter Wilson, writing in 1810, says that the nucleus of the congregation was the remains of an older one that met in the same place and became extinct about the year 1710. 'Mr Gabriel Sangar, who was ejected from the parish of St Martin's', gathered a Presbyterian congregation in St Peter's Court and 'preached to them as often as the turbulent state of the times would allow', till his death in 1678. 'We only know that a Mr Humphreys was the last pastor'[6]. A manuscript of the London Churches states that that congregation dissolved in 1714, but Wilson queries this, claiming that some of the Scots congregation in Peter's Court had been members of the old congregation, and the former was certainly in existence before 1711.

Confronted with such a profusion and confusion of stories one is inclined to paraphrase Robert Lawson's comment on the similar tradition of the Founders' Hall Scotch Church, and to say 'Not to lay any stress on this unauthenticated circumstance, it is certain that' the Scottish congregation in St Peter's Court, St Martin's Lane was in being by 1711 and was being ministered to by the Revs. George Gordon and Patrick Russell.

It was a good address. St Martin's Lane was one of the few streets in 17th century London that had a paved footpath. It was known as 'the street with the pavement', and two of its Coffee Houses later became meeting-places for famous figures and pioneers in the worlds of art, finance and insurance. St Peter's Court was reached through an archway, and an outside stair in the Court gave access to the meeting-house above the archway.[7] There the two ministers led their flock in worship, and the record of the early days is preserved in what is simply headed *'The Book of the Congregation Meeting in Peter's Court, St Martin's Lane'* — hereinafter cited as *The Book*. It contains a record of Baptisms (1711—46), Collections (1713—19), Accounts (1713—40), Charities (1725—45), and Kirk Session Minutes (1714—16). The first baptism is that of Russell's son, Thomas, by 'the Rd mr James Galloway minr of the gospell in Southwark'[8]. George Gordon baptised Russell's second son, Patrick, on Feb. 10th, 1712/13[9]. At the head of the first page of baptisms the ministers' names are shown as George

The Book of the Congregation meeting in Peters Cour.t in St Martins Lane under the pastoral care of the Reverend Mr George Gordon & Mr Patrick Russell

The Index.

The names of the Members with their Subscriptions from fo 1. to fo 6.

The orders of the several Sessions held for the Government of the said Congregation —————— from fol 50 to fol 150

The Account of the Collections made in the said Congregation & how disposed of —————— from fo 150 to the end

The Terms on which the Members of this Congregation under the Care of Mr Gordon and Mr Russell are admitted

Doe in the Presence of God sincerly with full Resignation Professedly give up my self to the Lord promising through Divine Grace to follow after and cleave to the Lord Jesus and his holy Gospel as is professed in this Congregation to my lives end. To Honour Love and obey my Reverend Pastors Mr Gordon and Mr Russell to Maintain Incourage and strengthen their hands according to my ability To Maintain Love Concord and Harmony in the Congregation as becomes an obedient follower of Christ.

Title-page of the earliest volume of records of the Scots congregation which later moved to Crown Court; and, from another page, the profession made by its members.

Gordon and Patrick Russell. If that order is not due to alpha-
betical considerations — which do not appear to rule elsewhere in the book — it may be deduced that Gordon was the
senior and that Russell came as his colleague.

Little is known about Gordon, other than that he is said to
have been licensed in 1675 and ordained in London in 1695,
and that he died in 1714. Russell became sole minister thereafter, as appears from page 4 of *The Book* where Gordon's
name is scored out and no other inserted, and from the entry
recording the Session's decision that Mr Russell be appointed
sole minister as from June 27, 1714.

We know more about Russell. He was born in 1676, and
ordained by the Presbytery of Peebles as minister of 'the
Paroch of Drumelziar' in January, 1700. That Presbytery
deposed him in 1702, but he was reponed by the Synod of
Lothian and Tweedale in 1711, largely through the solicitations
of Dr James Anderson of Glasshouse Street, whom we met in
the previous chapter. It appeared from Anderson's letter to the
Synod that Russell had already been ministering, on the
strength of a Testimonial from the Presbytery of Peebles given
in 1704, 'as a Gospell minister to dispense the Word and Sacraments, under divers worthy ministers in South Britain'[10], so it
seems that his part in the affairs of 'the congregation meeting in
Peter's Court' began between 1704, when he arrived in London,
and 1709, when he petitioned for reponement.

There exists an account of the early years, written by John
Jones (1700–1770), upon which Walter Wilson's chapter seems
to have been based, and which describes accurately enough the
Church of Scotland discipline. 'This church appears to have
been established about the commencement of the 18th century,
upon the principles and governed according to the discipline of
the Church of Scotland, the exercise of which is vested in the
Minister and Elders by the choice of the People, the Duty of the
one being to labour in the word and doctrine, and of the others
to assist in the Government of the Church and to provide for
the relief of the poor members, for which purpose they meet
together at set times to regulate its concerns'[11].

The elders in Peter's Court were John Maxwell, who was both
Secretary (or Session Clerk) and Treasurer, John Macgie,
William Gray, and Thomas Martin. In 1713 John Macgie moved

The names of the Children who have been
Baptized in the meeting house and else where
by Mr Gordon and Mr Russell since Septr
first 1711 yeares

1711
Septr 3d mr Pat: Russell minr had a son baptized by
the Rd mr James Galloway minr of the gospell
in southwork named Thomas.

1712
Septr 7th mr George Glover shoe maker in newport street had
a daughter baptized named Euphan.

feb: 10th mr Patrick Russell minr had a son baptiz'd by his
1712 2/13 Rd mr: Geo: Gordon named Patrick

1713 mr James Russell perewige maker in vine street in
april 10 St. martins in the fields had a son baptiz'd name
Patrick

Septr 20 Hugo Thomson Taylor in westminster had a daughter
baptized named Mary

Octr 11th Mr Walker Taylor in Bedford berry had a daughter baptized named Isobella.

1713 1/14 Mr Tho: Cagon tobacconist att the foot of the
feb 7th hay market in St martins in the fields had a
son baptiz'd named Alexander

june 27 Mr William Done Taylor in Duke Court St martin
in the fields had a daughter baptized named Marga
ret

Novr 30 mr Andrew Hudson in Halloway in the paroch of Is
lington had a son baptiz'd named Andrew

Jan: 16 mr Adam Horry perewige maker in the passage to
round Court St martins in the fields had a son baptiz
named Gavin.

The first baptisms recorded in St Peter's Court, including those of two sons of one of
the ministers.

to Ireland, taking with him a Certificate of Transference to the sister-Church there, and the Kirk Session offered to the congregation, for their choice as new elders, the names of Charles Maxwell, Adam Campbell, and David Watson, who were elected and ordained in proper Presbyterian form, 'having solemnly promised to be faithful and diligent in all their duties of that holy and honourable employment of Elders of Christ's Church'.

It would appear that the Meeting-house was in poor condition, and in 1714 it became necessary to repair the roof. The question of building a place of their own was raised, but the congregation was far from affluent, as certain entries in *The Book* reveal. Some furnishings, including pews, a noble mahogany 'extinguisher' pulpit, Sacrament Table and Cloth, and a Dyall (clock), had been acquired for £4 from Plaisterers' Hall in Addle Street, where an Independent congregation had worshipped from 1666 to about 1700. A debt to 'the joyners and workmen that had been employed in fitting up the Meeting' with those furnishings had been paid by Gordon and Russell, who were still not reimbursed when Gordon died. With a struggle the congregation paid Gordon's widow, and in 1715 the Kirk Session recorded its agreement with Russell that 'the pulpit, pews, Dayell, Sacrament Table and Cloth to be solely the property of the congregation on payment of the debt of £21 15s. to him or his Executors and Administrators'[12]. In such circumstances of penury it would be necessary to depend on outside help for the building of a new church, and arrangement to solicit subscriptions must have been expeditiously made, for in 1718 a site was secured on the Duke of Bedford's estate in Covent Garden. The draft of the original lease, now missing, made out to Rev. P. Russell, J. Brown, J. Maxwell, W. Walsh, for 61 years from Michs 1718, specifies that within two years there was to be erected 'One Chappell House or place for Divine Worship the same to containe Twelve Ground Squares upon the fflatt or more and in height of walls 20 feet or more' at a cost 'of £400 of lawful money of Great Britain or more'. Further 'The Chappell to be built with good well burnt bricks and good mortar made with good lime and sand and no loam or black-earth mixt therewith saving that the rubish of the walls of the old buildings now standing on part of the said ground may be used therein being well mixt with Lyme'. Also specified were

The First House of the Royal Academy, St. Peter's court, St. Martin's lane

Prior to housing the Royal Academy the large room over the archway was the place of worship of the Scots congregation, which moved thence to Crown Court in 1719.
The Archives Department of the Westminster City Library

'all Rates Duties and assessments to the Church parish and poor Trophy money and Taxes on Windows and Lights'[13]. On March 29th, 1719, the congregation began the next phase of its life with the opening and dedication of their new building on a site described in the lease as 'All that piece and parcel of ground lying and being in the parish of St Martin in the ffields aforesaid abutting upon a Court then commonly called Crown Court'.

The former meeting-house cannot have been irreparable, for it became a meeting place for the artistic community then centreing around St Martin's Lane. It was soon occupied as a studio by Louis Francois Roubiliac, the Hugnenot sculptor, who founded there his Academy for the Improvement of Painters and Sculptors.[14] There he himself may have fashioned his statue of Newton in Trinity College, Cambridge, and his striking figure of Handel, represented with the score of *Messiah* in his hand which always attracts the rapt attention of the visitor to Westminster Abbey. His bust of 'Lady Grisel Baillie, Aetat 81' (see below) is still to be seen at Mellerstain. Later, according to Kenneth Black, the building housed William Hogarth's Drawing School. Hogarth lived nearby in Leicester Fields. Possibly it was in Peter's Court that he painted the pictures which he gifted to his friend Thomas Coram for the latter's Foundling Hospital. It was at a charity sale of paintings at the Foundling Hospital in 1758 that Hogarth and some of his friends conceived the notion of a Society of Artists, and their St Martin's Lane Academy became, ten years later, The Royal Academy of Arts[15]. Some of the planning may well have been done where Russell's congregation had once worshipped, and where much later a Quaker one was to worship.

The new building in Crown Court was indeed designed for worship, but the terms 'Meeting-house', 'Chapel', and 'The Meeting' continued, from custom, to be employed. It was in 1727 that *The Book,* for the first time, referred to it as 'The Church in Crown Court'.

The full cost of the building was £619 10s. 11d., 'less half-year's rent returned, £23 16s 9d.' Appeals for subscriptions had been made in Scotland as well as in London, and a list of

'The Noblest Prospect which a Scotsman ever Sees'

donors and their contributions, covering six foolscap sheets, was still extant in 1928 although its present whereabouts is unknown. Fortunately Dr Moffett reproduced some of its contents in early issues of the Crown Court Church Magazine[16]. 'The first page', he says, 'records the names of "The most noble the peers of North Britain who by Mr Russell's interest did contribute to him for building of the chappell in Crown Court in Russell Street, Covent gardine" '. Eleven of these, in sums of three, four and five guineas, gave altogether £48 06s. The 'Right Hon'ble the Gentlemen of ye House of Commons', listed on the following page, outdid them with a total of £55 5s. Other five pages record 'The names of strangers who have contributed. . .', amounting in number to about 200, and the last page lists 'Y^e inhabitants of ye city of Edinb: who etc', and includes, amongst the names of many famous representatives of Town and Gown, that of 'the Rev. Mr W. Wisheart, principall of ye College', whose son, later to succeed him as Principal, was for ten years the minister of Founders' Hall Scotch Church in London.

This document contains its own reminder of contemporaneous events. 'The most noble the peeres of *North Britain*' were so designated not (as has been said) because of the official disapproval in England of all things Scottish after the '15 rebellion, but in a genuine effort to make the Union effective by naming the two nations as geographical parts of the new united kingdom. South of the border that effort was soon abandoned, although N.B. for Scotland was still in postal usage this century when S.B. would have provoked only a puzzled frown on an English brow. For a while, however, South Britain was an acceptable synonym for England in both countries: in 1711, as we have seen, the Synod of Lothian and Tweedale heard of Russell's assistance 'to divers worthy ministers in South Britain', and in 1723 that indefatigable traveller, John Macky, writes of Scotland as 'a Nation which if encouraged hath as many natural Commodities for Exportation as any whatsoever, and more than South Britain'. (He adds the cryptic comment 'but a finer Education than what is necessary for Trade hath been the Misfortune of this Kingdom; but perhaps the Union with England may open their eyes to their own interest')[17].

The Forty-Five was still to come, but the third section of the subscription list contains the name of one whose part — and death — in the battle of Prestonpans has been described for us in 'Jupiter' Carlyle's *Autobiography*[18]. 'The Right Hon'ble Coll. Gardiner in Westminster', as the list describes him, had been a great rake, but was converted by reading a book called Gurnall's *Christian Armour,* given him by his mother years before and unopened until he curiously picked it up to pass the time before the hour of an assignation. His estate was in the parish of Prestonpans, and his monument can be seen on the south side of the railway line near that station as the London train approaches Edinburgh.

Travel between the capitals in those days was not a matter of hours but of days, and the address 'att ye blew anchor in little britain' appended to a number of the names of subscribers prompts the conjecture that that was the hostelry where the Edinburgh coach arrived and departed and that Mr Russell shrewdly visited it to catch arriving Scots and press his interest upon them as one of high priority.[19].

Sir Patrick Johnston, another friend of Crown Court, had been Lord Provost of Edinburgh in 1706, and as such was one of the thirty-one Scottish Commissioners who worked out and signed the terms of the Treaty of Union along with the English thirty-one. His popularity with the Edinburgh citizens suffered from his advocacy of the Union, and on one occasion they 'threw stones at his Windows, broke open his Doors, and searched his House for him, but he having narrowly made his Escape, prevented his being torn in a Thousand Pieces'[20]. His interest in Crown Court and its work was no passing one. By his Will he left £10 in 1736 'for the poor Scots in London', and Mr Russell's distributions of this are duly recorded in *The Book.*

It is in the list of the 'Right Hon'ble the Gentlemen of ye House of Commons' that we come across what is perhaps the most interesting amongst all the distinguished names of Mr

'The Noblest Prospect which a Scotsman ever Sees'

Russell's contributors — that of George Baillie of Jerviswood. Since one of his ancestors has already appeared in Chapter one, and one of his descendants in this century was to play a cardinal part at a critical point in the story of the Scots Kirk in London, a brief sketch of the life and character of this remarkable man is not out of place.

His father, Robert Baillie of Jerviswood (sometimes spelt Jerriswood), a great-grandson of John Knox,[21] had been imprisoned in Edinburgh Tolbooth in 1676 after rescuing his brother-in-law, a minister, from the hands of the notorious Captain Carstairs. Then in 1683 he had been charged in London with high treason because of alleged complicity in the Rye House Plot, and removed to Edinburgh for trial because under Scottish law not only his movable but also his heritable property could be forfeited if he was condemned. The sea journey at his age, and his Tolbooth imprisonment (of which his wife left a harrowing description), brought the old man to physical collapse; but his spirit was strong and he faced trial and execution with calm faith. His son George was present at his execution, and the experience 'ever after gave that grave, silent thoughtful turn to his temper which before was not natural to him'[22]. Soon thereafter, in the company of his father's close friend, Sir Patrick Hume of Polwarth, he escaped to Holland.

Sir Patrick's daughter, Grisell, cannot be omitted from the story. At the age of twelve she had taken her father's messages to Robert Baillie during his first imprisonment. After Baillie's execution Grisell, now 21, ingeniously hid her father, first in the family vault in Polwarth Church, and then in a 'hole in the earth' below a room in the family home, smuggling food to him from the family table until her young brothers remarked on her gargantuan appetite. Grisell was no ordinary girl.

When William of Orange and Mary his queen arrived to assume the throne in England, Sir Patrick Hume and George Baillie came with him. Jerviswood and the other family estate of Mellerstain were restored to Baillie, and Hume became Lord Polwarth of Redbraes. Baillie was made Receiver General of Scotland, and in 1691, at Redbraes, he married Grisell.

Lady Grisell Baillie's name is well known, both for her poetry and song and for her *Household Book*, a detailed record of the Baillie expenditures and a mine of information about customs

65

and costs in those days. For example: 'For Defo's Book in defence of the Union, £1 10s [Scots, which was 2/6 sterling]' 'For Naphtali a book, 1s' (see chapter two); 'For the thirteen days' journey to London with five passengers, £22 10s., with expenses of £10 (sterling)'; 'For stoping Grisie's teeth with leed, and some things to clean 'em, 10s. (sterling)'. Grisie was one of her two daughters.

Baillie sat in the Scottish Parliament for Berwickshire. He was an early subscriber to Paterson's *Company Trading to Africa and the Indies,* of which he became a director, and the English last-minute withdrawal from which led him to join the new Country Party, 'standing stiffly by the interests of his country'. He was much consulted during the Union negotiations, and was one of the selected members who sat for Scotland in the first British Parliament. To the first elected Parliament of 1708 he was returned for the county of Lanark, and retained that seat even when the Tory party was victorious in 1710. The treatment which then began to be meted out to Scotland and her Church gave him serious doubts about the value of the Union, but he refrained from working for its dissolution, in order to help to foil the avowed Tory intention of attempting the restoration of the Stewarts after Anne. On the accession of George I he was made one of the Lords both of the Admiralty and of the Treasury, staying in office until 1725, when he and other Scottish office-holders were turned out by Walpole 'for not being sufficiently subservient to the English view of Scottish policy'.

He had always been active in the affairs of the Church, and in London he 'continued steadily in his own Church and principles'. His experience at his father's execution, and his own sufferings, had taught him a compassion which extended even to his opponents when they were in misfortune. After the '15 rebellion, English feeling was strong against the Jacobites, and he had good reason to share that feeling, for 'the Highlanders had plundered several country gentlemen's seats, particularly the houses of John Pringle of Stichel and Mr Baillie of Jerviswood, carry'd away what peuther they could get to melt down for Bullets, destroy'd their corn, etc.' Nevertheless Baillie risked his popularity and the retention of his offices by a courageous plea in Parliament 'for mercy for the poor sufferers by the rebellion', saying that 'he had been bred in the school of affliction, which had instructed him in both the reasonableness and the necessity of showing mercy to others in like circumstances'. Lady Grisell's accounts show that actions matched words: 'To Laird of Wedderburn when in prison, £5'; to Mrs Whitfield, £1 1s, 6d.', and at least half-a-dozen other gifts to wives, widows and dependants of prisoners who had been captured or of those who had been killed at Preston.

Several of his household staff, to whom he was accustomed to present Bibles and copies of 'Thomas of Kempes', worshipped at Peter's Court and later at Crown Court. *The Book* shows, for example, '8s. paid at Christ. 1715 for a sitting[23] for Mrs Jean Firsaith', who appears in the Baillie *Household Book* as 'Jean Forsith, engaged at Whit. 1713', her wage then being £2 in the year plus the two pair shoes always included. The same sum for a sitting was paid for Kathrin Hart, who appears as Katharine Heart in *The Household Book,* where she was 'entered to be Laundry Maid and washer at Whit. 1714, her wage in the year is 34s., and her two pair shoes at 2s. a pair — £1 18s 4d.' For her journey to London by sea when the household moved thence in 1715 the fare was £1, 'victualls furnisht by the skiper'. Her wages were 'highted' to £3 in London from Candles. 1715, and again 'I highted her wages at Whit. 1717 to £5.'

Lady Baillie kept all the household's financial records. Items noted as 'To Poket' or 'To my Dear's Poket' refer to Baillie's personal spendings, which varied from five to eleven guineas a quarter. A number of entries show the family's generosity to building funds, or for the upkeep, of dissenting congregations in England and Ireland. One or two of these have interest for us here. 'To Mr Anderson's meeting house building', 'For collection to build Anderson's Meating House', and 'To Mr Anderson's Bathel'[24] all indicate a close connection with Dr James Anderson of Glasshouse and later Swallow Street, already mentioned. There are also contributions 'To Earle's Mitting House', and 'To Church Bathel in Mr Earle's Meeting House'. This would be the Rev. Jabez Earle, who had been tutored at Bethnal Green[25], and whose name appears, along with that of James Anderson and next to that of 'Patrick Russell, St Martin's Lane, Westminister' in John Evans' *List of Dissenting Congregations (1715– 29).* Earle's congregation had first worshipped in Little Eastcheap, then in Drury Lane where he succeeded Abraham Hume in 1707, and later it removed to Hanover Street, Long Acre. Earle was one of the 27 Presbyterian 'Subscribers' at the Salters' Hall Synod in 1719[26]. He became a Trustee of Dr Williams' Foundation in 1723, was awarded a D.D. both by Aberdeen (King's College) and Edinburgh Universities in 1728, and 'remained vigorous until his death, although latterly blind'. His funeral sermon was preached by the minister of Founders' Hall Scotch Church. He himself had been the preacher at the funeral of John Cumming, an earlier minister there.

The question remains: to which congregation were the Baillies attached while in London? One entry in *The Household Book* sheds obscurity rather than light on that question. 'For 3 seats in a Pew in King Street Chapell at Lady Day, ½ year, 18s.' and 'For a Piew in King Street Chapel a quar. at Michels, 9s.' The mystery deepens, for no such chapel with such an address appears in any surviving, accessible record. King Street in Covent Garden originally ran up to Bow Street, where it would face the south aspect of Crown Court Church, but in 1715—17 when the King Street entries appear the congregation was still in Peter's Court. Both Drury Lane and Long Acre where Earle's congregation worshipped run within a stone's throw of Crown Court, but he was never its minister.

There is no doubt, however, that Baillie servants belonged to Crown Court, nor that Baillie himself was a generous contributor to the building there. The Baillie records do much to help us to understand the life of those stirring times in which the Scottish National Church in Crown Court came into being. Baillie died in 1738, aged 75, and was buried at Mellerstain. 'At one and the same time he was a most zealous patriot, a very able statesman, and a most perfect Christian'[27].

Patrick Russell was the almoner of several legacies, as well as of the periodical 'collections for the poor', the detailed distribution of which were carefully inscribed in *The Book*. Not all Scots arrivals in London found the streets paved with gold, and probably the elders found the congregation's charitable resources the more heavily strained in the periods immediately following the '15 and '45 rebellions, when the Scot was *persona non grata* in England.

There was no doubt where the sympathies of the Scottish church lay in that matter. They were naturally anti-Jacobite. Many of them, both ministers and members, like Fleming and Baillie, had suffered persecution. None had any desire to see the Stewarts return. We read, in *The Book,* of Crown Court Session's appointment in 1716 'that Thursday, ye 26 of January instant, be kept as a day of humiliation and prayers for the suppression of the rebellion that is on foot in Scotland against the King and government', and in the Accounts, when there was a 'collection for ye poor on ye 7 of June', a note that it was 'the day of Thanksgiving'[28].

Records of special offerings reveal the wide range of the congregation's benevolences. Mystery attaches to one: 'pay'd for a reckoning when the meeting was held about the French meeting-house in October 1718 — 1s 6d.' Was the meeting held to arrange help for a French congregation, or was it to negotiate for the taking over of a former French meeting-house, before the decision to build their own Church in Crown Court had superseded such a plan? Certainly when the congregation was in its own building Russell seems to have encouraged it in outgoing generosity. We find, in 1721: '2s 6d. to M. Hubert, minister of a french calvinistic congregation in the palatinate towards his journey to Edinburgh', and later, 2s 6d. 'to Mr Tubar, a french minister in charity'. A long list of 'Money collected upon Briefs'[29] during the next quarter-century includes aid to non-conformist congregations in almost every English county, in some cases because of loss by fire or flood. There were others for 'protestants in Copenhagen', for 'Folkstone fishery', for 'oyster dredgers (Kent)', and a strange reference, in part indecipherable, to 'Cobi and Villas (?) in valley Luzerne in Piedmont by inundation'. The congregation concerned was undoubtedly Waldensian[30], and the Luzerne of the entry cannot be the Swiss one but Luserna in the Pellice valley, opposite Torre Pellice. The inundation would be that of the Pellice river.

Nor was Scotland forgotten in those 'Briefs'. Abercromby Harbour, St Andrews Harbour, and 'Dunbar Harbour in E. Lowthian' appear in the list, although — perhaps owing to their secular nature — the generosity they evoked was below the average. At any rate this was no ingrowing congregation.

To judge by the occupations of the fathers of children baptised, its membership covered a wide band of the social spectrum. We find: watchmaker, engraver, haire-merchant, joyner, barber and periwig maker, stay tailior, mapstick-maker, leather-cutter, snuffmaker and chandler, moyhair merchant, labourer, stationer (this was Patrick Russell, son of the minister, himself baptised by George Gordon on Feb 10th, 1710), groom to the Lord Cardigan, bookseller, linnen-draper, attorney-at-law (this was John Maxwell the Session Clerk), gardner[31] to Squire Harvey at Islington, glover, gentleman to Lord Cowper, glass-grinder, lighterman, clerk to the justiciary in Scotland, tub-japanner, cheesemonger, stonecutter, silver-polisher, school-master, cordwainer, chaireman, pedlar, sugar-boiler, hosier and hatter, narrow-weaver, cap maker, souldier, sailor H.M.S. Yarmouth, yeoman cowman at Harrow, packman, surgeon on H.M.S. Chatham, Inspector of the highways,[31] apothecary, sword cutler, harpsichord maker, cabinetmaker, peruke maker, whip maker. With these we are at the half-century, when cabinetmakers, tailors, periwigmakers, bakers and tobacconists have become more numerous, one of these last being identified, when his third child was baptised, as 'tobacconist to His Majesty', his shop being in Holborn. Shoemakers then began to increase, but changes in fashion were about to put the peruke and periwig makers' fortunes at risk. In 1765 a petition was presented to George III by the master peruke makers of London, 'setting forth the distress of themselves and an incredible number of others dependent on them, from the almost universal decline of their trade, in consequence of gentlemen so generally beginning to wear their own hair'[32]

Entries respecting coach fares, meals and supply-fees show that there were frequent exchanges of pulpit, not confined to Scots or even Presbyterian but including ministers of other non-conformist denominations. Closest of all, naturally, were the links with the ministers of the other London Scottish churches, particularly in the baptism of one anothers' children. Co-operation in actions relating to the welfare of the neighbourhood is also evidenced by entries such as: 'Oct. 26, 1730, pay'd towards the charges on account of the meeting house in routing out those who kept disorderly houses, 12s 6d.' It is interesting, too, to find a receipt in 1722 which included 'twenty-one shillings and seaven pence towards building St Martin's

Church', but that, paid along with the ground rent to the Bedford estate, was an assessment, not a voluntary contribution from the Scots.[33]

Patrick Russell, as shown in the pages of *The Book,* was a man of initiative and energy who set firmly on its feet the somewhat shaky congregation to which he came as Gordon's colleague. He saw his people through the harsh disappointments of a period when the promises of the Treaty of Union were cynically disregarded by the party which came to power in 1710. He also helped the nonconformist cause through the great unsettlement following the Salters' Hall Synod of 1719, taking his stand firmly as a Subscriptionist[34]. One sermon of his, preached at the funeral of a brother minister, survives, entitled *The Deity of Christ.* It well represents the Subscriptionist position. At his own funeral on December 14, 1746, his friend John Mitchell preached on Zecharaiah 1:5. The sermon was entitled *The Mortality and Death of God's Prophets considered;* it was published at the request of his congregation, and was sold by Patrick Russell, Stationer, at the Bible and Crown in Panton Street, Leicester Fields. 'Remember', exhorted Mr Mitchell, 'with what fervour and affection he has set Christ before you in all His excellence and glory, . . . and the subject with which he finished his life and labours this day three weeks, when as if he had known what was so near he called upon himself and you to "run with patience the race that is set before you" '[35]. He had survived his wife Rebecka by five years, and both were buried in 'the nonconformists' cemetery', Bunhill Fields.

One point requires explanation before we move to the next stage in the story of what became known as the Scottish National Church, Crown Court. This concerns the use of that general title instead of 'Church of Scotland'. For over two centuries it was a tender point with Scottish congregations in England, and with the Presbyteries in which they came to be organised, that they were not accepted as being part of the Church of Scotland but only as being connected with it, the more so because most of their ministers had been trained in Scotland and ordained by the Scottish Church. Deprived of the title Church of Scotland, they declared their relationship with that branch of the Church Catholic by one which at least declared the dignity of their connection with it. Congregations called themselves Scotch or Scottish National Churches, and Presbyteries added to their designations the phrase 'in connection with the Church of Scotland'. By the end of the nineteenth century some were boldly, although without sanction, naming themselves Church of Scotland. That claim was legitimised, as explained in Appendix A, after the Union of 1929.

NOTES

1. James Boswell, *London Journal, 1762–1763*, p. 260.
3. Dissenting Meeting Houses were unobtrusive, economically built, and generally roofed for cheapness with red pantiles. Hence the label 'Pantilers'.
2. *To the Baptised of the Scottish Church resident in London and its vicinity*, a Pastoral Letter printed and circulated by the Scots Presbytery of London in 1827.
4. See Chapter twelve.
5. Kenneth Black, *The Scots Churches in England*, p. 78.
6. Wilson, *op. cit.*, iv, 4, 20. In *Fasti Ecclesiae Scoticanae*, vii, 467, however, 'the tradition that one of these congregations had worshipped in the chapel of the Scottish Embassy (Scotland Yard)' is accepted as 'probably correct', citing as authority Black, *op. cit.*, p. 78. But see Chapter twelve.
7. Macmichael, *Charing Cross and its Immediate Neighbourhood*, p. 193 (where also the location of the quondam Peter's or St Peter's Court is identified with the present nos. 110–111 St Martin's Lane, where now stands St Martin's House, opposite the National Opera House (London Coliseum), formerly the site of Old Slaughter's Coffee House and Thomas Coutt's residence.)
   See also Malcolm, *Londinium Redivivum*, iv, 288. The *St Martin's Scrapbook* contains a sketch of the old Peter's Court.
8. The name of James Galloway appears with some frequency in *The Book*. He was minister of a Presbyterian congregation which had originally worshipped from about 1689 in Parish Street. Horsleydown, and moved to St John in 1702, possibly uniting there with another English Presbyterian congregation. (Information from MS notes in United Reformed Church History Society Library) But see Wilson, op. cit., iv, 278, and Chapter four *supra*.
9. The Gregorian Calendar was belatedly introduced in Britain when the *Calendar (New Style) Act* was passed in 1750. At the same time the commencement of the legal year was changed from the 25th of March to the 1st of January — a change which had been made in

'The Noblest Prospect which a Scotsman ever Sees'

Scotland in 1700, before the Union. Thereafter the calendar and the legal year coincided on both sides of the border. But the 'loss' of eleven days in September, necessitated by the adoption of the Gregorian Calendar that year, furnished hecklers with a useful cry against unpopular parliamentary representatives — 'Who stole our eleven days?'.

10. *Minutes of Presbytery of Peebles*, Sept. 26th & Oct. 7th, 1711. *Minutes of Synod of Lothian and Tweedale*, Nov. 8th, 1711.
11. MS. in Dr Williams' Library, 12.64 (41, 46) London.
12. *The Book*, Oct. 10, 1715.
13. Draft of original lease, dated Feb. 1718, quoted in *Crown Court Church Magazine*, Sept. 1921.
14. Esdaile, *Louis Francois Roubiliac*, passim. *Dict. of Nat. Biog.* vii, 311. *London Journal*, Oct 12, 1723.
15. *Encyclopedia Britannica*, 11th. ed., artt. *Academy, Royal,* and *Hogarth, William.* Malcolm, *Londinium Redivivum*, iv, 298.
16. From 18th century copy kindly shown by Mrs Jean Stewart.
17. Macky, *op. cit.*, iii, 272.
18. *Autobiography of Alexander Carlyle of Inveresk*, pp. 21ff, 148ff., etc. Also *Funeral Sermon*, and *Life and Death of the Heroic Col. Gardiner*, by Dr Philip Doddridge.
19. By 1842 'The Blue Anchor' had disappeared from Little Britain in the London Directory, but the *Directory of Stage Coach Services, 1835* (reprint, Alan Bates; pub. David & Charles) shows 'The Bull and Mouth', just round the corner in St Martin's le Grand, as the arrival point of the Edinburgh-London Royal Mail Coach.
20. G. Lockhart, *Memoirs concerning the Affairs of Scotland, etc.*, p. 223.
21. 'A daughter of John Knox was married to one of the Baillies of Jerviswood' — Thos. McCrie, *Life of Knox*, i, 451.
   Countess of Ashburnham, *Lady Grisell Baillie*, p. xi.
22. Robert Baillie's body was quartered, and one part was exposed at Lanark, where William Leishman, a smallholder of Roberton, stole it away for burial. Years later, in gratitude, the Baillies sent Leishman's son and namesake to Glasgow University, of which he afterwards became Professor of Divinity, and eventually Principal. He forms one link in a chain connecting Glasgow with the First Scots Kirk in London, Founders' Hall. Gershom Carmichael, son of the first minister of that congregation, became Professor of Philosophy in Glasgow University. Two of his pupils were John Simson (see Appendix B) and Frances Hutcheson, who became "the founder of the Scottish School of Philosophy". Leishman (who later spelt his name Leechman), studied under Hutcheson, who said of him that he was "expected to put a new face upon theology in Scotland" when he became

Professor of Divinity. One of Leechman's early pupils was Robert Lawson, who became the eighth minister of Founders' Hall in 1751. (*Dictionary of National Biography*, xi, 832; *Fasti*, vii, 397).

23. A sitting: accommodation for one in a pew, for which 'seat-rent' was paid, the minister's stipend consisting, in the case of Crown Court and many other congregations, of the total amount of seat-rents collected.

24. The Bathel, or Beadle (from O.E. *bydel*, to announce), was the Kirk Session's officer, acting as its agent and under its orders. In Scotland he was often known as 'the minister's man'. Now he is too often just 'the Church Officer'.

25. One of the Dissenting Academies; see Chapter two, note 13.

26. See Appendix B; also Wilson, *op. cit.*, i, 169.

27. *Lady Grisell Baillie's Household Book*, p. xxiii. From this, and from the *Memoirs* of their daughter Grisell, Lady Murray, much of the foregoing information is drawn.

28. Similarly, in New Broad Street church, Petty France, John Allen preached a sermon in 1746, entitled *Rejoice with Trembling*, 'in Thanksgiving for the Suppression of the Rebellion'.

29. 'Collections upon Brief' were authorised by 'Church Briefs' or 'King's Letters', issued out of Chancery in the king's name, bearing the privy seal, and licensing the petitioners to collect, through clergymen, magistrates and churchwardens throughout England, money for the charitable purpose specified. In the reign of George IV they were abolished, having proved more profitable to the officials involved than to the charities themselves. The Anglican Book of Common Prayer, in a rubric between Creed and Sermon in the Order for the Lord's Supper or Holy Communion, still directs that at that point 'Briefs, Citations and Excommunications' are to be read.

30. The Waldenses were followers of Peter Waldo of Lyons, a pre-Reformation reformer of about 1170. They have been much persecuted, but survive as an active branch of the Church, particularly in the valleys of Piedmont, where their ancestors had found refuge in their earliest persecutions. Both Cromwell and Milton (sonnet *On the Late Massacre in Piedmont*) remonstrated against a seventeenth century persecution. The Church of Scotland has long been their friend, and many of their ministers have studied in Scotland.

31. Three baptisms and four-and-a-half years later Mr Inglish, the squire's gardner had become Mr Inglish, the king's inspector of the high ways.

32. *Gentleman's Magazine*, 11th Feb., 1765. The Petition goes on to explain 'the fatal necessity they are under of misemploying the Lord's Day', presumably under the necessity of engaging in other work that day to make ends meet, 'by which they and their families are become as those that know not God, whilst their fellow-subjects are happy

in the inestimable privilege of attending and discharging their religious duties and imbibing the precepts that tend to bear a conscience void of offence'.

33. St Martin's in the Fields, already dilapidated in Henry VIIIs time, was demolished and rebuilt, 1721–22. The cost was £38,891, of which £35,450 was raised by Act of Parliament imposing a levy of which landlords paid 4/5ths and tenants 1/5th. (Malcolm, *op. cit.*, iv, 193, 4).

34. See Appendix B.

35. John Mitchell, whose name appears frequently in *The Book* and in the subsequent volume, seems to have been minister of a congregation worshipping in Nightingale Lane, near the Tower — probably Independent. (T.S. James, *Presbyterian Churches and Chapels*, pp. 691 & 700; and *Congregational Historical Society Transactions*, iii, 72; iv, 358; & vi, 116).

CHAPTER 6

Politics, Theology, Medicine and Commerce

The Revolution of 1688 had brought relief to English nonconformists. Thereafter they were no longer subject to overt persecution, for although efforts were made in Anne's time to reintroduce penal legislation the two Acts concerned were repealed soon after her death. The *Test Act* of 1673, however, remained on the statute book, much to the disadvantage of nonconformists. It was not repealed until 1828, and the question of its repeal became a controversial issue even amongst the ranks of the nonconformists themselves.

In Scotland things were different. The old Tests had been annulled, and the Convention of 1560 restored by the Scottish Parliament, recognising Presbytery as the national form of Church polity and government. After the Union the Tory government of 1710, by its *Toleration Act,* gave the Scottish Episcopalians in 1712 the rights and liberties which its *Occasional Conformity* and *Schism Acts* would have denied to non-Episcopalians in England. But the oath, abjuring the Pretender, which was required of all holders of public office, bore heavily against the Scottish Episcopalians, since they were generally Jacobite in sympathy; and the anti-Jacobite legislation which followed the rebellions of 1715 and 1745 further handicapped them[1].

The Presbyterian cause in Scotland might therefore be said to hold a privileged position. But the misgivings of many about the transference of political power to London, and to a Parliament where bishops formed part of the Upper House, were realised, very soon after the Union, in legislation which was to have the most serious effects, not only in Scotland but ultimately on the Scottish National Churches in England. Patronage was the question at issue.

The pre-Reformation practice of Patronage had been re-

76

introduced after the Restoration, but in 1690 was abolished again under William, a pecuniary compensation being voted to the patrons. The second British Parliament, in 1710, with a cynical disregard for the *Act for the Security of the Church* which was indissolubly attached to the *Treaty of Union* and expressly safeguarded all the rights and practices of the Church of Scotland, once more imposed the system of patronage upon her. It was a plain breach of the terms of Union. 'In 1712, wrote Macaulay, 'five years after the Treaty, an Act restoring patronage was passed, the bill being hurried through both Houses of Parliament in a single month. The British legislature violated the Articles of Union, and made a change in the constitution of the Church of Scotland'[2]. No pretence was made of consulting the Church, nor did the patrons pay back the compensation received in 1690.

This flagrant breach of the Treaty, which even the influence of the Duke of Argyll and of William Carstares could not avert, justified the alarm already expressed in Scotland concerning the English indifference to Scottish Church rights. At the very meeting in 1711 when the Presbytery of Peebles considered Patrick Russell's petition to be reponed, it also resolved to overture the General Assembly 'that the General Assembly fall upon proper methods for giving a publick testimony against the incroachments being made upon this Church'. But the Act remained on the Statute Book until 1874. 'Year after year', continues Macaulay in the passage quoted, 'the General Assembly protested against the violation; and from the Act of 1712 undoubtedly flowed every secession and schism that has taken place in the Church of Scotland'. The Kirk in London was not unaffected by the blow, although a century was to pass before its full impact arrived there[3].

Scottish congregations in England were of course immune from the operations of the Patronage Act, since there were no patrons to claim such rights over a 'nonconformist' body. Nevertheless, for the reasons mentioned in Appendix C, numerous congregations of the 18th century Scottish denominations which resulted from the Act came into being in all parts of England where Scots settled in any numbers. What is to be remarked, however, is the general absence in the English situation of the bitter feelings which often marred the relation-

ships between those denominations in Scotland. Scottish
National and Secession ministers, in fact, sat together in the
Presbytery of London, as did more than one English Presbyterian minister. In 1794 Nathaniel Forsyth, a Secession (or
'Burgher') student from Scotland, applied to the Scots Presbytery of London for license. He was accepted 'according to the
principles and practices of the Church of Scotland' on the
personal recommendation of two Secession ministers in London.
(In the preceding year a Mr Forsyth, with two others from
Kensington, had sought the Presbytery's approval for the
erection of a church in that village. This was given: but there
is no evidence that the Forsyth who was licensed in December
1794 was the one who had sought that approval in June 1793.
Nor does anything further appear concerning a Kensington
Church). We have already noticed in chapter four the ordination
of Alexander Easton in 1792, and the Declaration in 1793
'as to their sentiments, both Religious and Moral', in both of
which Secession and English Presbyterian ministers took part
with their brethren of the Scots Presbytery.

Already, during Russell's ministry, signs of such interdenominational co-operation were evident in the Crown Court
records. His successor, a Scot, John Freeland, was in fact minister of an English Presbyterian congregation in Bromsgrove.
The Session Minutes record his Call, signed by six elders, and
attested by a visiting minister, as follows: 'I, Mr James Mackie,
minister of the Gospel at St Ninians in Scotland, being providentially upon the Spot, was desired to Moderate this Call, and
I do testify the above Call to be very unanimous, that the above
Subscriptions are genuine and signed in the presence and by the
desire of the whole Church present, and witnessed by me, James
Mackie'. The Session Clerk's letter accompanying the Call has a
touching postscript: 'dear Sir, May ye Lord clear up yor Way,
incline and determine you to us, and pray favour us with yor
agreeable answer as soon as possible you can, for you cannot
but believe our people will be longing to see you. Robt Wiseman'.[4] Freeland was inducted in June, 1747, but his ministry
was brief owing to his ill-health and early death in December
1751.

Wiseman's predecessor as Session Clerk, William Welsh, was
still on the Session, but must have been old and perhaps senile,

for four months after John Freeland's induction there is a minute dated October, 1747 — 'It was moved that as Mr Welsh was much indisposed in health in case of his death it might occasion some trouble by the loss or mislaying thereof [viz. the Lease for the site] or of its falling into the hands of his executors who might be strangers to our Church. It was ordered that Mr James Maxwell do get ye Lease registered before it should be delivered to Mr Welsh'. A creased and yellowed scrap of paper, the bottom third of which is missing, still to be found within the pages of the 1747—52 Minute Book, reads as follows:*

1. The first Leace was in 1719. The first Leace being [two words, indecipherable] Mr Welsh it was renewed 18 March 1746, and the new Laces put in for the remaining years. There is 28½ years of the Lace to com from Michelmes 1755. Which Lace is Registrated.
2. The House is inshoured for £475 in the hand and hand ofec on Snowe Hill for 7 years from 8 Febry 1747 and ends the 8 Febry 1755 in the then Elders names.[5]

Welsh and Walker of the Session both died in 1749, and when Messrs Edington and Paine were elected in their places they were 'acquainted with the State of the Church, viz.,

1st. Of the Lease of the Meeting House, the Form of yearly Ground Rent, and Registration.
2ndly. Of the Insurance of the Meeting House, the Time, Term of years, and for what sum of money.
3rdly. Of the cash belonging to the Church placed out in the Bank of England, the sum, in whose names, and how the profits are applyed.
4thly. Of the cash in the present Treasurer's hands and the sum as appears in the Churches books.
5thly. Of the rules agreed upon by the old Vestry as to the management of the Church and how the Christian charity is applyed.
6thly. Of the servants, the Salaries and Services of each one of them'[6].

It may be noted that ten years later, on the ordination of further elders, there was minuted 'A List of what belongs to the

*See page 83.

Church in Crown Court, Russell Street, Covent Garden, in the hands of Mr Stevenson, Treasurer.

1st. The Lease of the Meeting House.

2nd. 4 silver Cupps for the Sacrament with a mahogany case.

3rd. 2 Pewter Dishes, 2 Plates, 2 Table Clothes, 4 Napkins.

4th. A Book of the Receipts of the Ground Rent'.

Of these four items only the last seems to have survived, but it includes one particular receipt clearly relating to item 2:

Bought of Ph. Bruguier

To 4 Chalesses 75 x 13 at 6/2 per oz.	£23	6	7
Fashion at 9d per oz.	2	16	9
Ingraveing Ditto		10	0
	26	13	4

April 21
1753 Recd. by the hands of Mr Robert
Wiseman the Contents and All Demands   Ph. Bruguier.

The '4 silver Cupps for the Sacrament' were therefore but six years old when their existence was noted as item 2 in the List. The original chalices used in Peter's Court are nowhere noted, but when the congregation moved into Crown Court the 1719 record of payments includes 'payd for 2 dishes for ye elements — 5s.' These may have been the '2 Pewter Dishes' of item 3, and since there were also '2 Plates' the 'dish' may have been the archaic use of the word as signifying 'cup'.

On October 23rd, 1749, the Session appointed a special prayer-meeting on account of the prevalent 'mortality among cattle', which a much later minister referred to as 'interesting to no less an authority than the Board of Trade as being the first mention of that visitation on record'[7]. Already, however, in that year, *The Gentleman's Magazine*[8] had carried a report from Manchester, saying that 'The distemper among the cattle has reached this county'; and indeed Lady Baillie's *Household Book* contains an entry dated April 20, 1715: 'To tax for the death of the Cows — 5s.' These entries correspond with the dates of outbreaks, not of foot-and-mouth disease, which did not reach Britain until 1839, but of rinderpest, which arrived in Britain in 1713 and for over a century-and-a-half produced recurrent crises of great seriousness in the agricultural economy of these islands. In pre-industrial-revolution days whatever threatened that economy was cause for concern and dismay much more immediately in urban areas than is the case nowadays. The Crown Court Kirk Session knew well how closely life in the metropolis was dependent on what was going on down on the farm.

They had other worries as well. In December 1751 the Rev. John Mitchell performed the same sad office as he had for Patrick Russell, and preached the funeral sermon for John Freeland. The pulpit was hung with mourning, and December 26th was appointed as 'a day of humiliation and prayer for the Church in its present situation'. The vacancy, however, was brief. Mr Freeland's brother advised the congregation to consider a young man known to him, and by March, 1752 the Rev. Thomas Oswald had been elected and ordained to the charge of Crown Court 'by the Scots Presbytery of London'[9]. A letter written to Mr Jones of Fleet Street by Mary Oswald in 1810 states that her uncle, Thomas Oswald, was born in 1722 'of a very old and respectable family, having had the property of Dryburgh, near Denny, in their possession from the year 1547'. He was a Glasgow graduate, licensed by the Presbytery of Abertaff in 1748, and had assisted Principal Tullidaff at St Andrews until Crown Court called him. He married, in London, the daughter of an Alderman; they had two sons and two daughters; and after twenty-five years he resigned in order to return to Scotland, where his wife's considerable fortune enabled him to buy the family estate from his brother, who was childless. He became minister of Clackmannan Kirk, was appointed a Justice of the Peace, and died in 1787, aged 65[10].

It was a difficult, but not a discouraging situation to which the London congregation called him. The number of members had fallen during his predecessor's illness. The Precentor — then known as the Clerk — had been dismissed for scandalous conduct. But 'the church in its present situation' had benefitted from some good stewardship and forward planning by the Session. The lease was 'registrated'; the buildings were 'inshoured'; the elders, old and new, were well-informed; and a Crown Court tradition was growing. There were still family links with the early years: Patrick Russell's second son, whose baptism had been recorded in Peter's Court in 1713 and who was now a stationer in Panton Street, was a loyal member: his own daughter, named Rebecka after his mother, had been baptised at the same font in 1746[11]. And the congregation, although not large, was spiritually alive, meeting on Monday evenings for prayers and able to support weekly lectures. There was good hope for the new ministry.

A dinner — total cost, £1 11s. — was given to celebrate the ordination and induction, 'at the Coffee House'. This may have been Old Slaughter's Coffee House in St Martin's Lane, — 'the Coffee-house on the Pavement' — famed as the resort of artists and writers. Hogarth, Hayman, Roubilliac, Gainsborough, Wilkie, Haydon, Dryden, Pope and Goldsmith in their days were often to be seen there[12]. But if £1 11s. paid for a dinner to welcome the new minister, what was charged for a cup of coffee?

The indications are that the membership and vitality of 'The Presbyterian congregation at Russell Street in Covent Garden', as the ground-rent receipts at that time name it, picked up quickly under Oswald's ministry. Still closer co-operation grew up with ministers and congregations of other denominations. The minister of the English church at the Hague, the Rev. Mr McLane, took part in some services. The Revs. Messrs Hart of Doncaster and Bertram of Southampton, are mentioned as visiting preachers, with no indication as to their denomination. George Turnbull and John Patrick can be identified as the ministers of the Scotch Churches in Hammersmith and Peter Street respectively; and James Gordon, who appears as preacher twice during Oswald's time, was almost certainly the minister of Alford in Aberdeenshire; he had been Moderator of the General Assembly of the Church of Scotland in 1734, and was a firm encourager of the Scottish churches in England. The closest links, of course, were still those of personal friendship with the ministers of Founders' Hall — Robert Lawson, who baptised Oswald's children as Oswald baptised his, and whose funeral sermon was preached by Oswald — and Henry Hunter, who succeeded Lawson in the new building in London Wall.

The Baptismal Register, however, holds many other names than those relating to Oswald's fellow-ministers, and two of these have a more than passing interest.

One name which appears with some frequency — those were

The first Lace was in 1719 The first Leaces being...
it was Atcheved and The Lace put in for the Remaning...
Ther is 28½ years of the Lace to Com from Michelmes 1755...
Which Lace is Registrated.

2. The house is fnsshoured for £475 in the hand and hand
Ofsee on Snowe hill for 7 years from 8 Febry 1747 and Ends
The 8 Febry 1755 in the then Elders names

3. Ther is £16.. 19. 8½ in the Banck 3 p[er] Ct Enevelys of £26
in the naems of Robt Wiseman and Iowed Withing for the
youse of the Church for Which Mr Wiseman and Mr Wellan
have Granted their Obligation in the Churches Booke

4. Ther is .... at preasent in Robt Wisemans hands of
...apers in the Vestory Box Which ....

...By Thomas Oswald mawmudenser
William Smelling Son of Mr John Harvie & Anne
his wife in the Parish of St Anns Westminster
was born July 25th & baptised August 1st
14th by — Thomas Oswald min

Smellie Robert the Son & Eupsey the daughter of
Mr John Harvie Surgeon & man midwife in Meards
Street St anns Soho & Ann his wife were born Decr
the 27th & baptised the 31st —

.... Son of Doctor John Harvie & Ann
his wife in Warder Street near Soho was
born May 30th & baptised June 7th

The records of baptism in 1755, 1756 and 1758 of three of John and Anne Harvie's large family.

the days of large families, and of high infant and maternal mortality — is that of John Harvie. The entries against his name in the column 'Father's occupation', the Christian names of two of his children, and the address to which he had graduated by the time his third child was baptised, together provide clues to an interesting, not to say highly important, chapter in the story of British medicine. In 1753 there was baptised in Crown Court 'William Smellie, son of Mr John Harvie, man-midwife, and Ann his wife.' In 1755 'Smellie Robert and Euphy, twin son and daughter of Mr John Harvie, surgeon and man-midwife, Meard Street, Soho', were baptised. And by the time that 'John' was baptised in 1758 'Mr' had become 'Dr' and the address had changed to 'Wardour Street'. It was in that year that the famous Dr William Smellie retired with his wife Euphan to his home town, Lanark. He had settled in London in 1740, sharing his home for a while with William Hunter from East Kilbride, and with him revolutionising the practice of midwifery in St George's Hospital, the Middlesex Hospital and the British Lying-in Hospital. A major result of their pioneering and campaigning was the revolution they achieved in obstetrical practice, securing the acceptance of properly trained medical attendance and surgical aid at confinements, and the recognition of obstetricians as eligible for election to the Fellowship of the College of Physicians. Before their time the presence of a man in the lying-in chamber — and there were no women doctors in those days — was not to be thought of, unless obstetric operation was required and then only with the most careful regard to female modesty. John Harvie's adoption of the title 'surgeon and man-midwife' may be regarded as part of William Smellie's and William Hunter's campaign to have obstetrics accepted as a branch of medicine. The high infant- and maternal-mortality of those days must have been appreciably lowered by their campaigning.

It is interesting to trace the professional succession of Scot by Scot in this field. John Knyveton, 'latterly man-midwife to Middlesex Hospital', kept a diary in which he describes how, in order to graduate from the status of apothecary to that of surgeon, he sought out Dr Smellie only to find that he had just retired; but in his place he found 'Dr Harvie, recently stepped into the shoes of his old master, the famous Dr William Smellie. . .,

Dr Harvie taking over Dr Smellie's London home at Wardour Street, Soho, and all his equipment'[13]. Later he refers to an unusual caesarean operation at which William Hunter, his brother John, and Dr Garthshore were called in to consult[14]. He refers also to James Ford of Marischal College, Aberdeen, Physician Extraordinary to Queen Charlotte, to William Cruickshank of Edinburgh, partner to William Hunter and personal friend of Dr Johnson whom he attended in his last illness, and to Matthew Baillie, surgeon to George III, and nephew of the Hunter brothers, who had set up his practice in their house when they moved, his sister, the later-famous Joanna Baillie, coming to housekeep for him there. London medicine and surgery appear to have been largely in the hands of Scots in those days, and the toast which 'Jupiter' Carlyle heard William Hunter propose in 1758 reflected this: 'May no Englishman venture out of the world without a Scottish physician, as I am sure there are none who venture in'[15].

The other name which catches the eye in the Crown Court Baptismal Register may be seen to this day on imposing buildings throughout England. Thomas Coutts went south with his older brother James from Edinburgh in 1752. Their father, a corn factor and negotiator of bills of exchange, had been Lord Provost of Edinburgh in 1742. Their purpose was to found a London branch of the family business, Thomas being then seventeen. In James' house he met his brother's friend, James Boswell[16], and other of London's literary men and actors with whom he maintained lasting friendships. He also met, and later married, Susannah Starkey, nurse to his brother's daughter. As sole head of the firm after James' death in 1778 he brought the banking house of Coutts & Co. to the highest degree of efficiency and reputation, and with the great wealth it brought him he gave generous support to many good causes.

It was in 1769 that his son John* was baptised in Crown Court, the father being described as 'Thomas Coutts, Banker, next door to Old Slaughter's Coffee House in St Martin's Lane'. His three other children were daughters, and all 'married well', Susannah to the third Earl of Guilford, Frances to the 1st

*See page 98

marquess of Bute, and Sophia to Sir Frances Burdett, the great supporter of the Reform Bill. After his first wife died Thomas Coutts married the actress Harriot Mellon, to whom he left a fortune of nearly two million pounds[17]. She in turn bequeathed it all to Angela Burdett, Sophia's daughter, who then took the name of Burdett-Coutts, and made that name so famously respected through the range and generosity of her carefully administered benevolences that in recognition of her services to the nation she was created Baroness Burdett-Coutts of Highgate and Brookfield in 1871. She lived into this century and was buried in Westminster Abbey. One of the special objects of her charity was the Ragged School Union, and it is pleasant to learn, as a later chapter will show, that in this way some of Thomas Coutts' wealth returned to help his old congregation in the service it was to offer through its Ragged Schools to the neighbourhood where he made his first home[18].

We are not yet finished with Thomas Oswald. The accounts of his time show many points of minor interest. The ground rent was £14 p.a.; the premium for the fire insurance — still with the Hand-in-Hand Fire Office in 1769 — was £3 2s. 8d.; the Clerk (i.e., Precentor) was paid £1 10s. a quarter; 2 years' paving and lighting cost £5; the supply fee was 10s. 6d. for a service; a Spitting Box for the Vestry cost 6d., as did Repair of Hinges for the necessary; and 19 yards of Black Flannel for covering the Pulpit cost £1 3s. 9d. That last item was dated 26th January, 1761. George II had died on Oct. 25th, 1760. The *Gentleman's Magazine* in January 1761, announcing details of the Court's change of mourning, intimated that Friday 13th January was the day appointed for a general fast. Presumably that was the occasion when the pulpit was draped in mourning.

It was during Oswald's time that the peace of the nonconformist churches in London was threatened by the flaring-up of controversy about the Test laws. It will be remembered that, immediately after the Revolution, efforts to admit dissenters to civil quality with episcopalians by the repeal of the Test and Corporation Acts were thwarted, despite William's strong support, by the attitude of the established clergy towards those who forty years before had kept them in the wilderness for thirteen years. Now in the 1750s there arose one of those sporadic attempts, which were to recur at intervals during the next hundred years, to secure the repeal of the Tests. Oswald, like many of his nonconformist colleagues, feared that repeal would open the door for the return to power in politics and education of the Roman Church, and that fear 'led him to oppose the repeal, in which decision', says Walter Wilson, 'we are bound to pay greater deference to the sincerity of his motives than to the correctness of his judgment'[19]. But although he was one of the thirteen ministers, seven of them Scots, who printed a pamphlet opposing the 1772 application to Parliament *For the Relief of Protestant Ministers, Tutors and Schoolmasters,* his reconciling spirit led him 'to take a conspicuous part with some of his brethren in attempting to lessen the contention that then prevailed among the Dissenters respecting the Test Laws'[20]. It is an issue which we shall meet again in this story.

NOTES

1. Scottish Episcopalians suffered also from internal troubles. It was 1766 before they had organised themselves as the Scottish Episcopal Church. In 1784 Bishop Skinner of Aberdeen and two others consecrated Samuel Seabury, whom the Church of England had refused to consecrate, as Bishop for Anglicans in the U.S.A. On the death of Charles Edward Stewart in 1788, Bishop Skinner, against Church of England opposition but with support from Principal William Robertson and other Church of Scotland ministers, secured George III's official recognition for Scottish Episcopacy, and in 1792 the anti-Jacobite penal handicaps were removed.
2. Lord Macaulay, *Speeches,* ii, 180.
3. See Chapter ten; also Appendix C for an account of the effects of the Patronage Act of 1712.
4. *Crown Court Session Minutes,* 24th May, 1747.
5. 'Britain's oldest fire-insurance company', the Hand-in-Hand, was formed in 1696 in Tom's Coffee House in St Martin's Lane. Three Tooley Street wharfingers, Hay, Chamberlain and Beale, called 17 others there to combine in a mutual insurance venture, first called *Ye Amicable Contributors* but later named after Hand in Hand Alley in Tooley Street. The timber-built warehouses there near London Bridge held fats and tallow imported for chandlers and soapmakers, and were a high fire-risk, as the great Tooley Street fire of 1861 demonstrated — see Chapter ten. The motto of the Hand-in-Hand was 'Love as Brethren'. The Commercial Union Assurance Co.

is its descendant. Hay's Wharf is still on the London map. (Ayton Ellis, *The Penny Universities*, pp. 152–4).

Fifty years passed before Life Insurance followed, the pioneer society being the *Scottish Ministers' Widows' Fund*, launched in 1742 by two Edinburgh ministers, Robert Wallace and Alex. Webster, who persuaded the General Assembly to require complete statistics on mortality etc. from every Presbytery in Scotland. On these Webster based his Tables of Average Longevity and thus worked out an actuarially dependable scheme, followed by all subsequent life-insurance companies. Later, under the authority of Lord President Dundas, they sent schedules to every parish minister in Scotland, and thus made up the first Census Return in the United Kingdom in 1755. This work provided Wallace with material for two books, one of which prompted Malthus's *Essay on Population. (Encyclopeadia Britannica*, 11th Ed., vol. 28, p. 459, and *Dictionary of National Biography*, xx, 560 & xx, 1025).

6. *Crown Court Session Minutes*, 4th Mar., 1750.
7. Report of speech by Rev. A. Macrae at laying of foundation-stone of new church, Crown Court, in *St Columba's Church Magazine*, June, 1910.
8. *Gentleman's Magazine*, xix, 390.
9. *Wilson*, op. cit., iv, 8; *Fasti*, iv, 302. But no documents of the Scots Presbytery of London now exist prior to those begun in 1772: see Appendix D.
10. *M.S. 12.64 (73)*, 41–46, in Dr Williams' Library. Principal Tullidaff (or Tullidelph) became an advocate in 1742 of Wallace and Webster's Widows' Fund (see note 5 above). In Clackmannan, after 1777, Thomas Oswald had as an Elder Mr Bruce of Kennet, who had been tutored by Thomas Boston and was the great-great-great-uncle of Lord Balfour of Burleigh (see Chapter eleven).
11. The font in those days was a basin of silver or pewter, resting in a hoop or bracket attached to the pulpit. The accounts for 1719 include 'payd for ye iron to hold ye bason − 1/6d'.
12. Ayton Ellis, *op. cit.*, pp. 150ff.
13. Ernest Gray, *Man-Midwife*, p. 19. On Dec. 26th, 1783, Knyveton records his admission as a Licentiate in Midwifery of the Royal College of Physicians, 'the College having determined in Oct. 6th this year to recognise the art of midwifery by conferring a license in the subject'.
14. William Hunter made his name as the first great teacher of anatomy in England. Later he left surgery for obstetrics, and was appointed surgeon-accoucheur in Middlesex Hospital where he began his quiet revolution of obstetrical practice. His name and fame are preserved in

the Hunterian Museum of anatomical and pathological specimens which he bequeathed to Glasgow University. See Chapter thirteen for another London Kirk link with that Museum.

John Hunter's fame rests upon his work in bone-surgery, on the lymphatic glands, and on the treatment of aneurisms by tying off the affected arteries and leaving the circulation to reconstitute itself through collateral vessels. London's Hunterian Museum was his gift to the Royal College of Surgeons there. His wife wrote the lyrics for Haydn's *Canzonets*, including 'My mother bids me bind my hair'. She was left ill-provided for at his death, as Knyveton makes clear, and another Crown Court member came to her rescue as we shall see in Chapter nine.

15. Alexander Carlyle of Inversk, *Autobiography*, p. 362. Carlyle records his meeting with Garthshore on p. 546.

16. James Boswell, *London Journal, 1762–3*, pp. 262, 269.

17. Mrs Coutts, widowed in 1822, became a close friend of Sir Walter Scott and consulted him at length regarding her second marriage, with the Duke of St Albans, in 1827. (Scott, *Journal*, p. 414). Her Will provided that if Angela Burdett married a foreigner her interest in the Banking House was to pass to her sister Clara. She did, in fact, later in life, marry a U.S. citizen, and a compromise between her and her sister, Mrs Money, gave 2/5ths to Angela and 3/5ths to Clara, who thereupon took the name of Money-Coutts, inspiring *Punch's* quatrain: Money takes the name of Coutts?
> Superfluous and funny,
> For everyone considers Coutts
> Synonymous with Money!

18. Charles Dickens, who advised Baroness Burdett-Coutts about some of her philanthropic enterprises and who dedicated *Martin Chuzzlewit* to her, found the character of Martha in that book suggested to him by his own involvement on behalf of the Shepherd's Bush Home which, with his encouragement, she had founded for women of the streets. The prototype of Mrs Gamp, likewise, was a nurse whom the Baroness temporarily employed to look after an ill neighbour and friend. See Dickens, *Letters to Baroness Burdett–Coutts, with a Biographical Introduction*, passim. The effigy and fountain commemorating Greyfriars Bobby in Edinburgh was erected by her.

19. Wilson, *op. cit.*, iv, 8.

20. *Ibid.*

CHAPTER 7

'With United Earnestness'

Thomas Oswald's successor was one of the five Aberdeenshire men who have ministered to the congregation whose story we are now following. Since his name was Cruden the mind at once leaps to the famous but emotionally unstable Aberdonian of that name — suitor of Sir Thomas Abney's daughter, agitator for prison reform, self-styled 'Corrector of the People', erasor of *No. 45* (the badge of John Wilkes' party[1]) wherever a damp sponge would wipe it out, member of Swallow Street Scottish National Church, Sunday distributor of handbills on which was printed the Fourth Commandment, and — compiler of that monumental and indispensable work, *A Complete Concordance to the Old and New Testament*. But that was Alexander; our Crown Court man was William Cruden, and although the two have been said to be related we have come across no positive evidence that this was so.

Will Cruden — so he always signed himself — was born in 1725, the son of the beadle at Pitsligo. He graduated M.A. at one of the Aberdeen Universities[2], and was ordained at Logie Pert in 1753. He must have had misgivings about the operations of lay patronage and its effects on the spiritual life of the Church of Scotland, for in 1767 he demitted that charge to become minister of the first Relief Meeting House in Glasgow[3]. But on accepting the call to Crown Court he advised his Glasgow congregation to return to the Church of Scotland.[4].

By that time Crown Court had been vacant for two years, and according to a much later document 'had almost fluttered out of existence'. That it revived to a lively and growing condition was obviously due to the devotion and ability of Will Cruden, who is described in Walter Wilson's *History of Dissenting Churches* as 'a worthy and respected minister, of approved talents and piety, and he lived in London greatly respected by

90

his brethren'.

Cruden seems to have confined himself very closely to 'the life and work of his own congregation. No meeting of Presbytery was held at Crown Court during his time, and his name appears on none of its sederunts.[5] We would know more about his ministry and the witness of his congregation if Kirk Session Minutes were available, but unfortunately they have disappeared. We have other sources of information, however. Baptismal Register and congregational accounts survive, and other records help also to fill the gap.

Amongst the Bedford Estate records is a lease of the site and meeting-house dated 1774.[6] It appears to be an emendation of the first lease, and specifically includes permission to pull down the present building and erect a new one. Already in 1738 extensive repairs had been necessary. Now, apparently, something more drastic was required, and within three years, we find, the permission granted in the 1774 lease was being used. 'The Committee in Trust for the Rebuilding of the protestant Dissenting Meeting House in Crown Court, Russell Street, Covent Garden' had to raise over £1400 — more than twice what the original building had cost 55 years earlier. It is an indication of Cruden's popularity and capacity that the whole amount was contributed by members and their friends between February 1776 and March 1778. Some items in the accounts, such as *The Measuring Dinner,* and *The Raising Dinner for all the men,* are of interest as reflecting the practices and perquisites of tradesmen in those days. *Measuring ye Whitewash* cost 10s 6d. *Laying ye First Brick* was another half-guinea. A contemporary entry in the Treasurer's accounts discloses where the congregation worshipped while the rebuilding was in progress:

Rec'd June ye 26th 1777 of Mr Jas Stephenson five and twenty Pounds for rent due to the Helther of the Helvetique Chapel, I said receiv'd for the use of the s'd Chapel. Frans. Hobler.

The Swiss Chapel, now in Endell Street, then stood in Castle Street.

There must have been something of the poet in Will Cruden, but of what quality we do not know, having found no copy of his *Hymns on a Variety of Religious Subjects* which he pub-

91

lished in Aberdeen in 1761, or his *Nature Spiritualised in a Variety of Poems*, published in London in 1766. After his death in 1785, however, a number of his friends collected and printed fifteen of his sermons, under the title *Sermons on Evangelical and Practical Subjects*. These reveal a well-furnished mind, a warmth of human sympathy, an appreciation of the variety of spiritual need, and a deep conviction of the effective saving grace of God. He is depicted in a frontispiece, an engraving 'after a painting by W. Allan', and the whole edition was subscribed for by 500 persons, some of whom bought 6, 10 or 12 copies each.

We have evidence of the effectiveness of his preaching. In 1776 a young cabinet-maker from Fettercairn arrived in London. His name was Anthony Crole, and he was aged 22. One Sunday he turned into Crown Court Church, and thereafter 'was assiduous in finding opportunity to hear the Gospel'. Such was the effect of Cruden's preaching that ten years later, having been trained in Lady Huntingdon's College, Crole himself became a minister, in Cumberland Street Chapel. In 1797, the lease expiring, he moved with his congregation to Founders' Hall, where the First Scotch Church had worshipped for so many years. He died in 1803, and his funeral sermon was preached by Alexander Waugh[7].

Will Cruden died in 1785, and a depressing two years' vacancy ensued. It may have been that the congregation's books were lost sight of with the minister's death, for two notes of special collections taken during that vacancy are inserted, anachronistically, in *The Book*, which belonged to the St Peter's Court era. One, dated 1785, records the collection taken on 3rd July 'for the Relief of the Unhappy Sufferers of the late Dreadful Fire in Compton Street', amounting to £13; the other, on 23rd July 1786, a collection of £14 11s 6d 'for the assistance of the dissenting congregation of Bolton in Lancashire, to enable them to defray the Expence of enlarging their place of worship, & delivered to their Pastor, yᵉ Revd. Robt. Simpson'.

Two years without a minister, for a congregation to which the memory of a similar interregnum was only eleven years distant, must have been discouraging in the extreme. Had they read a poem by one Robert Burns, entitled *The Calf*, the vacancy might have been longer still, for they might not then have chosen the Rev. James Steven, whose sermon on Malachi vi:2 Burns so cruelly satirised in that poem. On the other hand if, reading it, they knew that when Burns heard the sermon at Mauchline in 1786 Steven had been but newly licenced by the Presbytery of Paisley — and even more if they knew that Burns wrote the poem only in order to win an incautious wager, which he had made with his friend Gavin Hamilton, they would probably have concluded that Burns was revealing more about himself than he was informing the reader about the potentialities of the young preacher. At all events they did call James Steven, and he was ordained by the Scots Presbytery of London in November 1787.

Steven, who had been born in Kilmarnock, was then twenty-six, and he spent sixteen years in London, during which the healthy state in which he maintained Crown Court was reflected progressively in the Kirk Session Minutes. A 'Receiving Book for Pews' was instituted as part of a scheme for systematising the congregation's financial affairs; pew rents varied from 10s. to 2 guineas a year, depending on the number the pew could accommodate; but one or two families paid five guineas, so the tendency to social discrimination attached to the pew-rent system was not wholly avoided. Certain pews were rent-free. The keeping of Baptismal and Membership Rolls was more carefully organised.

Relationships with other non-conformist ministers and congregations continued to be close, particularly of course those with other Scottish churches. When Crown Court was undergoing some repairs in 1795 members of the congregation took communion at Swallow Street. Close connection with the Presbytery was re-established. There was a care, also, for dignity and reverence in worship; latecomers had sometimes disturbed the congregation, and the pew opener was instructed not to admit people during prayers, while a notice was placed on the doors asking quietness from those who came in wearing pattens. And there was sufficient affluence, at least amongst the elders, to enable them to support Will Cruden's widow until her death in 1801, and to subscribe £14 14s. to provide furniture for a school which the widow of a member planned to open so that she might be able to support herself and her children.

The growing evangelical concern of the last decade of the 18th century did not leave Steven or his congregation untouched. There are two references in Session minutes to a sermon preached in Crown Court by the Rev. John Love, minister of Crispin Street, with whom Steven frequently exchanged pulpits. So impressed was the Kirk Session by that sermon that they arranged early in 1794 to print 1000 copies of it. Meanwhile their minister was involved, along with John Love, in an enterprise which was to have world-wide and lasting results.

In 1792 William Carey and eleven friends had met at Kettering and formed the pioneer *Baptist Society for Propagating the Gospel among the Heathen.* In 1794 Carey wrote to Dr Ryland from India; Ryland consulted with David Bogue, already mentioned, and two months later Bogue published an *Address on Missions,* which crystallised the thinking of a little group of London ministers and led to the calling of a meeting in the Swan tavern in Change Alley before the end of the year. To John Love was given the task of sending out the 'small letter' which brought eight ministers together, to consult respecting the formation of a Society to take the Gospel to other lands. Four of these were or had been associated with the Scots Presbytery of London — David Bogue, formerly in Camberwell, John Love of Crispin Street, Alex. Waugh, of Wells Street Secession, and James Steven of Crown Court. It was an interdenominational group, including Congregational, Episcopalian and Methodist representatives, 'whose strife shall be, not to promote the interests of a special section, since Christ is not divided, but with united earnestness to make known afar the glory of His person, the perfection of His work, the wonders of His grace, and the overflowing blessings of His redemption'. The date was the twenty-second of September, 1795, and James Steven has his place in history, as one of the initiators of that noble enterprise, *The London Missionary Society.*

Although in respect of missionary zeal those Scots ministers in London were ahead, of the leaders at least, of the home Church, when Love went to Glasgow as minister of Anderston Church he soon formed the Glasgow Missionary Society, of which, as of the L.M.S., he was the first secretary; and through it and its Edinburgh counterpart Scottish people found the opportunity they wanted to extend the Church's mission beyond these islands. When the Church of Scotland did officially recognise its missionary obligations in 1824 the Scottish Church ceased to be represented on the L.M.S., which ultimately became the missionary agent of the Congregational Church.[8]

It was in Steven's time that one of the earliest non-British missionaries of the London Missionary Society was ordained by the Scots Presbytery of London, 'at Mr Steven's Meeting House, Crown Court', on November 3rd, 1797. We read that several denominations of English and Scotch ministers, both in and out of the Establishment, were engaged in the act. The Rev. J. Theo van der Kemp, M.D. was a native of Holland. He had been 'a confirmed Deist, but on a party of pleasure a waterspout had overturned the boat, his wife and daughter were both drowned, and he in an extraordinary manner had been saved, which led to his conversion. At the beginning of the year a Moravian friend presented him with the first sermons preached at the London Missionary Society, the perusal of which led him to offer himself to that benevolent body'[9]. We can amplify the story, on either side of his ordination. The son of a professor of theology in Rotterdam, he had broken away to lead a dissolute life as an officer in the dragoons. After his marriage he steadied, and resumed his interrupted medical studies, taking a course in Edinburgh where he graduated M.D. in 1782. Then came the tragic loss of wife and child while sailing on the Rhine, and his own survival and conversion, followed by his offer of service to the L.M.S. in 1797. After his ordination he returned to Holland to found the Netherlands Missionary Society. In 1799 he sailed on a convict ship to South Africa, where he was welcomed at Cape Town by the governor and the Dutch Reformed Church. But 'he and his colleagues . . . advocated social equality between barbarians and civilised people', and when in 1811 they laid before the governor a list of brutalities and injustices inflicted on Hottentots the initial welcome turned to hostility and the colonists put every hindrance in their way. The opposition was doubtless sharpened when, identifying himself more closely with the blacks, he married a Malagasay girl whom he had purchased from slavery. The pulpit from which he had preached to the

Hottentots was publicly scrubbed after he had left Graf Reinet. He died in 1811.

After his death the London Missionary Society sent out John Campbell of Kingsland to advise as to the future. Campbell, orphaned in infancy and brought up by an uncle in Edinburgh, was a contemporary at the High School of Walter Scott and the Haldane brothers. Although fostered in the Relief Church, of which his uncle was an elder, he considered himself a member of the Church of Scotland; but his co-operation with the Haldanes led him to a dissatisfaction with the Moderate spirit then prevailing, to an association with John Love and the formation of the Edinburgh Missionary Society, and to an interest in the anti-slavery issue as co-adjutor and representative in Scotland of John Newton and William Wilberforce. While still an ironmonger in the Cowgate, Edinburgh, he became known as an able speaker and was invited as such to the May Meetings in Kingsland Chapel. In 1803, after completing a course of study under Greville Ewing in Glasgow, he became minister of the Kingsland Independent congregation. He was set apart to his South African mission in Miles Lane by the venerable Dr Waugh — 'As God was with Vanderkemp so will He be with thee, Campbell!' In South Africa he saw the stupidity of applying non-Christian standards and methods by whites to blacks, and having reported to the L.M.S. in London was sent back on their behalf, accompanied by John Philip of Aberdeen, to Cape Town, where they were joined by Robert Moffat, later the father-in-law of David Livingstone. John Philip stayed, as superintendent of the L.M.S. South African Mission. Campbell returned to Kingsland in 1820.[10] He preached more than once in Crown Court.

It was to be expected, of course, that Crown Court would rally to the support of the new enterprise in which its minister had been a pioneer, and on November 5th, 1795, we read, 'This evening a subscription was opened by the Session for supporting the Missionary Society for conveying the Gospel to the Heathen, to which all the members present chearfully set their hands'.

Nor was that overseas interest confined to subscribing money, or even to providing 'gospel ordinances for the Heathen'.

In the Crown Court Baptismal Register are the records of the baptisms in November 1792 of Sarah, and in June 1794 of James, the children of James and Susanna Mein, 28 Little Earl Street, Seven Dials, Parish of St Giles. Both were baptised by James Steven. James Mein their father was born in 1761 at Melrose, and when the *Coromandel I* set sail from Deptford with a group of Border Scots in 1802 as the first free emigrants to Australia, he and his wife were amongst them. On their arrival they were given grants of land on the Hawkesbury River in New South Wales. As they built their houses, cleared their land, and set about supporting themselves as a settlement, they looked amongst themselves for one who would unite them as a Christian community and lead them in worship. They found him in James Mein, in whose house they worshipped until they built their Ebenezer Church in 1809, and who continued to minister to the Ebenezer community for twenty-one years until Dr Lang arrived in 1823 and the Presbyterian Church was organised on a national basis. The church still stands, the oldest of any denomination in Australia, and is regarded as the cradle of the Church there. There is something in this story which is reminiscent of those other 'followers of John Knox' who built 'the oldest Free Church building in England' two-and-a-half centuries before.

James Mein and the other settlers received welcome help from Bligh of the Bounty, who had just been appointed Governor of New South Wales and who gave them aid after a disastrous flood in 1806. In turn Mein was able to subscribe liberally to a relief fund in 1817 for sufferers from a similar flood. He was a strong supporter of Governor Bligh in the Rum Rebellion.[11]

There were other, and more world-shaking, rebellions afoot in those days. Cruden's and Steven's ministries covered the years of both the French and the American Revolutions, in the latter of which the Presbyterian insistence on the equal worth of all men played no small part[12]. One searches in vain for any sign of awareness of those critical events in the Crown Court Session minutes[13]. Certainly they were days of great difficulty for some Scottish congregations in London, at least three of which became extinct towards the end of the century. Crown Court had much on which to concentrate its efforts in its own immediate neighbourhood, and its interest in overseas mission

1769

John Son of Thomas Coutts Esquire Banker next door to old Slaughter's Coffee-house in St Martin's Lane was baptised May 24th being born the 17th.

Robert Son of Robert Campbell Wood-merchant and Cabinet Maker in Queens Street 7 dials was born May 19th and baptised June 4th.

Mary daughter of the Reverend Mr Oswald minister of the Presbyterian Congregation in Russel Street Covent Garden was born in Little Ormond Street Queens Square May 30th and baptised June the 8th by the Reverend Mr Patrick.

John Patrick

Record of baptism of John Coutts by Mr Oswald, and, later, of Mr Oswald's own daughter by John Patrick, minister of Peter Street Scots Kirk. John Coutts, like his three brothers, died in infancy.

Sarah Daughter of James & Susannah Mein No. 28 Little Earl Street Seven Dials Parish of St Giles Born September October 5 Baptized November 18 1792 By the Revd James Steven

James, son of James & Susanna Mein No. 28 Earl Street 7 Dials born the 14 May & Baptized the 1 June 1794 — by the Revd Mr Steven —

did not distract it from the work at its own doors.

Covent Garden was a deteriorating area, with many slum properties and all the social problems associated with these. The children of families crowded into such dwellings could count on Steven's support and the generosity of his people. There existed 'The Friendly Society for Educating and Clothing One Hundred Poor Children who attend the Service at Crown Court", and the accounts of the congregation show a sum collected in 1797 at a week-night service when the sermon was a plea for Christian care for 'such as these'. This was the beginning of what during the next ninety years came to be one of the great achievements of the Scots church in Covent Garden.

The care of the poor continued to be an important part of the Kirk Session's work, and in 1800 a new set of 'Rules to Govern the distribution of the Charitable Funds of the Church' was drawn up. These provided that distribution should be confined to members or subscribers, 'that the Minister and Elders should not wait for the application of poor members but, as far as they are able in their intercourse with the congregation, to find out proper objects and bring their cases forward to be considered and relieved; that as cases frequently occur for immediate relief the Minister (and any Elder after conferring with another of his brethren) might offer relief, according to the circumstances, with a sum not exceeding half a guinea; and that families which because of age or other causes are no longer able to subscribe should be called upon by a delegation who would enquire into the circumstances and report'. On the same date it was reported that a number of bad coins, copper and silver, to the face value of £16 6s., had accumulated from the collection plate; it was agreed they be sold for the value of the metal.[14]

The new century saw an air of dejection fall upon minister and Session, and it is clear that when in 1803 Steven accepted a call to Kilwinning he was conscious of a decline in attendance and a sluggishness in his Session's response to his leadership. They on their part seem to have regarded his departure as sudden and unexpected. The difficulty they experienced in finding a successor, which may well have been due to the discouraging impression which a discouraged Session and a dwindling congregation made on the minds of possible candidates, seemed once again to put Crown Court's future at serious risk, and this for the third time in sixty years.

Although James Steven left under a sense of disappointment over the decline in membership during his last year there, he had achieved perhaps more than he realised. He ministered in Kilwinning for another twenty-one years, and died suddenly in 1824.

NOTES

1. John Wilkes was Radical M.P. for Aylesbury in 1757. Alexander Carlyle of Inveresk, in his *Autobiography*, pp. 176, 193, 451, describes him in his youth as 'a sprightly, entertaining fellow — too much so for his years; for even then he showed something of the daring profligacy for which he was afterwards notorious'. Ascribing the frustration of his ambitions to the Prime Minister, Lord Bute, he established a paper in 1759, called *The North Briton* in opposition to Smollett's *The Briton,.* It soon became anti-Scots as well as anti-Bute. The notorious No. 45 of his paper was caustically critical of the king's message to parliament, and Adam Smith, reading it, said 'Bravo! this fellow will either be hanged in six months or he will get Lord Bute impeached'. Wilkes was briefly imprisoned in the Tower, but continued his chequered career until his death at seventy. Lord Bute did fall, largely because of Wilkes' campaign. 'No. 45' became the slogan of the Wilkes party.

2. The two were King's College (founded in 1494) and Marischal College (founded in 1593). They were merged in 1860. 'You must know, Mr Speaker', said a Scots M.P. in the 1830s, 'that England has two Universities — and so has Aberdeen!' (Lord Cockburn, *Circuit Journeys*, p. 153).

3. See Appendix C *re* Relief Church. Cruden's Glasgow congregation numbered over 1000 — twice that of Crown Court. One of his members had been David Dale, the hard-headed, soft-hearted, paternalistic employer of women and children, whose cotton-spinning mills at New Lanark, Blantyre and Spinningdale were for their day models of enlightened employment and social care, harsh although later judgement of their conditions understandably became. Dale disagreed with Cruden in 1768 and joined an independent group newly formed in Glasgow, known as the Old Scots Independents. (Struthers, *History of the Rise, Progress and Principles of the Relief Church*, pp. 182ff.)

4. *Fasti*, v, 404 and vii, 468, where it is stated that Cruden was 'probably

of the same family as Alexander Cruden', but no evidence is stated for the probability. See also Wilson, *op. cit.*, iv, 9.

5. The Scots Presbytery of London, meeting at the Angel on July 9, 1776, *inter alia* 'Resolved unanimously that every member of Presbytery, unless in case of illness, shall pay for non-attendance two shillings and six pence, and for want of punctuality to the hour of meeting one shilling sterling'. Whether Mr Cruden avoided these heavy fines, and if so how, we do not know.

6. Greater London Record Office. *Bedford Estate Records, E/BER/CG/L/52*

7. Wilson, *op. cit.*, ii, 294–341.

8. The full story of Scottish participation in the founding of the London Missionary Society may be found in James Calder's *Scotland's March Past*, Livingstone Press, 1945. The L.M.S. became, in 1976, Christian World Mission.

9. *Minutes of the London Presbytery of the Scots Church in England in connection with the Church of Scotland*, Nov. 3, 1797.

10. Robert Philip, *Life, Times and Missionary Enterprises of the Rev. John Campbell*, passim. John Campbell, *Travels in South Africa* (1815 & 1822). Passim Drummond and Bulloch, *The Crown in Victorian Scotland*, pp. 156-61. A.D. Martin, *Doctor Vanderkemp*, passim. John Philip, *Researches in South Africa*, passim.

11. *Australian Dictionary of Biography*, ii, 221, which also gives (ii, 83) a fifteen-column account of that other Scot (and Aberdonian), Dr James D. Lang, who organised the Presbyterian Church of New South Wales, founded the Scots Church, Sydney, in 1823, and gave an account of 'the venerable James Mein', the pioneer of Ebenezer. (We find Dr Lang present as a visitor at the important meeting of the Scots Presbytery of London on 23rd Jan, 1834, when the statement concerning the churches in the Presbytery, which issued in *The Tabular View* referred to in Appendix D, was received). An article in *The Glasgow Herald* of May 3, 1817 speaks mistakenly of James Mein as having been an elder in Crown Court. *The Challenge of the Years*, by the Rev. C.A. Whyte, recording the history of the Presbyterian Church of New South Wales, gives a full account of Mein's work at Ebenezer. Apparently the Mein children did not accompany their parents to Australia. They may have died in infancy or, at the ages of 10 and 8, may have been left in the care of their grandparents, probably the Joseph Mein family of Seven Dials who were also members of Crown Court.

12. The American Revolution of course occurred during Cruden's ministry, of which we have no Session records. In the State of New York it was commonly known as 'The Presbyterian Revolution'. Horace

Walpole said of it that 'our American cousin had run off with a Presbyterian pastor'. This was with reference to the fact that John Witherspoon, son of the Yester manse, minister of the Laigh Kirk, Paisley, and later the President of Princeton College, helped to draft, and was the only minister to sign, *The Declaration of Independence*. Presbyterian enthusiasm for the Revolution is understandable when one learns of the difficulties to which they had been subjected under the episcopally-dominated British regime. The First Presbyterian Church in New York — on the pulpit Bible of which George Washington took the oath as first President — had, over half-a-century earlier, 'losing all hope of a charter of incorporation by which they might enjoy a right to their Church and cemetery, . . . and especially considering the invidious treatment they received upon all occasions from the Episcopalians', decided to vest the fee of them in the General Assembly of the Church of Scotland. The minutes of the Commission of Assembly dated 8th November, 1732, show that 'the forsaid Deeds being recorded in the Books of the Lords of Council and Session for probation writs, the first is kept here and the other sent to the Minister and Consistory of the Presbyterian Congregation there, whereby the said Church and Grounds it stands upon and belonging thereto are secured to the presbyterians there in all time coming'. When the Revolution finally succeeded the Vestry of Trinity Church changed its attitude, and even offered the First Church, whose building had been damaged, accommodation in Trinity Church itself.

13. But they may well have been referred to from the pulpit. A series of three addresses by a later minister of Crown Court, John Cumming, survives in print, entitled *Liberty, Equality and Fraternity*, the texts being John vii,32, Prov. xxii,2, and I Peter iii,8. They were delivered in April, 1848, soon after the French February Revolution of that year and the establishment of the Second Republic.

14. *Crown Court Session Minutes*, Nov. 19, 1800. The coins were probably 'bad' because they had been clipped, the silver coins of that period still representing the market value of the metal. It was not until 1816, when the guinea made way for the sovereign, that gold became the standard, and silver was reduced to the level of a token coinage, which made clipping unprofitable.

CHAPTER 8

Caledonian Asylum and Gaelic Chapel

Before we venture into the nineteenth century we must take note of a new element which appeared in the London Scottish community during the last quarter of the seventeen hundreds. The beginning of that century had seen a large influx from the Lowlands. Now, after General Wade's roads had opened up north and west Scotland, and when the bitter hostility to the Jacobites of those regions and begun to diminish as memories of the '15 and '45 faded, men from the Highlands increasingly made their way south.

In 1777 Crown Court church had been rebuilt; but Gaelic speakers from the Highlands pined for the word and praise of God in their own tongue. They had also other common interests which they felt they could express, as an ethnic group in London, to the advantage of their homeland and for the removal of handicaps still perpetuated thirty years after the last Highland rebellion. In July of that year a group of them met to form the *Gaelic Society of London,* whose membership was to consist solely of Gaelic speakers; and in the following year twenty-five Highland gentlemen founded the *Highland Society of London,* which accepted those of Highland descent whether Gaelic-speaking or not. Both had aims peculiarly important to Highlanders. The Highland Society stated these in plain terms: 'For preserving the language, dress, music and antiquities of the ancient Caledonians; for rescuing from oblivion the valuable remains of Celtic literature; for the establishment and support of Gaelic schools in the Highlands of Scotland and in other parts of the British Empire; for relieving distressed Highlanders at a distance from their native homes; and for promoting the improvement and general welfare of the northern parts of the Kingdom'[1].

Much could be done towards those ends in London itself.

103

Four years later the greatly-detested Acts, passed after the '45 and forbidding the wearing of the Highland dress, were repealed, and kilt and plaid in the wearer's clan tartan could be donned without penalty. *The British Society for Extending the Fisheries and Improving the sea-coast of this Kingdom* was founded in 1786, to purchase land and form free towns and villages and fishing stations in the Highlands. In 1807 the Highland Society published the poems of Ossian[2], and in 1859 'it originated and chiefly aided in forming and establishing the London Scottish Rifle Volunteers'.

Two other London foundations of the Society are of special interest to us here. Both are foreshadowed in a printed appeal — to be found, accompanied by a personal letter from the president to the Earl of Liverpool, in that Prime Minister's correspondence preserved in the British Library. The first indicates that a subscription list for the building of a Gaelic Chapel was being opened in 1809. It was headed by H.R.H. the Duke of Sussex, the Duke of Montrose, the Marquis of Huntley, the Earls of Nairn, Breadalbane, and Selkirk, and others, including Thomas Coutts, Banker, and not a few from Barbadoes, St Croix and Surinam, as well as various churches and others in Britain. The appeal contained the assurance that 'the Gaelic Chapel is distinctly and avowedly under the protection and guidance of the Society', and that 'this Chapel is no sectary but a recognised branch of the Established Church of Scotland'. One paragraph particularly refers to the fact that there were many parents 'destitute of religious instruction', and their children were consequently left in ignorance of evangelical knowledge and the great duties of morality. 'The Committee, anxious to check the destructive career of vicious ignorance [to which that must lead] consider the erection of a Schoolhouse in connection with the Chapel indispensably necessary'.[3]

The School

The Gaelic Chapel, in Cross Street, Hatton Garden, was dedicated on 30th May, 1813. Meanwhile the Highland Society was vigorously pursuing its other, educational, objective, with a contemporary need especially in mind. At a meeting on 18th

March, 1815, with its president, H.R.H. the Duke of Kent and Strathearn in the chair, it resolved to make a public appeal for subscriptions, the Prince of Wales, then Prince Regent, consenting to become a patron of the institution. Thereafter things moved rapidly. A large and influential Committee, headed by the three royal brothers, T.R.H. the Dukes of York and Albany, of Kent and Strathearn, and of Surrey and Inverness, with no fewer than 90 titled Scots and 70 others, subscribed as sponsors, and on 14th June, 1815 Parliament passed "An Act for establishing and well governing the Charitable Institution called *The Caledonian Asylum,* for supporting and educating Children of Soldiers, Sailors, and Marines, Natives of Scotland, and of indigent Parents, resident in London, not entitled to Parochial Relief". By the terms of the Charter of Incorporation H.R.H. Edward, Duke of Kent and Strathearn (later the father of Queen Victoria) became the first President of the Corporation, and in 1817 The Royal Caledonian Asylum was opened in Cross Street, adjacent to the Gaelic Chapel. The close connection between Asylum and Chapel continued for a full quarter of a century, despite the removal of the latter to Regent Square in 1827. After the Disruption broke the connection the Church of Scotland association was soon re-established by the creation of a new Scottish National church in Holloway, near to the Asylum's Islington home.

The Peninsular War of 1808-14 left many children in England bereft of their Scottish fathers, and from the beginning the Royal Caledonian Asylum met an urgent need as a residential school. Later it moved to Islington, and finally into the cleaner air of Bushey, where in 1917 its governors succeeded in dropping the now misleading term 'Asylum' and it became *The Royal Caledonian Schools.* Today the schools are purely residential, the children receiving their education in local schools at Watford. The Schools' kilted pipers appear at many London Scottish occasions, and a large contingent from the Schools attend the annual Scottish Festival Service in St Columba's. There was a time when the Presbytery of London conducted an annual examination of the children, and kept it in association with a Church of Scotland congregation, until in 1920 St Stephen's Watford, which had originated as a place of worship for the children as well as for Scots in that area, — and which the Schools still attend — transferred to the Presbyterian Church of England.

Generous support, through the Highland Society, the Gaelic Society, the Royal Scottish Corporation, the congregations of the Church of Scotland in and around London, and the various London Scottish clans and other organisations, helps to maintain this benevolent enterprise. An illustration of the spirit of the Schools is seen in the fact that when the Hall of the Clans was destroyed in world war two and lay in ruins for lack of funds, two brothers at the Schools began a rebuilding fund by taking holiday jobs, and their example stimulated such generosity that the rebuilt Hall of the Clans, opened in 1963 by Queen Elizabeth the Queen Mother, is more than worthy of its predecessor. The ministers and congregations of the two London Scots kirks maintain the historic link, and the Moderator of the General Assembly makes an annual visit.

The Church

The Gaelic Chapel in Cross Street soon changed its name, and became **The Caledonian Church** about the time that the Rev. James Boyd was inducted as its first stated minister.

James Boyd had two other claims to our notice. While in London, on 20th February 1818, at the house of John James Ruskin, 54 Hunter Street, he baptised the twelve-day old son of that family, John. A few years later, after Boyd's removal to be parish minister of Ochiltree, his own son, Andrew Kennedy Hutchison Boyd, was born. 'A.K.H.B.', as he later came to be known through his essays — mostly written after he became minister of the first charge at St Andrews, and signed only with his initials — was also a distinguished church leader, becoming Moderator of the General Assembly in 1890, and being the convener of the Committee which produced the first officially sponsored Scottish Hymnal in 1898. His own son, a well-known authority on South Africa, became a member of St Columba's, transferring to Crown Court in 1910 to help his friend, its minister, after the rebuilding of the church there.

James Boyd returned to Scotland after only a brief ministry in the Caledonian Church, and his successor, Alec Macnaughton, stayed less than a year. Plainly there were difficulties, not the least of these being financial. It became necessary, in fact, to transfer the Church trust deeds to the care of the Caledonian Asylum, whose directors somehow kept the church going for the next two years. The long vacancy, however, was caused mainly by the clause in the Trust that the minister should conduct services in Gaelic. The young man on whom the congregation finally set their eyes was on all counts remarkable, but he had no Gaelic. He was willing to spend six months learning it, but the congregation found another way. An Act of Parliament was passed, relaxing the Gaelic-speaking requirement of the Trust, and Edward Irving accepted the call to become minister of the Cross Street congregation in 1822.

Irving's schooldays in Annan had just preceded those of Thomas Carlyle. Later he was Jane Welsh's tutor in Haddington. Then a series of discouragements brought him to the point of contemplating service abroad, where patronage would not be a bar to his ministry. It was at that point that Thomas Chalmers claimed him as his assistant in the remarkable home-mission venture he was embarking upon in the newly-created parish of St John's, Glasgow, and from that exciting work Irving was called, three years later, to be minister of the Caledonian Church. In London he found his old friends, Thomas and Jane (née Welsh) Carlyle, and was encouraged by their welcome and loyalty.

To begin with there seemed to be no particular need for special support. From the beginning of his ministry Irving's preaching drew increasing numbers to the little church in Hatton Garden. Within two years the building proved too small to hold the throngs who came to hear him.

In the Peel papers is preserved another printed appeal. It records that a meeting of the congregation under the pastoral charge of the Revd. Edward Irving was held at the Caledonian Church on Monday, 19th May, 1823, when it was 'resolved that means be immediately taken for building a new National Scotch Church; that it be in connection with the Church of Scotland; that the doctrines, forms of worship, and mode of discipline of that Church shall be taught; and the same shall in all time coming be filled by a minister duly licensed to preach the Gospel by the Church of Scotland and ordained according to the rules of that Church'.[4]

The new building, the **Regent Square National Scottish Church**, was dedicated in 1827 — with a gallery for the children of the Royal Caledonian Asylum — and the preaching of the inspired young minister quickly filled it. His influence was also felt in the Presbytery. In 1827 the Scotch Presbytery in London printed and circulated a Pastoral Letter addressed 'to the Baptised of the Scottish Church resident in London and its vicinity' of which some passages strongly resemble in content and style parts of the Caledonian Church's 1823 appeal already mentioned. It estimates that of the 'no less than 100,000 [in that area] who have received Baptism at the hand, and are thereby members, of the Church of Scotland, not 1000 present themselves at the Table of the Lord to renew their Baptismal covenant and join themselves to the body of Christ, for their spiritual nourishment and growth in grace'. It refers to young people, 'left at large to folly, and in the end engulfed by the wickedness around them', and it affirms 'We are no bigots, though heartily attached to the Church of Scotland, and we neither approve of or practice proselytising courses, but would endeavour to carry ourselves as a portion of the Protestant Church, whereof we look upon the Church of England as a bulwark'. Nevertheless, it reminds all fellow-Scots, we are the heirs of dearly-bought privileges, for any misuse of which we will have to answer. The letter, which runs to about 17,000 words, ends on a fatherly note, and is signed by six ministers and seven elders. Apart from reflecting problems which are still familiar in the Church's pastoral work it shows something of the mind and mood of the Scots Kirk in London a century and a half ago, as well as of the hand of the minister of Regent Square.

To Edward Irving there did come a time when he was in need of the understanding and support of all his friends. From some he received this, but by others it was withdrawn just when the need was greatest. The crisis in his ministry arose partly because of the pentecostalist manifestations which began to appear, and which his own convictions compelled him to allow as tokens of the presence and power of the Holy Spirit amongst Christ's people, in Regent Square in 1832. Already in 1830 the Presbytery had had its attention drawn to his teaching on the humanity of Jesus as expounded in his book *The Orthodox and Catholic*

Doctrine of our Lord's Human Nature, and had found it unorthodox. But it was on an accusation by the trustees of Regent Square church, 'of abuses of worship and discipline by the minister', that the Presbytery of London, on the 2nd of May, 1832, declared that 'the Rev. E. Irving has rendered himself unfit to remain the minister of the National Scotch Church aforesaid, and ought to be removed therefrom in pursuance of the conditions of the trust-deed of the said church'. This was with reference to the clause in that deed, requiring that the church should be used for worship 'according to the doctrines, forms of worship and mode of discipline of the established Church of Scotland', which Irving, in permitting 'speaking in tongues', (and that by persons who were neither ministers or licentiates of the Church of Scotland) was held to have violated.[5]

The more serious charge of heresy — that in his book Irving had implied Christ's sharing of our *sinful* human nature — had been noted by the General Assembly in 1831, who had directed the Presbytery of Annan, as the Presbytery which had ordained him, to try him on a charge of heresy. There, with 2000 people crowded into the parish church, lit, as darkness fell, by a solitary candle, the Presbytery found the libel proven, and Dr Henry Duncan of Ruthwell, its most distinguished member[6], had, in duty bound as Presbytery Clerk, to make the most painful statement of his life and pronounce the fateful sentence of deposition.

A strange thread connects the four men who in that year found themselves under church discipline. Edward Irving was deposed because his teaching on the humanity of Jesus was held to impute sinfulness to Him. MacLeod Campbell of Rhu was deposed for teaching universal atonement through Christ. Alexander J. Scott, whose preaching at Rhu had delighted Campbell and had later resulted in the 'speaking in tongues' which so impressed Irving, was deprived of his license because he could not subscribe the Westminster Confession of Faith.[7] And Hugh B. Maclean, to whom Irving's ordination charge when he became minister of London Wall Church had been an inspired beginning to his ministry, was forbidden to exercise that ministry when called to Dreghorn, his license being suspended by the Dreghorn Presbytery because he could not satisfy them with his answers to a charge of heresy. A new age in theological interpretation was struggling to be born, and these four assistants at the birth were sacrifices of the struggle.

Eight hundred of Irving's members from Regent Square went out into the wilderness with him, and from that nucleus sprang the Catholic Apostolic Church — a Bible Church, a Praying Church, a Sacramental Church and a Pentecostal Church, as Dr Harry Whitley has said[8]. But Irving had little to do with its development. He died, perhaps the victim of his own intensity of spirit as much as of the tuberculosis which finally claimed his life, two years after his deposition. 'He set out' said Dr John Cumming of Crown Court in Irving's funeral sermon, 'like some warship with streaming pennants and majestic sway, but the storms beat and the waves arose and prudence was driven from the wheel; and perchance the seven spirits that are before the throne ceased to breathe upon the sails'. The consciousness of his genius 'made him fancy he could penetrate the arcana of eternity and gather to his bosom flowers that blossomed not on earth. Like the eagle he soared too near the sun and was struck blind'[9]. Whatever the eccentricities of his words and writings the Church could ill afford the loss of this loyal and gifted minister and it is one of the sad reflections on her judgement that she let herself be forced to shut him out. Sixty years later, in partial reparation, the Moderator of the General Assembly, Professor A.M. Charteris[10], unveiled a statue of him in Annan. There, beside the parish kirk in which he was ordained in 1822 and deposed in 1833, stands the representation of that courageous, single-minded man who in so brief a ministry served with such tireless devotion the Kirk he loved and the Master he owned.

The Scotch National Church in Regent Square survived the immediate sad outcome of the Presbytery trial. Eleven years later, with its minister James Hamilton, it left the Church of Scotland connection, as did most of the Scots congregations in England[11]. Since then it has played a notable role in what to begin with was the Presbyterian Church in England, later became The Presbyterian Church of England, and is now the United Reformed Church in England and Wales. In 1944 the church building, and the P.C.E. Headquarters beside it, were destroyed by a rocket bomb. Both were rebuilt in 1966, and the latter have been the Offices of the United Reformed Church since the Union in 1972.

Other Nineteenth Century London Scottish Congregations

The story of the Scots Kirk in London during the nineteenth century was dramatically shaped by the Disruption of 1843[12]. Of the sixteen congregations connected with the Scots Presbytery of London during the eighteenth century, ten had expired or lost that connection before the century ended; but within the first forty years of the new century nine others (including the one which became Regent Square Scotch National Church) had been added to the number. Immediately after the Disruption only four remained 'in connection with the Church of Scotland', six having adhered to the Free Church and become the Presbyterian Church in England, and the others having by that time re-united with their parent congregations or dissolved. Within the next half-century, however, nine new Scottish congregations came into being, some of them having a comparatively brief life; while of the four survivors of 1843 only one saw the twentieth century, being accompanied into it by five of the nine. Of this total of seventeen 19th-century-founded congregations we have dealt with Regent Square and shall reserve the story of three others for fuller treatment in later chapters. What follows here is a synopsis of the remaining thirteen, seven arising before, and six after, the Disruption.

Pre-Disruption

1. **Artillery Street** was a breakaway from London Wall Scotch Church in 1803. It re-united with London Wall in 1809. At that time it had called the distinguished Robert Simpson of Hoxton Academy, a Scot from Milnathort and later a D.D. of Glasgow, to be its minister, but the London Presbytery 'would not sustain the call until he should lay an extract of license as a preacher from some Presbytery of the Church of Scotland'. (*Fasti*, vii,486).

2. A second Scots congregation appeared in **Southwark** in 1822, and the London Presbytery came to its aid in 1824, when a place of worship was secured and James Miller, a licentiate, appointed to minister, 'under the care of the Rev. the Presbytery of London'. Later we find the congregation worshipping in a schoolroom rented from the British and Foreign Bible Society, with Archibald Millar as the missionary. In 1843 William Chalmers Burns was called, but declined, and later became the renowned pioneer Chinese missionary. John Thomson became minister in 1844, but the Church of Scotland connection appears to have become slight, and no trace of *Southwark, Prospect Place* appears thereafter in Presbytery records. *(Minutes of Scots Presbytery of London,* 1772-1843; *Fasti,* vii,499)

3. Nearby in Lambeth, close to the Elephant and Castle, the **Verulam Scots Church** in Walcot Place had been in the care of James Millar, a Glasgow licentiate, who had been ordained to this charge in 1826. He resigned in 1842, and the congregation, which had never thrived, disbanded. (*Minutes, ut supra;* and *Fasti,* vii,498)

4. A Scottish congregation was formed in **Chadwell Street, Pentonville**, in 1827, and was recognised by the Presbytery in the following year. In 1829 W.R. Taylor became its minister, and during his time it moved to **River Terrace** (later called Colebrook Row), **Islington**. John Macdonald was minister from 1831-37, and was succeeded by Peter Lorimer, who, with his congregation, severed the Church of Scotland connection in 1843. Two months later the minutes of the London Presbytery of the Presbyterian Church in England recorded that Mr Lorimer — who had played a leading part in the dramatic scene in Woolwich (see Appendix D) — had to report that the Trust Deeds of the congregation in River Street required connection with the Presbytery of London in connection with the Establised Church of Scotland and also that its minister be amenable thereto. This property difficulty affected a number of seceding congregations and ministers. Mr Lorimer was appointed first Professor of Theology at the newly instituted English Presbyterian College in 1844 — a chair which he occupied with distinction. He was the author of a number of books, including *John*

Knox and the Church of England; and his address at the opening of the English Presbyterian College on Nov. 5, 1844, is a masterly *apologia* for the 'English Disruption'; 'We look now' he said,' to be an English Church, taking its place amongst others — and not only for Scots and Irish (as generally at present) but for all'.

5. In 1832 a congregation had been formed in **Greenwich** in connection with the United Associate (Secession) Presbytery of London. It applied for admission to the London (Church of Scotland) Presbytery in 1842, its minister being John Millar, who was succeeded in that year by Adam Roxburgh, son of the minister of Kilmaurs. He, with his congregation, went out in sympathy with the Free Church in 1843.

6. A Scottish congregation in **Dudley**, although far outside the bounds of London, had been received into the London Presbytery on an appeal from influential men in Birmingham. Its minister, Samuel Blair, was Moderator of the Presbytery at the fateful meeting in Woolwich when the breach took place (see Appendix D). He was one of the four who remained in the Church of Scotland connection, but his officebearers and congregation were not of his mind and entered the Presbyterian Church in England the following year.

7. That Presbytery meeting in Woolwich had been called to arrange for the ordination and induction of the Rev. James Ferguson to the year-old charge of **Goodman's Fields, White-chapel.** The congregation had gathered early in 1842, and the church was opened in 1843, Mr Ferguson to be its first minister. But in June the majority of the Presbytery refused, and he himself declined, that he should be inducted 'in connection with the Established Church of Scotland' (see Appendix D), and he and his congregation became Presbyterian Church in England, being joined by a great number of like-minded members of St Andrew's Scotch National Church, Stepney. Later the congregation moved to Green Street, and became John Knox P.C.E., Oxford Street (now Stepney Way), Stepney.

The Rev. Alexander Fletcher, though his name is absent from the London Presbytery records, was a conspicuous figure on the London Kirk scene. Son of the minister of Bridge of Teith, and a Glasgow graduate, he became minister of Miles Lane Chapel, a Secession congregation, in 1811. His popularity as a preacher attracted so large a congregation that a new church, Albion Chapel, erected for him in 1816, was soon crowded. A law case, in which he was exonerated, led to the United Associate Synod in Edinburgh suspending him, but with his congregation he moved to a new and spacious place of worship — the largest in London — in Finsbury Circus, where he ministered for thirty-five years. His services for children were famous: his last sermon was preached to 3,000 children in 1860. He died, honoured with an American D.D., received back into the Secession (now the United Presbyterian) Church, and the author of 21 books, one at least of which sold 50,000 copies in England alone.

After the Disruption, Swallow Street, St Andrew's Stepney, and Crown Court remained in connection with the Church of Scotland, Crown Court alone being unimpaired in number of elders and strength of membership. In course of time they were joined by nine others, of which six fall to be briefly noted here.

Post-Disruption

1. The departure of Regent Square from the Church of Scotland connection left the Caledonian Asylum without a place of worship, but in 1846 the Duke of Buccleuch, Dr John Cumming of Crown Court, and Mr Pollok Black of St Andrews Stepney successfully negotiated for and bought Holloway Chapel from a dwindling Independent congregation and restored it as a place of worship under the name of **The Caledonian Chapel, Holloway**. It was conveniently located not only for the staff and children of the Caledonian Asylum which had moved to Holloway in the 1820s but also for the Scots families which were then resident there. It continued its chaplaincy arrangement with the Royal Caledonian Asylum until the latter moved to Bushey in 1903, but the brevity of many of its ministries indicates — or explains — the lack of vitality from which it suffered at least

The Queen has just laid the foundation-stone of the new St Columba's, in 1950. Note
the remains of the chancel mosaic of the old building. See also the picture of the
laying of the foundation-stone of that building on page 153. As the Queen Mother
her Majesty returned for the dedication of the London Scottish Memorial Chapel in
1956.   *The Associated Press, Ltd.*

St Columba's Church, interior.   *Photo: Pamela Chandler.*

Crown Court Church, interior.   *Crown Court Church.*

The New Church, Crown Court, built on part of the old site and dedicated on 29th October, 1909.   *Greater London Council Photograph Library.*

(a) St James Church of Scotland, East Dulwich, in 1972.

(b) The Foundation and Commemoration stones from the original church and Hall are arranged now as a feature in the garden of the 'sheltered housing' buildings, erected with the bricks of the old church and preserving its name as St James' Cloisters.

Photo: Bill Waddell.

The Old Church, Crown Court, at the end of its days in 1907.
Greater London Council Photograph Library.

The New Church in Pont Street (1884), which stood for 57 years at the head of Pont Street until destroyed in an air-raid, May 1941.

(a) The old Crown Court Scots Kirk Communion Table, now in the Isle of Tiree. See chapters 5 and 12. *Photo: Miss Anne Stuart, D.C.S.*
The Minister and Deaconess of Tiree Parish Church.

(b) The Crown Court Communion Vessels and Alms Dish; 1842-8.
Crown Court Church of Scotland.

The Royal Caledonian Schools. Originally known as The Caledonian Asylum, the Schools were situated first in Hatton Garden, then in Islington, and since 1903 in Bushey, Herts.

The Moderator, the Right Rev. Dr Peter Brodie, opening the new Library in the Royal Caledonian Schools, November, 1978. Pupils, young and old, guided by the Woodwork Teacher, built the shelving, panelled the walls, and redecorated the room.

Photo: Watford.

a. The Scottish Corporation's sheltered housing at Bawtry Road, North London.

b. St Columba's House, the Corporation's hostel for Scots in London, with a possible resident arriving.

The mouth of the Fleet Ditch at Blackfriars, possibly painted by Samuel Scott, the friend and fellow-artist of Hogarth. The Scottish Corporation's buildings are in the centre of the picture, to the right of the Bridewell Bridge.

Guildhall Art Gallery, City of London.

The Swallow Street Scots Kirk Communion Vessels. For the story of their presentation see chapter four. *Photo: Bill Waddell.*

King Edward VI presents to John a 'Lasco the Charter constituting the first Protestant Reformed 'Church of the Strangers', in 1550. This 17th century painting depicts, from left to right, Cranmer, Ridley, Edward VI, Northumberland, a'Lasco and Knox.
Courtesy of the United Reformed Church.

The Horningsham Meeting House, dated 1566, where those "Scots workmen, followers of John Knox and John Calvin", who were then engaged in the building of Longleat, were able to worship according to their own convictions. It is still in use.

The Founders' Hall Scots Kirk Communion vessels. The silver chalices were given by four Elders in 1694. The pewter flagons and paten are of a later period when the congregation had moved to London Wall.

The Museum of London and the United Reformed Church.

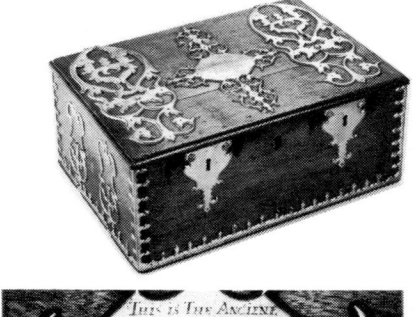

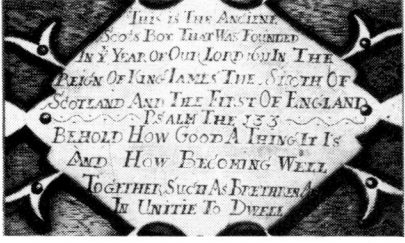

(a) The Scots Box, with (b) detail of inscription.   *The Royal Scottish Hospital.*
(c) The Commemoration Stone from the original Blackfriars Hall of the Scottish Hospital. A later hand changed SCOTS to SCOTCH at some period when the latter spelling became temporarily fashionable in England.   *Photo: Ian MacLeod.*

during the first twenty and the last forty of its ninety years of independent existence. Even during the longer ministries of Robert Mackersy (1870-77) and James S. Forsyth (1877-98) it was dependent on financial aid from other congregations; but these two at least made significant contribution to the work of the Presbytery and the life of the Scots Kirk in London. Forsyth particularly — one of the many Aberdonian ministers the London churches have known — figures prominently in that story, as a peace-making influence in the relationships of the Scottish and English Presbyterian Churches, as interim-moderator in the Crown Court vacancy of 1879-81 which had such a unexpectedly happy issue, and as adviser and encourager of the little group of Scots in East Dulwich about which we shall hear more in chapter fourteen. Dr Forsyth, as he became in 1894, was seriously injured in the disaster which befell the Scotch Express at Thirsk in 1892[13], but was able to return for duty three months thereafter.

The departure of the Royal Caledonian Asylum to Bushey in 1903 must have dealt a financial blow to the Holloway congregation, which had from its beginnings enjoyed a grant from the Asylum, as appears in a minute of the Kirk Session dated 17th Oct., 1877, stating that 'Mr Mackersey, late minister, had received £5 more of the Grant from the Caledonian Asylum than he was entitled to. The Treasurer was instructed to call on him for an explanation'. The matter was amicably settled before Mr Mackersey took up his new charge at Craiglockhart. The closing chapter in the tale of the Holloway church was written in 1950 and is related in chapter fifteen.

2. The Church of Scotland initiated a mission to Jews in association with the Presbytery of London in 1846, Henry Douglas being the first missioner and minister of the congregation established that year in **Halkin Street**, Belgrave Square. The work went on successfully for twenty years, Douglas's successor, Lawrence McBeth being given a D.D. by Glasgow University in 1864; but on his dismissal two years later the congregation merged with the Presbyterian Church of England congregation from Ranelagh Gardens, which then moved into the building and became Belgrave Presbyterian Church. Successive unions took it to South Kensington, Emperor's Gate, and Kensington

St John's, which still flourishes. The original building in Halkin Street, renovated, still stands, and is occupied as a private residence.

3. A Presbyterian Meeting-house had existed in **Croydon** from about 1800 — probably English Presbyterian, although under the ministry of yet another Aberdonian, John Calder, who became librarian of Dr Williams' Library, having already made his mark in literary London through a much earlier controversy with Dr Johnson. In 1865 James Bonthorne, who had been a Church of Scotland missionary in Cochin, India, and later an assistant in Crown Court, conducted services in Croydon 'in connection with the Church of Scotland' for some years after he left Crown Court in 1865. (*Fasti*, vii,522,585,714)

4. **Wood Green, St James'**, came into being in 1871 as an off-shoot of a congregation, probably English Presbyterian, in Lordship Lane. It joined the Presbyterian Church of England in 1875.

5. Dr Robbins was the first minister of a new charge set up by the Church of Scotland in Watford about 1896. It was later named **St Stephen's, Watford,** and became the place of worship for the children of the Royal Caledonian Asylum when the Schools moved from Holloway to Bushey in 1903. In 1920 St Stephen's transferred to the Presbyterian Church of England.

6. Various references in the Crown Court Session minutes and those of the Scots Presbytery of London show that a Scottish chaplaincy at **New Brompton** in connection with the garrison there was maintained from about 1864, when the Rev. George Walker, a licentiate of St Andrews Presbytery, was ordained as chaplain. New Brompton, or Gillingham, is now in effect part of Chatham. By 1910, when the Rev. George A. Selbie became minister, it entered upon a more settled existence than its earlier succession of very brief chaplaincies had allowed, and Selbie remained for ten years. In 1920 it was linked with St James', East Dulwich, and remained under the pastoral care of the minister there until 1929 when it became an Extension Mission, being granted full status in 1949. Since 1952 it has

116

been known as **Gillingham, St Margaret's,** and continues its work and witness there under the name of Scotland's 'patroness saint', the English-born Scottish queen.

NOTES

1. *Report of the Highland Society of London,* 1872.

   The Society also took up and much encouraged the cause of education in the Highlands, which for various reasons had lagged far behind that of the rest of Scotland. Neither Scottish nor Irish Gaelic had ever appeared in printed form until Carswell, the Reformation Superintendent of the Isles, published *John Knox's* Liturgy in 1567. Thereafter, as we have seen (Chapter three), Robert Kirk supplied the first translation of the Psalms, and went on to rewrite and publish in Roman type the Irish translations of the Old Testament by Bishop Bedell and of the New by O'Donell. The first Assembly after the Revolution, in 1690, received and distributed a gift of several thousands of these Irish Gaelic Bibles. Progress in Highland literacy, however, remained slow until the evangelical revivals of the 18th century stimulated a demand in the Highlands for the Bible in Scots Gaelic, and the Synod of Argyle in particular took the lead in supplying this from 1751 onwards. (Rev. A. Fletcher, art. in *Life and Work,* Aug. 1951). 'The records of the General Assembly in the second half of the 18th century . . . tell of unceasing endeavours to provide ministers, schoolteachers and Gaelic religious literature'. (Drummond & Bulloch, *The Scottish Church, 1688-1843,* p. 136). Frequently mentioned in Session and Presbytery minutes in London is 'The London Board of the Society for the Propagation of Christian Knowledge in the Highlands and Islands of Scotland', and most of the London Scottish ministers seem to have been active in its support. This 'Scottish Society for Propagating Christian Knowledge' had been formed in 1708, planted its first school in St Kilda, and was supporting 109 schoolmasters by 1832. (Drummond & Bulloch, *The Church in Victorian Scotland, p. 85).* Both the Gaelic and the Highland Societies of London gave further encouragement to the cause.

2. This was a publication of Gaelic material in MS left by James Macpherson, the genuineness of whose published Ossianic translations had been questioned by Dr Johnson. The Highland Society was able to establish that Ossianic ballads did really exist and that Macpherson had used them; but its conclusions as to the authenticity of all his work were somewhat negative. (*Highland Society Report*).

3. *Letters on Behalf of the Gaelic Chapel, Correspondence of 2nd Earl of Liverpool, British Library, MS. Addnl. 38255, f.105, and 38256, ff. 162,3.*

4. *Ibid., Peel Correspondence, British Library, MS. Addnl. 40356, f.136.*
5. *Minutes of Scots Presbytery of London,* 2nd May, 1832.
6. *Minutes of Presbytery of Annan,* 13th Mar., 1833.

    Dr Henry Duncan, besides being the preserver and restorer of the unique Runic *Ruthwell Cross,* was the originator of Savings Banks. There still stands in Ruthwell the whitewashed cottage where he and his parishioners realised his dream of enabling them to 'save for a rainy day'. In those days no bank would accept a deposit of less than £10. 'If any method could be devised for giving to the honest and successful labourer or artisan a place of security free of expense for that part of his gains which the immediate wants of his family do not require, with the power to reclaim all or part of it at leisure, it would be a most desirable thing', he wrote, 'even if no interest should be received'. He himself devised the method, and opened his penny savings bank in 1810. It did pay interest, from its first year. A great-granddaughter of his is a member of St Columba's church in London. He was also the stepfather of Mary Lundie, later the wife of another Duncan, minister of Cleish, and authoress of the favourite children's hymn, 'Jesus, tender Shepherd'.

7. See Chapter four, note 12.
8. H.C. Whitley, *Blinded Eagle,* pp. 82ff.
9. Andrew L. Drummond, *Edward Irving and his Circle,* p. 276. Whitley, *op. cit.,* p. 34, ascribes the image of the blinded eagle to Carlyle, citing an account by P.E. Shaw of a conversation between Carlyle and a visiting American thirty years after Irving's death.
10. A.H. Charteris, whose influence on a later stage in the story of the Scots Kirk in London was considerable, was Professor of Biblical Criticism in the University of Edinburgh. He was the founder of the Church of Scotland Magazine, *Life and Work,* of the Young Men's Guild, and of the Woman's Guild of the Church of Scotland. He also revived the ancient Order of Deaconesses. For their training he founded the Deaconess House in Edinburgh, and, for those requiring nursing training, the Lady Grizel Baillie Deaconess Hospital, built and equipped and maintained by the Church of Scotland, but since 1946 under the Hospital Board.
11. See Appendix C.
12. See Appendix C.
13. This railway disaster, which was due to the conditions under which the signalman at Thirsk had had to work, resulted in a reduction of working-hours for signalmen and a better system of relief. (See L.T.C. Rolt, *Red for Danger,* pp. 164-66).

CHAPTER 9

In a Time of Social Revolution

Just about the time that James Steven left London for Kilwinning a young Scottish probationer, George Greig, was accepted by the London Missionary Society for service abroad. He and his wife set sail with a number of other missionaries for their appointed field, but the voyage was interrupted by a French privateer, who captured crew and passengers and eventually set them ashore somewhere in South America. With very great difficulty and after many months the Rev. and Mrs George Greig at last succeeded in returning to Scotland[1].

Meanwhile Crown Court church was once more finding difficulty in securing a minister. But this time the congregation was not in such a depressed state as it had been in 1785; and although again two years were to pass before a successor was found, the Kirk Session kept careful records, gave the congregation an encouraging lead, and even played some part in the wider Church life of London. In 1803, for example, we find the elders going in a body with Wilberforce to the House of Commons, to support him in his protest about a clause in a Parliamentary Bill which would have appointed part of Sunday for the training of men in military exercises, giving as the grounds of their objection that the clause 'would offend many loyal subjects of the king'.

Nor were they idle in their search for a minister. They wrote to various ministers in Scotland, including John Love, now of Anderston in Glasgow, asking for recommendations. Several suggestions were made, but none proved suitable. At last in 1805, they heard of George Greig, fully recovered from the privations of his 1803 ordeal; the congregation elected him, and he was inducted in October of that year.

The Kirk Session minute recording his induction prompts a question which is underlined by the fact that neither Greig's

119

name nor that of Crown Court church appear in the minutes of the Presbytery during the whole term of his ministry. The query is raised because we find Mr Brocklebank taking the prayer and reading the scripture, Mr Simpson of Hoxton putting the questions and giving the address to Mr Greig, Mr Campbell of Kingsland taking the intercessory prayer, Mr Townsend of Rotherhithe preaching the sermon, and Mr Collyer of Peckham taking the concluding prayer[2]. None of these names appear on the roll of the London Presbytery, although Mr Simpson's name appears once as a visitor in 1791. They were in fact all Independent ministers, assembled *ad hoc* for the induction, George Greig himself being of that denomination. In consequence of this Crown Court remained isolated from the Presbytery and virtually independent for nearly thirty years.

Education

Despite that handicap the first twenty years of Greig's ministry were active and by no means ingrowing. The congregation's care for the children of the neighbourhood took a practical form in 1812, when the Session decided that their education was a Christian responsibility, and 'that with all convenient speed a Sunday School be accordingly established'. Two years later the necessary premises were found when three rooms and a loft adjoining the back wall of the church fell vacant, and arrangements were made to lease them. Finance was, as usual, the problem, and the School was to be opened 'at as little expense as possible', while the minister agreed to arrange preachers for three services on the first Sunday of the year, the offerings to be devoted to the Sunday School, the theme of the sermons.

Considerable information remains concerning the operation of the School, although it is uncertain whether the teaching was confined to Sundays or extended to weekdays. The Sunday School movement, started in 1780 by Robert Raikes in Gloucester, was by that time concerned to further the general as well as the religious education of the deprived children of the land, and this involved the organising of day-school teaching. In Crown Court, during a later ministry, the Day School became an established part of the congregation's work. During Greig's time the need for this may not have been strongly felt, but there is some implication of day-school teaching in the regulation that

TO THE
MASTERS and MISTRESSES
OF
SUNDAY-SCHOOLS.

I. ENDEAVOUR to know and practice the best Method of Instruction.

II. Be diligent in teaching the Children to read well.

III. Take Pains to make them understand all they are taught.

IV. Neither Writing nor Arithmetic are to be taught on *Sunday*.

V. Require nothing of the Scholars but what they can and should do, but see that all is done that is required.

VI. Keep exact Accounts of their Attendance every Sabbath-Day; and if any absent themselves, enquire the Reasons of their Parents.

VII. Make faithful Reports to the Visitors both of the Improvements and Behaviour of the Scholars.

VIII. Range your Scholars in Classes according to their Ages and Abilities, in order to raise such to a higher Class whose Care and Improvements merit Advancement, and to degrade others who by Negligence have deserved it.

IX. As much as possible avoid corporal Punishments----try Advice—Persuasion—Encouragement—Disgrace—Confinement, &c. more especially aim to inspire them with a Disposition to excel; and contrive honorary Rewards to confer upon such as deserve them.

X. Above all, keep the Religious Ends of the Institution always in Sight; and be constantly reminding all under your Care that SUNDAY-SCHOOLS are designed
—To check and reform vicious Habits, and all Tendencies towards them in the rising Generation.
—To inculcate upon them a becoming Regard for the Word and Worship of Almighty God.
—To require their keeping holy the Sabbath-Day.
—To warn them of the Evil of Sin in general, and of youthful Sins in particular, such as Pride, Pilfering, Idleness, Swearing, Lying, Disobedience to Parents, &c.
—To set before them the Excellency and Importance of Justice, Diligence, Humility, and a conscientious Regard to Truth in all they say, and a respectful Subjection to those whom the Providence of God has set over them.
—Finally, to explain, in a Manner suited to their Understandings, all the Truths and Duties recommended in the Holy Scriptures; and promote a believing and obedient Regard to them for their Happiness both here and hereafter.

Sunday School teachers, as well as pupils, were under advice, if not instruction, in 1814 — and surprisingly good advice it was. *Crown Court Church of Scotland.*

'Writing and Arithmetic were not to be taught on Sundays; but, in order that the children might be able to read the Bible for themselves, Reading was a subject on the Sunday curriculum'[3].

The children were set in classes according to age and ability, and might be moved up or down a class as the staff judged wise. Parents of absentees were to be visited and asked the reason for absence. Corporal punishment was to be avoided in favour of advice, encouragement, persuasion, and if necessary confinement or disgrace. The teachers were to keep the religious aims of the school in mind, and 'To check and reform vicious Habits and all tendencies to them in the rising Generation: To inculcate upon them a becoming Regard for the Word and Worship of Almighty God: To require their keeping holy the Sabbath Day: To warn them of the Evil of Sin in general, and of youthful sins in particular, such as Pride, Pilfering, Idleness, Swearing, Lying, Disobedience to Parents, &c: To set before them the Excellence and Importance of Justice, Diligence, Humility, and a conscious Regard to Truth in all they say, and a respectful Subjection to those whom the providence of God has set over them: Finally, to explain, in a manner suitable to their Understandings, all the Truths and Duties recommended in the Holy Scriptures; and promote a believing and obedient Regard to them for their Happiness both here and hereafter'.

But the 'Masters and Mistresses' were not themselves exempt from discipline. It came to the Session's notice in December 1814 that the nine male and ten female teachers were having tea together in the vestry on Sunday afternoons! After solemn discussion on 'the impropriety of the practice and the unpleasant consequences which might result from it', the Elders decided that 'the Teachers be desired to discontinue the same'[4].

An interest in further education is marked by the Session's congratulations to one of its number, Mr William Reid, on his election as a Trustee for the London University in 1827[5].

Amelioration

Meanwhile, amidst all the external confusions of the Peninsular War, the Luddite outbreaks, the insanity of George III, Waterloo, and the rise of the movement for parliamentary reform, an old issue, of much concern to non-conformists, had again arisen. The penalties of the Corporation and Test Acts still debarred dissenters from office, and in 1811 a Joint Committee had been formed 'for Protecting the Civil Rights of Dissenters', as was noted then in the Crown Court Session minutes. The following year the Committee prepared a petition to Parliament for the repeal of those Acts. There were two opinions amongst the dissenters themselves on this matter. Some would have resorted even to extreme measures to secure the abolition of the hated Acts. Others, although smarting under the deprivation of their civil rights, nevertheless believed the Acts should remain as the only safeguard against the Roman's Church's recovery of political and educational power. The elders of Crown Court decided not to sign the Committee's petition since the Roman Catholics were involved it, and their signatures might be construed as approval of 'the ardour with which the Roman Catholics have lately pursued their claims'.

The Acts were in fact repealed in 1828, and instead of the test of receiving the Sacrament according to the forms of the Church of England there was substituted a declaration containing the words 'on the true faith of a Christian', thus entitling Protestant dissenters to office. It is good to be able to record that in Scotland the campaign for including Roman Catholics in this relief, which came about the following year with the Catholic Relief Act, was strongly and ably supported by Whigs and Tories together, Thomas Chalmers being prominent in that support, with men like Lord Cockburn, Judge Jeffreys, and Lord Moncrieff.

One of the congregation's best-known members at this time was Dr Maxwell Garthshore, son of the minister of Kirkcudbright, colleague of the famous Hunter brothers[6], Fellow of the Royal Society, and Physician to the British Lying-in Hospital. He died, aged 80, in 1812, and we learn from Greig's sermon on March 15th something of his character. Every year he spent more than £1000 on charity, and gave free advice, three days a week, to poor people. He had literary as well as professional abilities, and used these, like his time and money, as 'means of bestowing blessing and comfort', knowing, as his diary comments, 'that their misuse brought contempt, self-condemnation and heartfelt misery, and that divine assistance was necessary for their right use'. On his deathbed he gathered his domestics around him to share his minister's prayer[7].

Expansion

The missionary interest of the congregation had spread amongst its young people, and a Juvenile Branch of the Auxiliary Missionary Society was formed in 1815. Through this a considerable number of subscriptions swelled Crown Court's generous support of the missionary cause, but that was not the limit of its interest. In August 1829 a special service was conducted by a group of ministers, at which a young man, son of the William Reid already mentioned, was ordained before departing for Bellary in the East Indies as a missionary.

In 1819 Queen Charlotte died, and the pulpit in Crown Court was draped in customary mourning. The drapes were stolen, along with the Baptismal Basin and a looking-glass from the vestry. A reward of £20 was offered, indicating the high value attached to the stolen property, but nothing was recovered[8]. In 1822 the tenant of the property next door left ladders against the railing, and thieves used them to climb to the roof and steal the lead guttering. These incidents may be taken as reflecting the unsettled state of the country, when poverty had become almost endemic amongst the labouring classes, and as indicating how acutely the pinch was felt in the Drury Lane area of London, with a corresponding increase in crime there. This in turn may explain the fall in evening attendances, which caused much concern to minister and elders in the latter part of that decade. They tried a variety of expedients to remedy the situation, without much success.

Morning and afternoon services, however, were well-attended, and the Sunday School flourished. In 1818 additional accommodation for the girls' school had had to be found. When the Sabbath School celebrated its seventh anniversary 1,379 children had passed through the teachers' hands, and in that year, 1821, there were 77 boys and 93 girls on the roll. It might be safe to assume that these were mostly children of the neighbourhood and that their parents had little connection with the congregation other than through their children's attendance at Sunday School. The children of members in those days received their Christian education at home[9]. The Sunday School movement was begun by those who saw what was happening to the children of parents with no connection with the Christian fellowship, and who counted it a duty to offer what parents were failing to provide.

The vexed question of 'psalmody' had engaged the Session's attention since 1776. In that and the following year a proposal to introduce the Scots Paraphrases had been turned down because of the 'aversion of many members to alter the Psalmody statedly used in the Church'[10]. In 1797 a wish had been expressed by some members that in the Public Worship in future the reading of the lines of the Psalms by the Clerk might be omitted[11], but a decision on the matter was 'deferred for the present'. On 3rd March, 1812, however, the Session 'agreed that Additional Psalmody might be used in public worship at the discretion of the Minister in conjunction with the Scots Psalms, and approved for that purpose the version of Dr Watts, with the Hymns by that author'[12].

Litigation

Greig and his Session seem successfully to have escaped involvement in the kind of dispute which in the case of at least two Scotch National churches culminated in Court proceedings. In 1815 division arose between the elders of London Wall and a 'Committee of the Congregation' over the question of the formers' nomination of a new minister and the latter's preference for another. Each accused the other of irregularities in procedure, and voluminous printed statements by both were widely circulated. In 1826 a case was heard in Chancery concerning alleged irregularities in the election of a successor to John Marshall of Swallow Street, the one party claiming that only members had the right to elect and the other that subscribers should also have that right, while a third party apparently claimed that in any case the terms of the Trust had been broken at the ordination of William Crookshanks ninety years earlier, and therefore the property should be forfeited and the congregation dissolved.

Both cases seem to indicate the beginnings of a rank-and-file re-assertion of the democratic spirit which has always informed the Presbyterian tradition. This was no doubt provoked to stronger expression by the increasing indifference to the rights of congregations in Scotland by those to whom Queen Anne's Act had given patronal rights. Ten years later that issue was to bring Presbyteries and the General Assembly into conflict with the Court of Session, and eventually to the point of disruption and the emergence of the Free Church.

Crown Court was not involved, as London Wall and Swallow Street were, in such litigation. Other litigation, in fact, evoked its generosity. Law suits had been taken out during the first decade of the century against a number of dissenting congregations, and the newly-formed *Society for Protecting the Civil Rights of Dissenters* found itself quickly out of funds when appeals for help in defending such cases were made to it. Crown Court was able to make a generous donation in 1811 and again in 1820.

Attenuation

The vitality of the early years of Greig's ministry showed signs of ebbing in the mid-twenties of the century. The Sunday School started to decline; expenses were rising; the Adelphi Day Schools which had been renting the buildings terminated their agreement at the end of 1824; by 1827 there was difficulty in finding sufficient male teachers, and a meeting with the Superintendent of the Western Sunday School Union brought no encouragement. In August that year the School was suspended.

About this time there seems to have been an awareness of the need to tighten up the Session's control of its affairs. In March 1828 it was resolved to bring the Baptismal Register up to date and to repair omissions in it from Mr Greig's personal memoranda; further, 'to obtain, from Dr Williams' Library in Red Cross Street, 2 doz. of the blank printed forms recommended for the registering of Births and Baptisms'. Two years later, after a further discussion on the accurate recording of baptisms and the safe keeping of records, it was resolved that 'A tin box of sufficient strength for the above purpose be provided forthwith, and that the whole of the Register Books be brought to Crown Court and being placed therein be deposited together in the Iron Closet in the Vestry'. This was duly done, as reported to the Session on 9th June, 1830. The 'tin box', or perhaps its successor, will appear later in the story.

Mr Greig resigned that year. Suggestions for the imrpovement of the life of the congregation had been left unacted upon; his income was not in proportion to his necessary expenditure; his health had deteriorated and after nearly 25 years he felt the time had come for him to retire. Two months later, before his resignation took effect, he died, and the minutes of November 19th contain full details of the arrangements for the funeral, where Campbell of Kingsland, who had taken part in his induction, delivered the address.

It was the year of the death of George IV, the accession of William IV, the opening of the first public railway, the first balloon flight, and the first serious proposal of a reform in Parliamentary representation.

Interregnum

In the course of 'desultory conversation' amongst the elders that month, 'the state of the Scots Presbytery in London was adverted to, which for years had been declining from the respectable state it formerly held and was reduced to a mere nullity'. This may have had reference to the lawsuits mentioned above; it certainly was relevant to Crown Court's own anomalous position in regard to the filling of its vacancy. They considered the possbility of some 'respectable ministers from the North who had recently come up to preach to the vacant congregations of Swallow Street, Wells Street, and other Scots churches'. Apparently it would not matter whether they were of the Church of Scotland or the Scots Secession Church. Later a meeting of the congregation was called 'to consider the propriety of connecting it with some respectable denomination, as more likely to conduce to its prosperity than by standing aloof from intercourse with other Churches and their presiding Ministers'[13]. The idea was 'deferred', and shortly thereafter the Rev. John MacNaughton was elected, and inducted in August 1831.

It had been a relatively brief vacancy. Unfortunately his ministry was briefer still. Seven months later he announced that he had received a call from the High Kirk, Paisley, which he had decided to accept. We know little about him, though what we do is all to his credit. To paraphrase a wry saying, he was a good minister, as ministers go; and as ministers go he went. The only monument to his short ministry — and it was set up rather in preparation for, than as a result of, his coming — was the fixing of a plate naming Crown Court at its Russell Street end, and of another at the Bow Street end of Martlett Court, pointing towards the church so that people might more easily find it.

127

Not many wanted to find it in 1832, and Session and congregation seem almost to have lost heart. Attendances fell, membership dwindled as the vacancy continued, and possible candidates turned away from a prospect which must have seemed beyond hope of recovery. Crown Court Session can have had little attention to spare for the two epoch-making enactments which received the royal assent, while their despairing search for a minister was continuing without success.

But even as the First Reform Bill, and the Bill for the Abolition of Slavery throughout the British Empire, were becoming law, in June and August of 1832, they found themselves, as a last hope, preparing a Call, and approaching the Scots Presbytery of London so that they might legitimately present it to a young man who was by God's grace to reform and liberate the remnant of the Scotch National Church in Covent Garden and lead the congregation into the days of its greatest fame.

NOTES

1. *Fasti*, vii,468. Wilson, *op. cit.*, iv,10, says that Greig had been assistant to Greville Ewing at the Tabernacle in Glasgow, which was the training-college set up by the Haldane brothers. A confusing reference to Mr Greig is found in the Kirk Session minutes, Nov. 1804, referring to correspondence with Mr Greig, stating that he was 'of Dunfermline', and reporting his reluctance to accept Crown Court's call because he was engaged 'to a lady averse from leaving our country' although she was well acquainted with England. Elsewhere, however, another reference identifies this minister as Christopher Greig.

2. Campbell of Kingsland appears several times in the Crown Court records of this period. See Chapter seven for extended reference to him.

3. *Crown Court Sabbath School Institution Minutes*, 6th July 1817.

4. *Crown Court Kirk Session Minutes*, 19th Dec., 1814.

5. *Ibid.*, 7th March, 1827. Preparations for the institution of a University not subject to the denominational restrictions of Oxford and Cambridge were at this time being initiated by London nonconformists connected with Dr Cox's congregation in Hackney and with other congregations, backed by prominent men such as Thomas Campbell, Lord Brougham and Joseph Hume. (*Encyclopedia Britannica*, 11th Edn., xxvii, 772). With William Reid as a fourth sponsor London University had at least four Scots helping to further English higher education. The preface to its first charter affirms the royal aim 'to

hold forth to all classes and denominations of our faithful subjects without any distinction whatever an encouragement for pursuing regular and liberal courses of education'. But that privilege 'was grudgingly conceded and until 1900 confined to the question of holding examinations and conferring degrees' (Lord H.P. Macmillan, *A Man of Law's Tale*, p. 254.)

6. See Chapter six.

7. George Greig, *The Death of Believers precious in the sight of God* — 'A Sermon on the death of Maxwell Garthshore, M.D., Physician to the British Lying-in Hospital, preached on March 15, 1812, in the Scots Church, Crown Court, Covent Garden'. Garthshore, son of the minister of Kirkudbright and colleague of William Smellie and the Hunter brothers in London (see Chapter six), is mentioned in 'Jupiter' Carlyle's *Autobiography*, p. 546, his wife being Carlyle's cousin. It was Garthshore who came to the rescue of John Hunter's widow when she was left in straitened circumstances. A letter from 'Dr M. Garthshore, M.D., St Martin's Lane, to Sir Joseph Banks, President of the Royal Society', dated 27 April, 1791, commends to the latter's generosity the Library of the Fellows of the Royal College of Physicians at Edinburgh. (Brit. Libr. MS.Add.33,979,f92)

8. See Chapter six, note 11, *re* Baptismal Basin. Kirk Session minutes further record, Mar. 3, 1819: 'It being necessary to procure a Baptismal Basin in lieu of that stolen from the vestry, which was a present from Mr George Purse, it was resolved that an order be given to Mr Purse to furnish the church with a Baptismal Basin similar to the former one'. The cost was £4 18s.

9. The post-Reformation tradition in Scotland included family worship, conducted by the father, as a daily meeting of the basic social unit, the family, with the Father revealed in Jesus Christ. Since this was firmly based on Bible reading and Christian prayer, the growing child learned naturally the fundamentals of the faith, while the parents, imparting them, gained firmer grasp of them themselves. The abandonment of family worship has much impoverished the communion of the saints, leaving a void between private devotion and public worship which the development of small groups for Christian fellowship and action during the last twenty years is now beginning to fill. When family worship was the practice, church doors needed to be opened only on Sundays and other occasions when the whole Christian community worshipped together.

Though parents have now largely resigned the Christian teaching of their children to Sunday Schools, that was not the reason why the General Assembly banned Sunday Schools in 1799. Under the influence of the Moderates at that time, afraid of the radicalism encouraged by the French revolution, and not discerning the social changes which the industrial revolution was forcing on the rapidly-growing towns and cities of the land, it suspected Sunday Schools as 'possible agencies of sedition', having already disapproved of 'missions to the heathen' as being 'examples of unreasoning zeal'. A wiser view later prevailed.

10. *Crown Court Kirk Session Minutes*, 1 Dec., 1796, and 2 Feb., 6 Apr., & 16 May 1797.

11. The Clerk or Precentor — in Scotland, the Letter-gae — led the people's singing of the Psalms. The practice of 'lining' the Psalms consisted in the Precentor's reading or intoning a metrical line and the congregation then singing it to the appropriate part of the tune, sometimes with all kinds of grace-notes; and so, 'line upon line', to the end. It spread from England to Scotland after the Westminster Assembly, but only under certain provisos. In the section 'Of Singing of Psalms', *The Directory for Public Worship* said that everyone who could read was to have a psalm-book, . . . 'but where many in the congregation cannot read it is convenient that the minister or some other do read the psalm, line by line, before the singing thereof'. In 1746 the General Assembly recommended that in private worship, families 'in singing the praise of God, go on without the intermission of singing the line'; but that return to older practice came slowly in public worship. *The Scots Brigade in Holland* (III, xiv, xvi, & 198-205) relates that one chaplain, following the Assembly recommendation, discontinued the practice amongst the Highland regiments. His colonel ordered that the practice of Lining be resumed, but received a respectful — and firm — note in reply: 'It will give us pleasure to be informed that you are satisfied with our conduct, though as a session we conceived we were accountable only to a superior court'. The practice lasted long in the Secession Church. The precentor of the Infirmary Street congregation in Edinburgh was reckoning without the minister when, as a half-way house he gave out two lines instead of one, 'for the worthy Mr Paxton, rising in the pulpit, dealt him a few weighty knocks with the Psalm-book'. R.L. Stevenson, in *Weir of Hermiston*, speaks of 'the nasal psalmody, full of turns and trills and graceless gracenotes'. And Walter Scott (*Journal*, p. 173) declares: 'Scotch psalmody . . . should be heard from a distance. The grunt and shuffle, the whine and the scream, should all be blended in that deep and distant sound, which, rising and falling like the eolian harp, may have some title to be called the praise of our Maker'.

12. When a special meeting of the congregation was called to be informed of Greig's resignation, the proceedings opened with the singing of the 107th Hymn in the *Second Book of Dr Watts' Collection:* 'Lord, we adore Thy vast designs'.

13. *Crown Court Kirk Session Minutes*, 17 Aug., 1830.

CHAPTER 10

'A Luminary Blazing in the Mid-Heavens'

John Cumming was born in 1807, in or near Aberdeen. He was educated at a school whose history can be traced back to the 12th century, Aberdeen Grammar School; and after graduating in Arts at Aberdeen's King's College in 1826 he secured a post as tutor to a family in Kensington. In London he attended Regent Square Scotch National Church where Irving was then at the height of his fame, but was called to preach one Sunday to 'the dwindling congregation of Scotch folk' in Crown Court. It was only the fourth time he had ever conducted a service or preached a sermon, but there seems to have been no doubt on the part of the congregation that he was God's man for them, or, on his, that he must accept the challenge of this unpromising call.

But there was an obstacle, and the Presbytery had to remove it. Meeting in August 1832 in Chadwell Street church, only three months after it had removed Irving from his ministry in Regent Square, the Presbytery heard a petition from the Kirk Session of the Scotch Church in Crown Court, that they might be taken again into communion with the Presbytery. They were formerly united, they said, 'but upon the abrupt resignation of the late Dr Steven of Kilwinning all efforts of their Presbyterian and other friends having been unavailing to discover a successor, they had made choice of a minister who, though not in immediate communion with the Church of Scotland, they considered as providentially cast in their way', and with whom the Session stipulated 'that he should conduct ye worship of ye Church and adminster ye Sacraments and in conjunction with ye Elders maintain discipline as heretofore had been done by his predecessors'. Their petition was granted, their Call to John Cumming was sustained, and the Presbytery arranged for his trials[1]. These were duly sustained, and on Thursday, 27th September, 1832,

131

he was ordained and inducted to the charge, and embarked upon what was to be not only the longest but the most famous of the ministries in that building.

It was an inauspicious beginning. In 1838 James Hamilton, a friend of Cumming's, worshipped in Crown Court, and later remarked 'I should fear that Presbyterianism does not thrive in London. I question how far it is worthwhile to struggle for its lifeless existence'. London Wall and Swallow Street had had their internal disputes. Regent Square was still suffering from the shock of Irving's deposition. And in Crown Court, although the seeds of recovery were then being planted, little sign of their germination had as yet appeared. Hamilton's pessimism is understandable. But it must have been only temporary, for it was not long before he himself became minister of Regent Square, and soon thereafter saw it begin to move steadily into a new and influential phase of its history, completely belying his own earlier qualms about the future of the Kirk in London.

Already, in fact, the revival of Crown Court had begun. Cummings' preaching was slowly attracting larger congregations. In the very year of Hamilton's jeremiad the Bedford Estate recorded the completion of a lease to Mr Thomas Mitchell, bricklayer, Dalziel Street, acting for the Scotch National Church in Crown Court, of 'a messuage or tenement therein erected situate on the west side of Crown Court (formerly called Old Crown Court)', for the rent of a peppercorn for the first half year and thereafter of £1. Four years later, and again six years after that, further leases allowing extensions of the site were negotiated, the latter at an annual rent of £70 and for 100 years.

The story behind these reveals the initiative and popularity of the new ministry.

After Cumming had been four years their minister, a deputation had suggested to him that the time had come to re-start the Sunday Schools, mentioning a dilapidated stable adjacent to the church, in Kingshead Yard. Cumming raised £146 for necessary repairs — a sum equal to the whole of his salary during his first two years — and the building was opened in 1836 with ten teachers and twenty-three children. The 1838 lease gave permanency to that Sunday School. In the same year the Session found it necessary to address a memorial to St Paul's Vestry, that the entrances to Crown Court should be improved. In 1838 Cumming's public disputation in Hammersmith with a Roman Catholic lawyer, Daniel French, attracted great crowds to hear the arguments, which lasted several days. The wide admiration for Cumming's part in them was expressed in the presentation to him of a polyglot Bible in ten languages and by the growth of the number of those who went to hear him in his own church. His life-long opposition to the papacy was further expressed in his encounters with Cardinal Wiseman at his palace in Golden Square[2]. his (unanswered) request to be allowed to argue with the Pope at the Vatican[3], and his 'claim to attend the Oecumenical Council at Rome in 1869'[4].

After 1841 the familiar tallow candle disappeared from the lists of sundries in the monthly order for church supplies: gas lighting had been installed. The evening service was re-introduced; and the practice of sitting while singing and standing for prayers was reversed. The possibility of having to build a new church was being considered for the first time.

Similar stirrings of new life were noticeable in other churches of the Presbytery, paralleling the renewed vitality of the home Church. With the encouragement of the General Assembly the Scots Presbyteries in England combined to form the English Synod, which all seven had joined by 1842; and undoubtedly their congregations shared the spirit which was animating the home Church in its 'Ten Years' Conflict' for freedom from state control and secular patronage.[5] In 1843 that struggle reached its climax. The Disruption took place, and 450 ministers surrendered manses, glebes, stipends and church buildings, and with their congregations went out and brought into being the Free Kirk.

It was at this point that the delayed effects of Westminster's breach of the Treaty of Union by the re-introduction of patronage in 1712 were belatedly but dramatically experienced by the Scots Kirk in London. At a meeting on 13th June, 1843, summoned to deal with the call to a minister for the new Scots Church in Whitechapel, the majority of the Presbytery decided to sever connection with the Church of Scotland — a step which was being taken also in all the other Scots Presbyteries in England. London was left with a Presbytery of four congregations, one being in Dudley, Birmingham. Later that year the Dudley minister, Dr. Blair, who had been Moderator of the fateful June meeting, requested to be loosed from his charge, and the Presbytery agreed, 'owing to the peculiar circumstances of the congregation', which had proved unsympathetic to its minister's views and erased the words 'in connection with the Church of Scotland' from its title. Of the three remaining London congregations two soon found themselves in great straits. The majority of the Swallow Street congregation departed, and in 1845 its minister had to issue an appeal, backed by the Moderator of the General Assembly, the Principals of Glasgow and Edinburgh Universities, and the two other London ministers. In that *Appeal to the Scottish Nobility and Gentry in England on behalf of the National Scottish Church, Swallow Street.* the signatories state: 'Had not the Elders of Swallow Street Church stood forward and at great personal trouble and expense vindicated this Church, it had been added to others in London wrenched from lawful connection and illegally and forcibly held by the Free Seceders or English Presbyterians. As this is the only church in the west end in connection with the Church of Scotland it is of great importance to disburden it of its present liabilities'[6]. Apparently it was disburdened, for Swallow Street continued for another forty years.

St Andrew's, Stepney, also lost more than half its members, but surmounted its difficulties and survived until the changing nature of the population and the replacement of sailing ships by steamships left few Scots seamen in the area and removed the need for it. It dissolved in 1889.

Crown Court, however, lost only one elder, and probably few members. Cumming, clearly, had no difficulties about patronage or state control of the Church. We find him boldly crossing swords with Thomas Chalmers on those issues, although he always had the warmest admiration for Chalmers and preached a memorial sermon in Crown Court when he died. One speech of Cumming's on the subject was published in 1837 with the title *An Apology for the Church of Scotland,* winning the public approval of the Archbishop of Canterbury and the Bishop of London. Not unnaturally he attracted those Scots in London whose sympathies were with the Establishment. These would include those who in Scotland were patrons, and therefore well-to-do.

THE REV. JOHN CUMMING, D.D.

The Rev. Dr. John Cumming, minister of Crown Court Scottish National Church,
1830-1879.   *The British Library, M.S.S. Dept.*
(From *The Penny Pulpit*, No. 2, 1858)

Crown Court, then, far from being weakened by the Disruption, continued to grow and extend its influence in the metropolis. Dr. Cumming — he became a Doctor of Divinity of Edinburgh University in 1844 — enjoyed growing popularity as a preacher, and shortly afterwards his congregation presented him with a silver tea-service, selected by Sir Francis Grant, President of the Royal Academy.

Two contemporary accounts give impressions of the building, and of the man who was drawing so many hundreds to it.

'The building has few claims to architectural consideration, being a mixture of all orders. The gallery is reached by stairs from the outside, a feature probably necessitated by considerations of space. Inside, the building is of the shape of a large oblong, the gallery being deep and commodious, with the pulpit in the centre of one of the long sides. The only national emblems to be seen are the thistle-shaped ground glass shades of the gas lamps, and a thistle or two on the painted glass windows. In all other respects it resembles an English Dissenting Chapel'.

'Dr Cumming is tall and well-formed. Across a high forehead sweeps a flow of dark hair. The whole head is a type of intelligence, from which shine a pair of dark, flashing eyes. His matter is deeply embued with evangelical truth, and always evinces intellectual superiority. He has the somewhat rare merit of being easy of comprehension to the humblest while he gratifies and instructs those posessing the most cultivated minds . . . His hearers include the Duchess of Wellington, Lady Ducie, the Countess of Listowel, Lord Keane, Lord Alfred Paget and others, together with the poor widows and labouring people of the neighbourhood'.[7]

Wylie of China

Its minister's power as a preacher was not the only influence exercised by Crown Court: nor indeed was that influence confined to London. Here, for example, is the story of Alexander Wylie.

Wylie's father had come from Scotland in 1791, and set up as an oil and colour merchant. When Alec was born in 1815 he was a delicate child, and was sent to Scotland before his first birthday to be brought up by relatives in Drumlithie, returning to London to complete his education in Chelsea. He was then apprenticed to a cabinet-maker, under whom he worked on the repair of Hatfield House after a fire. He became a Sunday School teacher in Crown Court in 1840. By that time his ambition was to go to China as a missionary. Nothing seemed less possible, but he was a determined young man, and resolved to be ready for the chance if it came or he could make it. He secured a copy of Primare's *Notitiae Linguae Sinicae,* brushed up his Latin in order to read and understand it, then made his way to the British and Foreign Bible Society and bought a copy of the Gospel according to St John in Chinese. What was he to make of that? He began at the beginning. He knew that in the very first verse the word 'God' appeared twice, and the word 'Word' thrice. He identified thereby the two characters representing them, and with that beginning went on to compile a large vocabulary of Chinese characters.

How far this would have taken him without further help it is impossible to say. But meanwhile Dr Legge[8] in China was urging on the London Missionary Society the need for a printing establishment in Shanghai, and on his return to England in 1846 secured the British and Foreign Bible Society's help in defraying the cost and finding a printer. They suggested Alec Wylie, and after six months studying printing during the day and learning Chinese with Dr Legge in the evenings he went to Shanghai and set up the printing concern. There he printed and from there he disseminated copies of the Gospels in Chinese and Manchu, and other publications in these and other languages, for he learnt French, German, Russ, Manchu and Mongol, as well as some Greek and Sanscrit. He had some amazing adventures and escapes on his journeys as a colporteur, and on other expeditions on which he guided Lord Elgin and Griffith John. He took an interest in Chinese mathematical literature, and in 1852 showed that Horner's method for solving quadratic equations of all orders, published in 1819, had been anticipated by Chinese mathematicians in the 14th century. He took an equal interest in Chinese astronomy, and besides his translations of Christian classics he published, in 1858, *A Compendium of Arithmetic* and *A Popular Treatise on Mechanics,* and in 1859 *Elements of Analytical Geometry and of the Differential and Integral Calculus,* and an *Outline of Astronomy* — all in Chinese. The Tokugawa

Government of Japan had these reprinted and distributed amongst the sons of the Samurai between 1860 and 1870, and in the Restoration period they became the foundation of the development of scientific education in the new Japan. Similarly a periodical founded by Wylie, the *Luh-ho-tsung-tan,* reprinted by the Japanese government, became the forerunner of modern journalism in that country[9].

This remarkable man, who was also an agent for the British and Foreign Bible Society for fourteen years, became blind and returned to London (where his daughter was now a member in Crown Court) in 1877. When he died later that year the Bible Society said: 'In the person of Mr Wylie they effected an entrance into the heart of China'.

Alterations and Enlargements.

By that time much had happened in Crown Court. The Bedford Estate records contain a total of 18 documents relating to leases in the name of the Scotch Church. Two of these pertain to a matter of much concern to the Kirk Session of the 1840s. Repairs to the old building had been carried out at a cost of £145 in 1835. When the lease was due to expire in 1841 a new lease was offered for 42 years at a ground rent of £25 per annum and a payment of £600. The Session would have preferred to build a new church on another site, and a suitable one was found in King Street, but the rent was adjudged too high so a scheme for alterations in Crown Court, costing £980, was approved, on a new lease, for 63 years. The customary printed appeal for subscribers brought enough, in addition to the congregation's givings, to meet the final bill of £1,607, although £200 had to be borrowed to attain the £600 for the new lease. These alterations had been completed about a year before the Disruption.

It was not long before the inadequacy even of this increased accommodation raised again the question of erecting a larger building on a new site, and in 1845 a majority approved this course. Promises of subscription, however, fell short of the estimates for site and building, and it was decided to buy two adjacent buildings, demolish them, enlarge the church once more, and build a school. The document for the enlarged site shows a lease of 100 years and an annual rent of £70.

During the alteration and extension the congregation worshipped in Exeter Hall. It was regarded as something remarkable that the Bishop of London had granted a license for its use 'by an assembly or congregation of Protestants, being a section of the National Scotch Church'. What was more remarkable was that during the six months in which it was so used the congregation commonly numbered around four thousand people, including many notables, as for example Lord Russell, then Prime Minister.

Back in the enlarged church Dr Cumming's activities increased. In the interests of proper order in church worship he had published, in 1840, a new edition of 'Knox's Liturgy', the *Book of Common Order* of 1561. Of the preface to this Andrew Drummond and James Bulloch say that it marked a general wish for liturgical reform, and they credit Cumming as giving the lead in that direction[10]. Now he became a frequent contributor to *The Times,* and produced a constant flow of publications on varied subjects. Some of these had a great vogue across the Atlantic. The catalogue of Union Theological Seminary in New York shows no fewer than 103 of them, fourteen on prophecy, and many printed (or pirated) in Boston.

Before long the larger church was filled to the doors, Sunday by Sunday. It was said that ordinary traffic could not move in Russell Street, Bow Street and Drury Lane, for the throng of carriages making their way to Cumming's church. In 1861 the Session resolved to engage a Commissionaire 'to attend on Sunday, morning and evening, and on Friday evenings, to keep order'.

It must have been around this period that Charles Henry Purday became conductor of psalmody in Crown Court Scots Church. He was a vocalist of some note, had sung at the coronation of Queen Victoria, became a publisher of music, and was a pioneer in the movement for the reform of the law in regard to musical copyright. In 1854 he published *Crown Court Psalmody: one hundred Psalm Tunes and Chants,* and in 1857 *The Church and Home Tune Book,* from which his tune *Sandon,* so long associated with Newman's 'Lead, kindly Light', comes.[11] If any of Dr Watts' hymns were of the 10 4 10 4 10 10 metre, *Sandon* may well have been sung for the first time by the congregation of Crown Court.

'To Teach — '

The carriages may have imparted an air of affluence to the neighbourhood, but the reality was much different. A study of a section of Covent Garden made in 1841 and covering 354 houses in the neighbourhood of Drury Lane had produced disquieting facts and figures. Forty-nine people had been taken into custody in one month. The 354 houses were inhabited by 1216 families. 262 adults were unable to read or write. Of the whole population only 134 persons attended public worship. The boys were trained for thieving, the girls for the streets.

John Cumming and his Session were not content to welcome the rich and respectable within their walls, and leave the poor and disreputable outside them unhelped. As we have seen they re-started the Sunday School in 1836, and the 1845 extension had provided a school building. Crown Court church was now in the business of day-school education, and the schoolrooms were full to their capacity of 500 children. Even this was not meeting the need. The annual cost of running the school was £600, towards which each child brought a penny a week, and the government gave a grant. But for the children of the area whose parents could not or would not provide the modest penny-a-week something must be done as well.

For such children a Portsmouth cobbler, John Pounds, had started a school early in the century. Sheriff Watson in Aberdeen and Dr William Robertson in Edinburgh did the same independently. But it was left to Dr Thomas Guthrie, with his *Plea for Ragged Schools* in 1847, to elicit nationwide sympathy and support, on the basis of the convincing statistics which he furnished, and persuade the government to subsidise the Ragged School movement. The genius of Guthrie's contribution to the movement was the added provision of clothing, and of training for useful employment. Within five years 216 former pupils of his Edinburgh schools were earning their living by honest industry[12]. In England the Ragged School Union was established in 1844, continuing its work until it became unnecessary when the Education Act of 1870 introduced universal compulsory schooling. To no-one did the Ragged School Union owe such generous support as to Baroness Burdett-Coutts, and it is good to think that Crown Court's Ragged School in Brewers'

Court was aided in that ministry by the bounty of one whose mother had been baptised at its font.

'To Heal — '

Mrs Haldane of Cloan, mother of a famous statesman, recalling at the age of 99 her childhood, and remembering the stir caused by the passing of the Reform Bill in 1832 (when the Chevy Chase coach to Newcastle was cheered, mile by mile, as its passengers shouted out the news all the way), remembered also the alarm caused by an outbreak of cholera that year, 'an unknown disease, and perplexing to the medical faculty'. It was to become very well-known, especially around the middle of the century, until improvements in sanitation and public water-supplies dealt with its causes. In 1832 the Presbytery appointed a 'Day of Thanksgiving for the Removal of the Scourge of Cholera.' Congested areas such as Covent Garden were particularly liable to its visitations, and when another occurred in 1849 the Scots congregation, on 'the fast-day observed in consequence of the prevalence of cholera', gave £149 13s. for the relief of families bereft of a breadwinner by that epidemic. Even more practical was the maintenance of a Dispensary, frequently mentioned in the minutes, where some education in hygiene seems to have been given. Prevention as well as amelioration was Crown Court's approach to this and other social problems.

Elsewhere prevention was not always considered. Crown Court had a member who on one occasion drew attention to a fire-risk which required attention, and on another wrote to the minister suggesting that the entrance doors should be altered so as to open outwards in case of panic. This was James Braidwood, who had founded the Edinburgh Fire Brigade and had been brought south in 1832 to organise and superintend the London Fire Brigade. His preventive advice doubtless saved the church building from being the scene of tragedy, but failure to follow it elsewhere led to the greatest fire since the Great Fire of 1666. This was the Tooley Street Fire in 1861, which burned for four days and nights, 'when the Thames glowed as if it were molten gold, and two and a half million pounds worth of goods fed the flames' The Sunday School records of Crown Court record the absence, on 23rd June, 1861, of the three Misses Braidwood.

Their father had been killed by a falling wall the previous day 'while at the post of duty directing the men of the Fire Brigade'. Dr Cumming's sermon, *The Last Fire,* preached on June 30th, pays tribute to this London hero and his work for the Crown Court Schools. It reveals also his own familiarity with the writings of contemporary scientists such as Lyell, and contains an apocalyptical passage of the kind that was then beginning to characterise his preaching. It speaks of those living virtues which no fires can annihilate, and ends with the words 'A cup of cold water, a visit to a mourner, the sympathy you have expressed, the help given to a poor ragged boy or girl to educate, cheer, and help them on the rough way of life — these shall survive that last fire and be mentioned with your name by Him who will say "Forasmuch as ye have done it unto one of the least of these, you have done it unto Me"'[13].

'And to Proclaim the Gospel'

The record of Dr Cumming's ministry and its appreciation by his congregation and a wide constituency beyond it — of which many instances could be given — reads like a romantic success-story. His friendship with the well-to-do and influential certainly helped him to achieve much. It was Lord Kinnaird who chaired his committee to erect new schools at the cost of £2500; and it was the Duke of Buccleuch who in 1851 joined with him and Mr Pollock Black of Stepney to buy from the dwindling Independent congregation in Holloway their Chapel, which then became the Caledonian Church, Holloway[14]. But equally he earned the confidence and even the affection of the ordinary man, whether in the pew or on the street — particularly for the sincerity and passion of his presentation of the Gospel.

To be sure, he had his critics, and savage some of them were. Tennyson's mother's favourite reading was Cumming's books, but Tennyson himself thought him a mountebank, and it is said that his picture of the 'heated pulpiteer' in *Sea Dreams,* who 'Announced the coming doom, and fulminated Against the scarlet woman and her creed' was drawn from his own reading of Cumming's sermons. Thackeray went to far as to call him a bigot and a blasphemer. And the genius of another writer first came to public notice through her bitterly critical essay, 'Evangelical Teaching', which appeared in The *Westminster*

James Braidwood, first Superintendent of the London Fire Brigade. He died under a falling wall in the great Tooley Street blaze in 1861, when melted tallow, ablaze on the river, made it seem that the Thames itself was on fire. Members of the Fire Engine Establishment, as it was called, 'sadly pocketed buttons from his tunic', after his body was recovered days later, as mementoes of their beloved Chief. A fortnight passed before the fire was finally out. *He died at the post of duty - the holiest place on earth on which to live or die.* – Dr John Cumming.

Guildhall Library, City of London

Review in October, 1855. Its theme was the printed sermons of the famous preacher of the Scotch Church in Covent Garden. According to her they consisted merely of 'wholesale assertion, vague declamations, and unctuous platitudes', were 'devoid of charity and hyman sympathy', and 'distinguished only by the prophesyings' which formed such a singular feature of their contents[15].

Possibly it was in answer to such attacks that Cumming felt entitled to speak of the 'thousands who had testified that they had got good here, not because there was eloquence or logic or something marvellous, but because there was the gospel in its simplicity and the love of God in all its transforming influence preached here[16]. George Eliot, after all, had never heard Dr Cumming preach, and in her intellectual rebellion against the narrow orthodoxy in which she had been brought up she probably read into the printed page a simplicity which she labelled platitudinous. The judgement of another contemporary — who *had* heard the preacher — was quite different. 'He never preached for less than an hour, sometimes an hour and a half, and yet I never felt bored. I always looked forward to them, . . . because his sermons, instead of consisting of a string of platitudes interspersed with trite ejaculations and irrelvant quotations, were one long chain of closely reasoned argument. I suppose that the inexorable logic of it all appealed to the Scottish side of me. His preaching had the same fascination for me that Euclid's propositions exercised later, even on my hopelessly unmathematical mind'[17].

George Eliot's comment on 'prophesyings', however, touches on a point which was to become critical in Cummings' later ministry. As a young tutor in Kensington he had been an assidous worshipper in Regent Square Church, and in 1834 he had preached a funeral sermon upon Edward Irving, its famous minister. In his later years the extravagances of the Irvingites began to colour his preaching and writing. His sermons expressed the conviction that the seventh vial of the Book of the Revelation was being poured out from 1848 to 1867. 'Cumming had fixed a date in 1867 as the exact date of the Great Catastrophe. His influence with his flock rather diminished when it was found that Dr Cumming had renewed the lease of his house for 21 years only two months before the date he had fixed with

'A Luminary Blazing in the Mid-Heavens'

absolute certainty as being the end of all things'[18]. He himself outlived that date by twelve years. His ministry did in the end outlast its usefulness, and its last few years suffered a decline during which, as in earlier ministries, the membership dropped until no more than fifty might be expected in the church where at one time more than four times that number had sought admittance in vain. He retired in 1879, and died two years later.

It was the sad end to a long and splendid story; but the value of his ministry is attested by the facts that in Crown Court itself not only had the buildings been twice enlarged, schools built and extended, an assistantship established to help in running the Sunday School and visiting poor Scots and sharing in the Brewers' Court Mission, a regular Elders' Prayer Meeting constituted, and a library for children built up; but also that largely through his leadership the Presbytery of London had been re-established, a new Scottish congregation founded, and an inspired lead had been given in the matter of Christian care for the uncared-for London child[19]. The memory of his preaching remained with all who had heard him during the years of his greatest vigour, and in an obituary notice *The Times* described him as one who had been 'a luminary blazing in the mid-heavens and outshining the light of day'.

NOTES

1. It may be of interest to some to know that at his Trials for Ordination Cumming had to cope with: **An Exercise** on Romans x:10; **A Lecture** on John iii:14-17; **A Popular Sermon** on Hebrews ii:14; and Examinations **in Hebrew** on Psalm xxiii, **in Church History** on the 14th century, **in the Greek Text** *ad aperturum libri*, and **in Theology**, *passim*.
2. *The Penny Pulpit*, No. 2, 1858.
3. Lady Frances Balfour, *Ne Obliviscaris*, i, 175-7, which includes an impression of Cumming's preaching.
4. Kenneth Black, *op. cit.*, p. 106.
5. See Appendix C.
6. *Correspondence of Sir Robert Peel*, British Library, MS. Addnl. 40,564 f.73 dated 4th April, 1845. There had been a law-case to recover property from those who had seceded to form the Presbyterian Church in England. Regent Square congregation, despite the provisions of their Trust Deed which had so firmly ruled the issue in the matter of Irving's dismissal, retained possession of the property although

those provisions had been violated. Sixteen years later the *de facto* possession, amicably enough conceded, was recognised *de jure*. But in Swallow Street, where the minority still retained the Church of Scotland connection, naturally no such concession was made.

7. British Library, MS. Additional 28,509, ff. 375-384 — *A Biographical Sketch*, appended to a sermon by Dr Cumming in *The Penny Pulpit*. The paragraph describing the building is quoted therein from *Half-hours with our Metropolitan Ministers*, No. 3, dated Jan. 1, 1828.

8. Dr James Legge, an Aberdeen graduate, went in 1839 to Malacca and in 1841 to Hong Kong as a missionary. He became widely known as an outstanding Chinese scholar, and in 1876 a Chair of Chinese Language and Literature was constituted at Oxford, to be occupied by Dr Legge. His achievements were far more than merely scholarly. In Poc-lo, while he was in Hong Kong, an ugly situation arose and he set out on a mission of reconciliation. As he left he said to a colleague: 'If news comes that I have been murdered, go at once to the British Consul and tell him it was my wish that no gun boat should be sent up the river to punish the people for my death'. A great-niece of his is now an elder in St Columba's, Pont Street.

9. The information about Wylie's mathematical and other textbooks appears in the introduction to a Japanese publication of 1935, printed by The Alexander Wylie's Posthumous Publications Association, Tokyo.

10. Drummond and Bulloch, *The Church in Victorian Scotland*, pp. 190ff.

11. James Moffatt, *Handbook to the Church Hymnary, Revised Edition*, pp. 469f.

12. Oliphant Smeaton, *Thomas Guthrie*, passim. Guthrie's own account of the encounter near Arthur's Seat which prompted him to do something for such ragamuffins as the two he met there, is quoted: 'I said 'Would you go to school if beside your learning you were to get breakfast, dinner and supper there?' ... The boy leapt to his feet and exclaimed 'Ay will I, sir, an' bring the hail land too!', and then . . added 'I'll come for but my denner, sir!' ' (p. 46). Guthrie took a leading part in all kinds of philanthropic endeavour in Edinburgh, where his ministry in St John's took him down into the dens of the Cowgate and stirred him to arouse public concern over the conditions under which children were growing up there. He was one of the leaders in the Disruption. The statue depicting him with his protective arm around a ragged-clothed child stands in Princes Street Gardens, looking up Castle Street towards that of his friend and co-worker, Thomas Chalmers.

13. *'The Last Fire', a Funeral Sermon on the late Mr Braidwood, superintendent of the London Fire Brigade, preached by Dr Cumming on Sunday June 30th, 1861, in the National Scotch Church, Covent*

Garden. After Braidwood's death the authorities belatedly gave effect to some of the preventive measures he had advocated. See also *Life and Work; Scottish National Churches in England* Suplement, Sept., 1886.

14. See Chapter eight.
15. George Eliot, *Westminster Essays*, pp. 145-199. With equal cruelty, when Cumming's publication *The Next Tribulation, or Things coming on the earth* was selling at the rate of 8,000 in three months, *Punch* commented on 'The Great Tribulation which is Cumming on the Earth'.
16. *The Last Fire,* ut supra.
17. Lord Frederick Hamilton, *My Yesterdays*, pp. 43-46.
18. *Ibid.*
19. The claim that Crown Court's was the pioneer Ragged School in London appears to be well-founded, and counters the implication in Charles Dickens' otherwise balanced reference to Ragged Schools: 'They who are too ragged, wretched, filthy and forlorn to enter any other place; who would gain admission to no charity school, and who would be driven from any church door; are invited to come in here, and find some people not depraved, willing to teach them something and show them some sympathy'. (Quoted by John Burke, *History of England*, p. 228).

CHAPTER 11

Survival and Revival

When Dr Cumming retired it was the end of an era. It seemed, in fact, that it might be altogether the end, and not for Crown Court alone. In January of that year the Presbytery of London, deeply concerned about the state of three of the four London congregations, had appointed a committee 'to inquire into the position and prospects of said churches with a view to transmitting a full report to the General Assembly's Committee on London Churches'[1]. Two months later the Presbytery considered the committee's report, which judged only one congregation, Holloway, to be healthy, and proposed that the buildings in Swallow Street and Crown Court be sold. The proceeds would go to assist the recently projected plan, proposed by Dr Badenoch[2] and sponsored by a number of London Scots, for a central church, with an institute for young men and a Presbytery Hall attached, on the Thames Embankment. The Convener of the General Assembly's Committee met with the Presbytery ten days later. He was convinced that it was best to aim at creating a new church in place of those which had ceased to prosper. Swallow Street, Crown Court, and St Andrew's he regarded as hopeless; the congregations of the first two should be concentrated elsewhere, and the third transferred to a more suitable location in the east end. The Presbytery accepted this advice, but modified its decision when Mr J. Macvicar Anderson moved that Crown Court, if 'a good man from Scotland' could be found, might be allowed to continue for a time, 'with a view of ultimately transferring it to the new church'. This was agreed[3]; the Synod concurred[4]; and in August Dr Cumming intimated his resignation[5]. The 35 members of Swallow Street accepted the recommendation to sell and were permitted to meet in Crown Court until the future became clearer. They and their minister, in fact, joined Crown Court before the year was over[6].

148

Nothing thereafter was heard in Presbytery about the projected new church on the Embankment, but in all likelihood its influential sponsors were waiting to see what the outcome of this remission of sentence on Crown Court might be. The prospects were not encouraging. The contrast with the fame and influence of earlier years was particularly dispiriting. A thousand names had been on the roll in 1861, but in January 1881 the Session had to record that only 77 members had communicated that month. It also heard a report from the Vacancy Committee that despite much help from the Committee of Advice in Edinburgh it was still impossible, after eighteen months, to nominate a successor, the last minister approached, George Matheson of Inellan, having declined nomination[7]. Discouragement had evidently affected the Session itself, for its regular meetings consisted of Mr Forsyth of Holloway who was interim-moderator, and no more than three elders.

But further negotiations were initiated, and on May 29th of that year, 'with no small satisfaction and with heartfelt thanksgiving to Almighty God', the Kirk Session presented to the congregation the committee's nomination of the Rev. Donald MacLeod to fill the vacancy. Mr Macvicar Anderson, the Session Clerk, outlined the conditions on which he had good reason to believe that Mr MacLeod would accept a call, and further explained that 'the Rev. Mr MacLeod considered a new church in a better locality than Crown Court essential to a really successful ministry in London, and although in the present circumstances of the congregation he would consider it unreasonable to extract from them any pledge on the subject he yet expected that every effort would be made to attain this end'. Mr Anderson added that he and some others were already pledged to work for it. Mr James Campbell, M.P., an associated elder, moved Mr MacLeod's election on the conditions arranged by the committee, and this was unanimously agreed[8].

It was no young man who on those terms and in this unpropitious situation committed himself to what had been called a 'hopeless' cause. Donald MacLeod, son of the minister of Laggan and graduate of King's College, Aberdeen, had already served twenty years as a minister, in Dornoch, Dumfries, Montrose, Dundee and Jedburgh. He was inducted to the charge of Crown Court on June 10th, 1881, and publicly welcomed at a meeting chaired by the Earl of Aberdeen and addressed by Dean Stanley, Canon Fleming, Professor Charteris and the Revs. Oswald Dykes of Regent Square, J. Marshall Lang of the Barony, Glasgow, and James Stevenson of Jedburgh[9] — a distinguished interdenominational company. Such encouragement was needed. Swallow Street was gone. St Andrew's Stepney was dying on its feet. Crown Court's call to Mr MacLeod had been signed by less than a hundred, and 'even this remnant was by no means Scottish'.

Mr MacLeod's first actions were to strengthen his congregation's links with the mother-Church and restore her alignment with her traditions and practices. In this he found his Session had already done some sound planning, and soon after his arrival the new Scottish Hymnal was introduced[10], the offering was uplifted during the service instead of at the door, and it was decided that members should have the opportunity of contributing to the schemes of the Church by special offerings. It was also resolved to instal an organ. Two objections were made to this innovation, one being declared invalid because the objector was not a member, and the other being withdrawn — possibly because an offer to meet the whole cost had been made by Mrs Whitelaw of Alangrange![11].

Those early reforms might have suggested an abandonment of the intention to build a new church; in fact under MacLeod's leadership the congregation had quickly begun to recover strength and financial solvency. But Covent Garden was no longer a focal point of Scottish life in London. The 'Scotch Corner' had moved westward, and even Swallow Street had not been westerly enough to serve it. And only four months after MacLeod's induction the Session heard a report from its Clerk which sent it into urgent consideration of ways and means. Negotiations with Earl Howe for the acquisition of Curzon Chapel, he reported, had broken down because of the excessive sum of £30,000 demanded. But he had found a site on the Cadogan estate[12], available on a 96-year lease for £6,000, with a ground-rent of £70 per annum. On the strong recommendation of James Campbell of Stracathro the Session unanimously agreed to the transaction, all the more readily since the site was 'conveniently near the residences of practically all Crown Court's Scottish worshippers'[13].

This bold decision, which was to involve it in finding at least £20,000, might well have alarmed so small a congregation; but its minister and his Session had by now the support of a number of men of vision, courage and influence, and in those days the churches leant heavily on such leadership and aid. There were three Scottish members of Parliament — James Campbell of Stracathro, Sir A. Orr-Ewing of Ballincrain, and Sir Robert Jardine of Castlemilk. There was the Duke of Argyle. There was Lord Balfour of Burleigh, whose wife, a daughter of the Earl of Aberdeen, was a great-great-granddaughter of the George Baillie of Jerviswood to whom the early St Peter's Court congregation had owed so much. And there were men like Alexander Whitelaw of Gartshore, Major William Ewing of Brindley Manor, and 'that non-such for a Clerk', John Macvicar Anderson. Five of these contributed a total of £12,000 to the building fund, and two of them later undertook heavy financial commitments in aid of another Scots congregation in London.

Such vision and purposeful vigour were needed, for before the year was out a special meeting of the Session had to be called to consider an additional, unsought responsibility. A group of Scots living in and near East Dulwich had been meeting privately for worship, and believing that the time had come to establish a congregation they approached Mr MacLeod with the request 'that Crown Court Session and congregation take up the cause at East Dulwich and [give] their aid and co-operation, as meanwhile a Mission Station in connection with Crown Court Scots Church'[14]. The Session accepted that responsibility in December 1881, with the understandable proviso that they could not incur any pecuniary liabilities in connection with the Dulwich congregation. At the same time they expressed the hope that the money which would soon become available from the sale of the lease of the now defunct Swallow Street congregation might be invested in the building of a church in Dulwich, 'on condition that the Site and Building should be inalienably in connection with the Established Church of Scotland, and held by Trustees appointed by the Session of Crown Court Church'[15]. After considerable delay the Swallow Street Trustees decided that 'in no circumstances would [they] consent to the money now in Chancery going towards the new church at Dulwich, but that . . . it should be handed over to the Session of Crown Court, to be applied by them towards the building of the new Scottish National Church . . . on the Cadogan Estate'[16]. It was at this point that the two referred to above went to Dulwich's rescue, wisely — as we shall see — including the condition which the Crown Court Session had proposed.

Meanwhile, within eleven months of Mr MacLeod's arrival, £6,000 had been raised; and Mr Anderson — who was a distinguished architect as well as being Session Clerk — had been appointed honorary architect for the new building. It had been decided, also, that instead of being designated merely by the name of the street in which it was to stand it should bear the name of Scotland's patron saint, St Andrew.

Other responsibilities were not being neglected. It was resolved to circulate the Church of Scotland's new magazine, *Life and Work*, and to co-operate in initiating a 'Scotch National Churches in England' Supplement to it. Fifty copies were ordered for Crown Court and twenty for Dulwich. A branch of the Young Men's Guild was formed in 1882. A musical Committee was appointed. Detailed arrangements for the orderly administration of the Sacraments were approved. Steps were taken to appoint and ordain new elders. Forty pounds was contributed for the Schemes of the Church. Steadily the congregation was emerging from its slough of despond; and after it had raised over £10,000 the Session felt justified in opening the Building Fund for public subscriptions.

It had been hoped that with the imminent dissolution of the St Andrew's congregation in Stepney the monies accruing from the sale of the building might be available for the Crown Court and Dulwich building funds. The St Andrew's Session, however, had other ideas. Not only was it determined to continue, but its minister and clerk wrote 'objecting to the name of St Andrew's being given to the new Scottish National Church'[17]. The Building Committee was instructed to choose another name, which it took over two years to do. Only after the new building had been in use for three months was the notice-board authorised, identifying it as *St Columba's Church of Scotland, Pont Street, Belgravia*. The incorrect 'Belgravia' remained for a long time before being dropped. The north end of Pont Street is in Chelsea.

By that time St Andrew's was in serious difficulty, but it

The date was May 3, 1883. The building was eventually named St Columba's. *Guildhall Library.*
Illustration from The Pictorial World, May 18, 1883.

stumbled on for five more years before expiring. A debt which it had long owed to Crown Court—St Columba's was generously liquidated. Finally in 1891 the balance of the fund arising from the sale of its buildings, less two sums owed to its minister and beadle, was applied towards the erection of the church in East Dulwich.

Retracing our steps to 1883 we find in the May issue of *The Builder* the following report: 'On Wednesday afternoon the Rt. Hon. the Earl of Aberdeen, Lord High Commissioner to the General Assembly of the Church of Scotland, laid the foundation stone of St Andrew's Scottish National Church of Scotland in Belgravia. The church . . is intended for the congregation for so many years worshipping in Crown Court, Covent Garden, made famous by the ministry of the late Dr Cumming. The members of the congregation are for the most part resident in the locality of the new church. . . It will accommodate 900 persons without galleries. . . The exterior will be of red brick and Doulting stone; the interior of Corsham Down Bathstone. The pillars of the porch and the shafts of the chancel arch and of all the windows will be of dark grey Aberdeen granite, polished, with carved capitals, and those of the nave of Peterhead polished red granite. The style is early English 13th century, and the church has been designed and is being erected under the superintendence of Mr J. Macvicar Anderson, F.R.I.B.A., who not only gives his service as Hon. Architect but has contributed £1,000 to the building fund. The cost of the building will be about £12,000 and the cost of the site is about £8,000, making a total of £20,000.'[18].

Before the church was finished the Kirk Session had been spending much time and thought on two other matters. One was the urgent need to provide some place of worship for the Dulwich congregation. The story of that cause belongs to another chapter, but Mr MacLeod's responsibility for it continued until its first minister was inducted only a week before his own congregation moved to its new building. He was not to know that the responsibility would be re-imposed within sixteen months[19].

The other, equally urgent, was the question of what the Session minutes refer to as 'the ultimate destination of the buildings in Crown Court', once the congregation had moved to Pont Street. After repeated discussion[20], the question was remitted to a special committee in January 1884, and the Session heard its report of February 11th two days later. Three earlier suggestions — that the buildings be offered to the London School Board; that the Brewers' Court Mission might be asked if they could use them; and that Messrs Moody and Sankey might be interested in having them for their evangelistic meetings — had come to nothing. The Committee were unanimously against 'the continuance of Crown Court as a separate Church with a minister wholly disassociated from the Church in Pont Street'. Nevertheless the congregation's responsibility for the needy residents of Covent Garden could not be lightly abandoned with its removal to a more salubrious area, and the Committee's mind was summed up and justified by its convener, Lord Balfour of Burleigh, in a statement which merits extensive quotation. On the question of continuing Mission work in the district he pointed out 'the advantage that the Minister in Pont Street would derive from having someone engaged at Crown Court on whom he could rely for assistance to take services at stated intervals and in cases of emergency, and the undesirability of following the example of some congregations which in moving from a poor to a rich district had left the poor district spiritually unprovided for. He also expressed the opinion that in continuing Crown Court as a Mission the congregation would be working in harmony with those principles which actuated the Church of Scotland at home'. Their report unanimously recommended 'that the existing building at Crown Court should be maintained as a Mission Station under the Kirk Session of Pont Street Church or a Committee appointed by that body; that there should be a Morning Service there conducted by an assistant to the Minister of Pont Street Church or otherwise as the Kirk Session shall deem best, and in the Evening special Mission services; and that such scheme should be conditional upon £300 being first raised or guarranteed towards the first year's expenses'. The Session accepted these recommendations, and at once appointed its members as a Committee to carry them out, James Campbell, an associated elder, being convener and Lord Balfour, soon to be so associated, being co-opted[21]. Eight days before the dedication of the new church the Session appointed the Rev. Alfred M. Philip, a licentiate, to be assistant to Mr MacLeod at a stipend of £250. Crown Court was to be closed for repairs and cleaning, and re-opened for services on Sunday 20th April, when Mr Philip would commence his duties[22].

It was on March 28th, 1884, that the new church was dedicated. Its simple dignity was emphasised by the enriched arcade of stone and granite with marble mosaic which decorated the end wall of the chancel. Below the church was a hall capable of accommodating 400 people, and on the south-west corner of the building the tower, 113 feet in height, made a landmark at the head of Pont Street. There was no 'institute for young men', or 'Presbyterial Hall', however, although Crown Court's Young Men's Guild soon flourished in the new building, and the Hall was in fact immediately put to Presbyterial use, for the Presbytery itself met there that evening to appoint Mr MacLeod, Dr Souttar and Mr Macvicar Anderson as Assessors to the recently-inducted Dulwich minister to enable him to form a Kirk Session[23].

Later that year the Presbytery received Mr Philip's Presbyterial Certificate and duly admitted him as a preacher within the bounds. At that meeting, 'some conversation having taken place about the Presbyterial status of Crown Court and Pont Street churches', it was stated 'that an appropriate minute about this would be submitted at the next meeting of Presbytery'. It was further stated that the church in Pont Street 'was henceforth to be designated 'St Columba's (Church of Scotland), Pont Street, Belgravia'.'[24]. The promised draft was duly submitted at the next meeting, and read as follows: 'The Rev. Donald MacLeod and J. Macvicar Anderson Esq. appeared on behalf of the Kirk Session of Crown Court Church and acting also now in St Columba's Church. They represented that as the Presbytery were aware the New Church called St Columba's in Pont Street had been successfully completed, and had been formally opened with the sanction and in the presence of the Presbytery of London on the 28th day of March last, the preacher being the Very Reverend Principal Tulloch of St Andrews: further, that by regular deed of Constitution the new Church was inalienably connected with the Church of Scotland, and that according to agreement at the time when Mr MacLeod accepted the call of

the congregation to Crown Court Church, the said Mr MacLeod
had become the minister of St Columba's Church, while retaining his former position as Minister of Crown Court Church:
further, that the Kirk Session, to prevent any future misunderstanding, the Kirk Session were desirous to have Mr MacLeod
formally inducted to the new Church, in which the large majority
of the Crown Court congregation were now worshipping: and
further, that owing to the success which had attended the
continued ministry with the assistance of Mr Philip, a licentiate
of the Church of Scotland, during the past six months in Crown
Court Church, the Presbytery would be pleased to sanction the
continuance of Crown Court as a Mission Church in connection
with St Columba's in London'. This was approved, and the
Presbytery appointed that day week for the induction in St
Columba's[25].

The Presbytery plays a considerable part in the affairs of the
congregation at this period, mainly in connection with Mr
Philip. As Mr MacLeod's assistant his duties lay mostly in the
Mission Church, where he was supported heartily by the Kirk
Session's Crown Court Management Committee of 13 members.
That Committee's reports soon suggested that he might be
ordained, and the Session approved of an approach to Presbytery for the purpose, at the same time resolving that for the
present Crown Court should not be erected into a separate
charge[26]. The proposal met with opposition in Presbytery[27],
and was taken to the Synod[28], the grounds of objection being
that the ordination of one not about to be inducted to a charge
was contrary to the Church's practice and would be apt to
encourage *ministerium vagum*. Mr MacLeod countered that
objection by citing two cases in Scotland where ordination had
been granted to a licentiate in the same position as Mr Philip,
that is, an assistant engaged, under direction, in an important
ministerial work. The Synod granted the plea, and later events
justified it, for the General Assembly in 1896 called 'the attention of Presbyteries to the discretionary power which may be
exercised in granting under suitable conditions ordination to
probationers who are of sufficient experience, and are engaged
in regular service'[29].
The St Columba's Kirk Session was canny, however, and

discreetly decided at its next meeting 'that the subject [of Mr Philip's ordination] be postponed for further consideration with the view of learning what arrangements could be made for creating Crown Court into a separate charge'[30]. Action was swift. Next month they met specially to consider a memorial from their Crown Court Committee, who stated that they 'were of opinion that the time had arrived for the church to be erected into a separate charge, that such a step would have an immediate effect in increasing the success of the work, and that they were willing themselves to raise a yearly sum of not less than £250 towards the necessary expenses, the whole sum required being estimated at £500 a year'. After careful consideration the Session 'resolved to make application to the Presbytery of London for the Ordination and Induction of the Revd. A. M. Philip, B.D., as Minister of Crown Court as a separate charge; that the Kirk Session agreed to use their best endeavour to raise the sum of £250 a year, or such less sum as may be required for five years towards the maintenance of the Church and Mission at Crown Court, the Committee of Management of Crown Court having undertaken to raise a similar sum; and that in arriving at this Resolution the Kirk Session are influenced by the belief that Mr Philip has the full intention of continuing his ministry at Crown Court for at least two or three years to come'[31]. The Presbytery, being thus satisfied that the application was for Ordination *and Induction*[32], and having sustained the congregation's Call to Mr Philip and appointed his Trials for Ordination[33], duly ordained and inducted him on 13th November, 1885[34]. Under his leadership, and now as a separate charge, Crown Court set out to take up a new part in the story of the Scots Kirk in London, on the site first acquired 116 years before.

Although Mr MacLeod's responsibility in Covent Garden was now ended, another had already been re-imposed by the Presbytery when it accepted the Dulwich minister's resignation and named Mr MacLeod interim moderator of the Kirk Session there[35]. Not until 1888 do we find him finally free of care for the Dulwich congregation, by which time the University of Aberdeen had honoured him with a Doctorate of Divinity. Meanwhile in St Columba's another assistant had been appointed.

Fifth in the line of now over fifty assistants, the Rev. W.P. Paterson, B.D., was one of four who later became Professors and of three who later became Moderators of the General Assembly. His son, a distinguished psychiatrist, maintains the St Columba's connection as a member. Much of his work was necessarily concerned with the Dulwich congregation, but he was involved, also, in some of the distinctive features which now began to mark St Columba's contribution to the ministry of the Scots Kirk in London.

Some of these had in fact been launched before the congregation moved. In 1882 a branch of the Young Men's Guild had been set up, and in the new building it added vitality to the congregation's life. The annual collection for the London Hospitals continued to evoke its generosity, which over the years has much exceeded that of any other congregation of any denomination in London. Another new organisation of the Church of Scotland, the Woman's Guild, was soon being considered by the Session, which in January 1886 approved the formation of 'a Guild for Young Women'; but owing to the difficulty of finding 'a lady capable of taking charge of it' it was a full year[36] before the existence of a St Columba's branch of the Woman's Guild was noted in Session minutes, under the heading of permission to place in the hall a cupboard 'for the work to be made at the Young Women's Guild Meetings'[37]. The first church parade of the London Scottish Rifle Volunteers was held in St Columba's on May 9th, 1888, beginning an association which has continued ever since and is symbolised by the beautiful London Scottish Memorial Chapel incorporated in the present church. The Literary Society, which began as a section of the Young Men's Guild in 1893, has had a varied history and still flourishes. There was a Boy's Club, which was succeeded much later by the Scouts: its Cricket Club, formed in 1899, subsequently widened its membership, but became a casualty of the Second World War, by which time a flourishing Tennis Club, still active and with its own private courts, had been established. Musical aids to worship had early been encouraged by Dr MacLeod, and a more reverent celebration of the Sacrament of the Lord's Supper had been achieved with the adoption of the traditional Scottish practice of the Great Entry, when the Communion Elements are solemnly carried in by the

159

elders and laid upon the Table prior to the Action of the Sacrament[38] .

It is a surprise, however, to find that one new organisation for London Scots was not initiated by the Scots Kirk. The Caledonian Christian Club owed its existence to the initiative of an English Presbyterian, the Rev. William B. Alexander, minister of Whitefield Presbyterian Church, Drury Lane. It opened its first premises in Southampton Street in 1887, but apparently it did not come to the attention of St Columba's until 1889, when Dr MacLeod called a special meeeting of his Session[39] to hear Mr Arthur Robertson, first Secretary of the Club; and they appointed a committee to give guidance as to what action might be take in support of this 'Scottish Home for providing kindly welcome, temporary lodging, protection, direction and helpfulness to fresh arrivals in London'. Later the Club moved to Endsleigh Gardens; later still it was taken over by what is now the Social Responsibility Committee of the Church of Scotland; it was finally wound up in 1975 when the need for it had gone (or changed — see Chapter three). By then it had served three full generations of young Scotsmen, and thousands have had reason to be grateful for the Caledonian Christian Club and the welcome and encouragement it offered them on their arrival in London. A continuing committee in London, under the convenership of an elder of Crown Court (which had in later years a very close association with the Club), and including representatives of both London congregations, is examining the changed situation and exploring new possibilities[40] .

When Dr MacLeod retired in 1901 his twenty years' ministry in London had built up a strong and influential congregation, characteristically Victorian in its acceptance of the social *status quo ante bellum,* but by no means indifferent to the obligations of Christian service. He had directed the generosity of his members to the home and overseas missions of the Church and enlisted their support of the three other Scots congregations in London. He had strengthened the Church's links with such helpful agencies as the Royal Scottish Corporation, the Royal Caledonian Asylum, the Caledonian Christian Club, and the London Hospitals Sunday Fund. His preaching and persuasion had opened the eyes of numbers of his people to the civic and social needs where men and women of Christian conviction could make a distinctive witness and contribute their personal service. He enjoyed several years of retirement, and died in Edinburgh in 1911.

One of Dr MacLeod's elders, whose name will appear again in this story, should be specially mentioned here because of the crucial part he played in regard to 'the ultimate destination of the Crown Court building'. Lord Balfour of Burleigh had been tutored as a boy by Horatius Bonar[41], as his great-great-great-uncle had been by Thomas Boston[42]; and the fact that his wife's mother, Lady Aberdeen, was a Baillie of Jerviswood and a descendant of John Knox[43] may have added to his interest in Crown Court and to his concern for the welfare of the Scots Kirk in London. He was Secretary for Scotland from 1885 to 1903, Rector of Edinburgh University from 1896 to 1889, and chairman of several parliamentary Commissions relating to industrial relations and colonial affairs. His great-great-great uncle, Boston's pupil, had courageously dissented from the General Assembly's censure of the Erskines in 1733. He himself took as courageous a minority-stand in the Assemblies of his day on matters about which he felt deeply, particularly in regard to the re-union of the Scottish Churches. Almost as soon as he was commissioned to sit in the Assembly, 1875, he made a speech on the subject in which he said that, while not sanguine of present success, if they did not try they certainly would never succeed in achieving it. He lived to see the second reading of the Church of Scotland Bill pass through the Commons in 1921, and when he died suddenly soon thereafter his minister, Dr Fleming, in an obituary notice, dwelt on that vision to which he had contributed so much. 'He went through life — this strong, gritty man — with feet nevertheless shod with the gospel of peace; that is why he was recognised in all the Churches as the great peacemaker, the go-between of reconciliation. . . . As a young laird and elder of twenty-four he stood up in the General Assembly of 1874 and supported the Bill — patron though he was himself — for the abolition of Patronage. It would make for peace and re-union, the young elder made bold to say; it would remove the cause of the disruption of 1843, said this young statesman in budding sagacity; it would set at rest once for all

The Scots Kirk in London

the quarrel that had for so long been productive of such mis-
chief. And in 1875, and practically every year thereafter, in
spite of his having to hold the sword of Church Defence in one
hand while the olive branch was in the other, he joined his
mind and voice with those of Dr Charteris in planning and
commending one *eirenicon* after another, in order to bring back
Church peace to sect-distracted Scotland. It was the parable of
his lifetime; it was the dream and vision of his age'[43]. On July
9th, 1923, the Prince of Wales unveiled a memorial tablet
which the Kirk Session had erected in memory of their colleague,
and gave a brief address[44].

NOTES

1. *Minutes of London Presbytery*, 13 Jan., 1879.
2. *Ibid*, 10th Mar, '79.
3. *Ibid*, 21st Mar, '79.
4. *Minutes of the Scottish Synod in England*, 7th May, 1879.
5. *London Presbytery Minutes*, 19th Aug., '79.
6. *Ibid*, 13th Oct., '79.
7. Matheson may well have felt that his blindness would be an insuperable
   handicap in London. It was in the following year that he wrote the
   hymn, 'O Love that wilt not let me go', and four years thereafter he
   became minister of St Bernard's Edinburgh, with a congregation which
   grew to 2,000.
8. *Crown Court Session Minutes*, Mar. 29th, 1881.
9. Marshall Lang had been Dr Cumming's assistant for six months. (Lady
   Frances Balfour, *Ne Obliviscaris*, i, 175f).
10. *Crown Court Session Minutes*, 22nd Apr., 1881, at which meeting also
    the Session discontinued the singing of an anthem. This may have been
    because, despite Dr Cumming's concern for order in public worship
    (Chapter ten, note 9), the introduction of the anthem had had an
    opposite effect. Lord Frederick Hamilton in *My Yesterdays*, p. 44,
    describes it thus: 'Dr Cumming had recently introduced the anthem',
    not to the benefit of his congregation's worship. 'It was the singular
    custom of his congregation to leave their pews during the singing of
    this anthem and to move about in the aisles — whether as a protest
    against this daring innovation or merely to stretch their limbs or seek
    better places I could never make out'.
11. *Crown Court Session Minutes*, 14th June, 1881.
12. *Ibid*, 21st Oct., 1881. Only part of the site was on the Cadogan Estate.
    A portion was leased from the Trustees of Smith's Charity, and a
    letter from Macvicar Anderson in the Charity's archives refers in

162

passing to a strong campaign of opposition to the Scotch National
Church mounted by the local Anglican vicar. (Dorothy Stroud, *The
South Kensington Estate of Henry Smith's Charity*).

13. *St Columba's Magazine*, Feb., 1911.
14. *Crown Court Session Minutes*, 11th Dec., 1881.
15. *Ibid.* The stress on 'Inalienable connection with the Church of Scotland' was a heritage from 1843 when, with the Disruption, many
church buildings in England became the property of the newly formed
Presbyterian Church in England. See Chapter ten.
16. *Ibid*, 17th May, 1882. It was not until April 1883 that the Presbytery
was asked to approve, for the Court of Chancery, the allocation of the
residue funds of Swallow Street church, including £100 bequeathed
for the benefit of the poor of that congregation, to be disposed of
'for the sole benefit of the new Scottish National Church now being
built for the accommodation of the united congregations of Swallow
Street and Crown Court' (*Presbytery Minutes*, 30th April, 1883). The
bequest referred to was *The Charity of Mrs Margery Whitworth*, and is
still administered for that purpose by the Kirk Session of St Columba's.
17. *Crown Court Session Minutes*, 25th Oct., 1882.
18. *The Builder*, May 5, 1883.
19. See Chapter fourteen.
20. *Crown Court Session Minutes*, 31st Oct., 16th Nov., 1883, & 28th
Jan., 1884.
21. *Ibid.*, 13th Feb., 1884.
22. *Ibid.*, 20th Mar., 1884. After this date they became the Minutes of
the Kirk Session of St Columba's.
23. *Presbytery Minutes*, 28th Mar., 1884. In a duly sanctioned congregation with no elders, or an insufficient number to form a quorum,
the Presbytery appoints one or more of its own number as assessors
to act with the minister as a Session till an election has been held and
a Kirk Session has been regularly constituted. (*Practice and Procedure
in the Church of Scotland*, p. 112).
24. *Ibid*, 14th July, 1884.
25. *Ibid*, 13th Oct., 1884.
26. *St Columba's Session Minutes*, 17th Mar., 1885.
27. *London Presbytery Minutes*, 13th Apr., 1885.
28. *Scottish Synod in England Minutes*, 5th May, 1885.
29. *Practice and Procedure &c.*, p. 210.
30. *St Columba's Session Minutes*, 26th June, 1885.
31. *Ibid*, 13th July, 1885.
32. *Presbytery Minutes*, 12th Oct., 1885.
33. *Ibid*, 27th Oct., 1885.
34. *Ibid*, 13th Nov., 1885.
35. *Ibid*, 22nd July, 1885.

36. *St Columba's Session Minutes*, 28th Jan., 4th Mar., 1st Apr., & 2nd Dec., 1886.

37. *Ibid*, 19th May, 1887. But that it may have been formed before 1886 ended is suggested by the fact that Lady Victoria Campbell, a member of the branch, preserved with pride to the end of her life her Guild membership card, 'signed by A.H. Charteris in 1886'. Both the Young Men's Guild and the Woman's Guild were founded by Professor Charteris, who was a close friend of Mr MacLeod and had spoken at his induction. An early member of the St Columba's branch, Mrs Ratcliffe, offered for service as a Deaconess (an Order revived by Charteris), but ill-health caused her to withdraw. The first Deaconess of the Church of Scotland, commissioned in 1888, was Lady Grisell Baillie, an aunt of Lady Balfour of Burleigh and descendant of her famous namesake whom we met in Chapter five. The Church of Scotland's Deaconess Hospital in Edinburgh was named for her, The Lady Grisell Baillie Hospital.

38. *Session Minutes*, 26th Apr., 1884. The Little Entry, at the beginning of every service, is the bringing in of the Bible, symbolic of the Word to be proclaimed. If the people stand at that point it is as an act of reverence for the word, not for the minister.

39. *Ibid*, 23rd Oct., 1890.

40. Information from the Rev. John Miller Scott, B.D., minister of Crown Court Church.

41. Horatius Bonar, one of three brothers famous in the ministry of the Church of Scotland, and afterwards of the Free Church of Scotland, has been termed 'the prince of Scottish hymn-writers . . . . The best of his hymns rank with the classics; one or two have been claimed by exacting judges to be the best hymns ever written' (*Moffatt, op. cit.*, pp. 273f.)

42. Thomas Boston (see Appendix B) dealt faithfully with the household to which, as tutor to the young heir of Kennet in 1697, he was chaplain. He recorded in his memoirs several incidents and encounters of his Kennet period, particularly a crisis in his spiritual life which took place while he meditated under a walnut tree in the garden there. (See G.H. Morrison, *Memoirs of the Reverend and Learned Thomas Boston, A.M.*, pp. xii,xiv, & 29). The present Lord Balfour has kindly shown the writer a beautifully fluted walking stick, with a silver band engraved: *'In memory of Thomas Boston, 21st January 1697. From the tree mentioned in his memoirs, then growing at Kennet, and blown down 1862'.*

43. *St Columba's Magazine*, August 1921.

44. Five years after that the Prince's brother and sister-in-law, the Duke and Duchess of Kent, later to be king and queen, visited St Columba's for the unveiling and dedication of a memorial to another elder, Field Marshal Earl Haig.

CHAPTER 12

'No Mean Heritage'

Crown Court became a full charge at the end of 1885, when the Rev. Alfred Morison Philip, B.D., was ordained and inducted as its minister. He was the son of the minister of New Deer, a graduate of Aberdeen University, and had been working in Crown Court for eighteen months as Mr MacLeod's assistant. It was understood that he would continue there for at least two or three years. In fact he remained for six, and they were years of slow but steady progress, during which the roll increased from under 150 to over 250 members. It was no easy task he undertook, but he had trustworthy assurances of help. At the service of ordination and induction the charges[1] had been given by Mr MacLeod who, reminding him of the stature and renown of Dr Cumming, his own predecessor in that pulpit, added the somewhat intimidating admonition: 'You have succeeded to no mean heritage'. But, he went on, 'Here is a sweet strong word which the Master gives you, on which you may now and always rest — "I will make My grace sufficient for thee!" '

Encouragement and practical help from Mr MacLeod and his members continued to support the cause in Crown Court, and the relationship between the two congregations was close and strong. The last meeting of the St Columba's Crown Court Management Committee was held on Nov. 10th and reported to the St Columba's Session on the 12th. At its meeting the following day the Presbytery appointed Mr MacLeod and Mr Macvicar Anderson of St Columba's and Mr J. Cochrane Murray of St Andrew's as Assessors for Crown Court,[2] and they met with Mr Philip on Dec. 3 and agreed to ask the congregation to send in signed lists for nomination to the eldership. On the second day of the new year, meeting in St Columba's and examining these lists, they nominated Matthew Jackson, Henry Edward Morgan, Thomas Thomson, James Wright,

David Stewart and Hugh Williams as elders-elect, who, being duly elected, were ordained, and the new Kirk Session constituted, on the 7th of February, 1886. Four of them had been members of the St Columba's Crown Court Management Committee. Three other such members later accepted the important offices of Session Clerk and Joint-Treasurer, George Macdonald becoming the former and Samuel Murray and David Gerard Laing the latter.[3] Laing was an elder on St Columba's Session and also its Treasurer, so that financial appeals by the one congregation to the other were smoothly and favourably dealt with.

Soon after Mr Philip's induction the experiment of a Gaelic Service drew between 500 and 600 Highlanders to Crown Court to worship in their native tongue. It was decided to make this a quarterly occasion. Later an arrangement was made with those responsible for the Gaelic Service instituted by the Highland Society of London in 1813[4], so that, with the four services a year in Crown Court and the others in Regent Square, Gaelic-speaking Londoners might hear the word and sing the praise of God together in their native tongue every month of the year. Now only the quarterly services in Crown Court remain.

The Education Act of 1871 had dispensed with the need for the Crown Court Schools, but the Ragged School Union's annual donation continued, for there was still ample scope for work amongst the young in the neighbourhood. Soon full use was again being made of the class-room accommodation, by such organisations as a Girls' Society, Youth Club, Juvenile Missionary Society, Band of Hope, Mothers' Meeting, Library and Visitors' Association. The last-named had about 153 families under its care at any one time. There was also a Costermongers' Club, later re-named the Friendly Benefit Society, but it was short-lived. The Sunday School was one of the most flourishing agencies, to begin with under the superintendence of one of the Laing brothers and later of Mr William Tibbs, when it attained a strength of 464 scholars and 38 teachers. The Mothers' Meeting, of about 250 members, ran two savings clubs — the 'Clothing and Coat' and the 'Boot and Shoe' Clubs. A Night School for Girls was in being by 1888 and continued for many years to provide social recreation as well as domestic instruction for the girls of the area. Evidently the spirit of Lord

Balfour's warning against 'leaving the poor district spiritually unprovided for' was being wisely applied to include the material as part of the spiritual welfare of that still underprivileged neighbourhood. In all this work a number of St Columba's members were actively involved, and Crown Court could always depend on support from that quarter.

An amusing misunderstanding arose over one appeal for help. The Crown Court Session decided to organise a charitable service for the neighbourhood, under the name of *The Needy Nook*[5]. In agreeing to contribute and to help in the staffing of this venture the St Columba's Session anxiously added that it hoped this name was not meant to replace the time-honoured one of Crown Court as the designation of the congregation. Anxiety was relieved when it was explained that *The Needy Nook* was a soup kitchen. It functioned on Wednesdays and Saturdays; soup was sold at ½d. a quart, and about 135 quarts were prepared each day. A 'dinner of bread and soup' was distributed free to destitute children, of whom there might be a dozen each week. Volunteers from the two congregations staffed *The Needy Nook,* which continued its work for twelve years until increasing deficits and lessening need led to its abandonment in 1898.

In April, 1886 the Session discussed the advisability of setting up a stipend endowment fund, and found speedy encouragement from St Columba's. The Session there had heard a report some months before[6] from Mr T. Nicolson, who had been Treasurer until shortly before Mr MacLeod's arrival, that there existed a fund amounting to £150, dating from the 1860s, and that although there was no clear record as to its purpose he believed that Dr Cumming had had in mind the establishment of an endowment fund. The St Columba's Session resolved to treat it as the nucleus of a stipend endowment fund for Crown Court, and retain it for that purpose 'until the church of Crown Court is independent of St Columba's and Trustees are appointed'. That time had now come, and in addition to the £150 the sum of £1000 was promised by Sir Robert Jardine and the Rt. Hon. James A. Campbell so soon as the congregation had raised an equal amount[7]. One of the achievements of Mr Philip's ministry was the securing of the congregation's £1000 within four years. A considerable sum was raised at a bazaar held in

Edinburgh, and in 1891 some of the endowment of the dissolved congregation of St Andrew's Stepney became available, and the Fund could then yield £80 per annum for stipend.

It had always been difficult for the stranger to find the location of the church in Crown Court. Once again we find the Session tackling this problem, and hearing, in April 1886, that their decision to instal a lamp in Russell Street, bearing the name of the church, had been implemented. But the subject was to appear on the Session's agenda several times in succeeding years.

The membership of the congregation had grown by the time that St Columba's five years' guarantee had expired in 1890, but began to shrink. When Mr Philip accepted a call to Avoch[8] in 1892, the future of Crown Court church seemed uncertain, particularly as the financial position in St Columba's at that time seems to have been unsettled. The Crown Court Session, however, was confident that Crown Court was needed, and sent a deputation to St Columba's to say that if a successor to Mr Philip could be found they wished to continue as an independent congregation, provided that they could count on a contribution each year from St Columba's, as before.[9] The St Columba's Session was able to guarantee £150 each year from its own membership, and promised to put Crown Court on its schedule of special offerings from the whole membership of the congregation. A successor was found, in the person of the Rev. Alexander Macrae, a native of Kingussie on Speyside and a graduate of the University of St Andrew's. He had been ordained to the ministry at Greengairs near Airdrie in 1888, and was inducted to Crown Court in December, 1892.

Mr Macrae ministered there for a quarter of a century before resigning upon his appointment as Officiating Chaplain to the forces in London during the first world war. He took a prominent part in the affairs of the Presbytery, and for a number of years was Clerk to the Scottish Synod in England. His appointment as Officiating Chaplain in 1917 followed immediately upon his three-years' active service to the 2nd Battalion of the Scots Guards, during which he was mentioned in despatches.

In the course of his ministry considerable improvement took place in the Covent Garden neighbourhood. The deteriorating condition of the church buildings was causing concern, and there was considerable pressure from the Bedford Estate authorities to take remedial action[10]. In 1904 a scheme for removal to a new site was being discussed with the Duke of Bedford's Estate, but had to be abandoned because of a radical alteration in the larger Estate plan of which the scheme had been part. One of the neighbourhood improvements is reflected in a Bedford Estate document of the same year, where a plan prepared by the City of Westminster for the widening of Russell Street from 15 to 50 feet shows a necessary encroachment on the area occupied by Crown Court's schools, together with an altered access to the church itself[11]. The Session's own minutes show that an offer of £3,005 was originally made for the surrender of that area, but was turned down on the grounds that something better could be expected. A sealed offer of £1,850 was later made by the City of Westminster, but again rejected because the Session was advised that a claim could be made for £3,750[12]. In the end £1,850 had to be accepted, and it proved impossible immediately to use this for a reason which will appear in Chapter fifteen.

The next document in the Bedford Estate: Crown Court Scotch Church collection of leases is dated 1909[13], and marks an episode in the congregation's story which must have been as alarming as it was necessary. It shows the surrender of the leases of two parcels of ground, one dating from 1847 and the other from 1858, both having 38 years still to run, at a total rental value of £3,500. The circumstances leading to this transaction might have spelt failure and extinction for the congregation of 223 members. Instead, with the distinguished help which the crisis enlisted, they led to new beginnings and positive advance.

In 1904, and again in 1907, reports on the structural weakness of the old building, and its final condemnation as unsafe, had faced the congregation with a choice between repairing, rebuilding, removing, or renouncing its place in the London scene for ever. It was a bold decision which authorised the signatures of the five Crown Court Church Trustees to that document of 1909. They were The Right Hon. Lord Balfour of Burleigh (Chairman), the Rev. Alexander Macrae (Minster),

Henry Morgan (Session Clerk), The Lady Frances Balfour, and Sir George Alex. Cooper, Bart. The signature of one Trustee is missing — that of the Right Hon, James A. Campbell of Stracathro. He had died the previous year. It was to him that Lady Balfour ascribed the principal credit for the bold suggestion which had such a happy outcome — the building of a new Crown Court Church. 'There were plenty of arguments for patching up the old fabric and continuing it with all its burdens for the remaining years of the lease. There were many reasons for selling the site and leaving the congregation to gather where they would. . . The story of the new Kirk of the Crown really lies in the decision given by Mr Campbell [who] decided that the right course was to rebuild on part of the old site, with a new lease and a reduced ground-rent, and [who] started the rebuilding fund'[14]. One of his last actions was to contribute £1000 to that fund, and it was probably due more to his example and persuasiveness than to any cause other than Lady Frances Balfour's own persistent advocacy and personal generosity that it grew to a figure almost sufficient to meet the total cost by the time the new church was dedicated in October 1909. In the interval the congregation worshipped in the Newton Hall of the Royal Scottish Corporation in Crane Court[15].

The cost was £11,000, and the congregation, now of 352 members, had perforce to rely on such friends to raise the amount. The Duke of Bedford's Estate had granted a ninety-nine years' lease of the site, which was only the rear half of that on which the old church and schools had stood, with a ground rent of about one third of the previous one; and the Duke himself had subscribed £1000. St Columba's Kirk Session, 'in order not to interfere with the effort now being made on behalf of Crown Court', postponed for more than a year its own long-planned scheme for a £10,000 stipend-endowment fund[16], and 'the old Communion Plate having become redundant through various presentations of new vessels by members, presented it to Crown Court'[17]. John Burdett-Coutts[18] was a subscriber, and other names from the past appeared on the subscription-list, for as Lady Frances Balfour records: 'One of the church records revealed a list of original donors in 1718. I conceived the idea of asking their descendants. . ., and also the

45 Scottish Ministers, past and present, 5 Scottish Prime Ministers among them, to become subscribers. . . Almost none refused, and these few perished miserably within a year or two'![19].

Some interesting details about the building and its furnishings are noted by the Lady Frances Balfour in the article already mentioned.[14] The organ was a gift from Mr Andrew Carnegie, who broke his customary pound-for-pound rule and met not only the entire cost but also the bill for the carving of the organ-case. The Communion Table, of oak, with a slab of Iona marble as its top, was presented by the Woman's Guild of St Columba's. The Font, of the largest piece of marble ever cut out of the quarries of Iona, was given by the St Columba's Young Men's Guild. The Lectern was gifted by the architects. Nothing of the old church could be preserved for the new, except the distinctive 'extinguisher' pulpit which the original congregation had acquired from Plaisterers' Hall in 1710. This was eventually replaced by the present pulpit, given in memory of Dr Cumming by his granddaughters[20]. A wooden plaque bearing the royal arms, which had at some time been fixed below the gallery of the old church, and some of the stained glass presented by Dr Cumming when the church was renovated in 1845, were placed in the hall. The original 1710 Communion Table was given to Tiree Parish Church, where it was later joined by a gothic Lectern Chair from the new building.[21] That chair had become redundant in 1924 when Lady Frances Balfour, on the death of her husband, replaced it with a handsome Jacobean oak chair which the builders had fashioned from the timbers of the old church and presented to him in 1908[22]. This is the one remaining physical relic of the original church. The restricted site determined some architectural peculiarities of the building, and accounts for the long stairway giving access to the place of worship above the hall, and also for the lofty windows above the gallery, admitting all possible light from above the level of surrounding buildings.

The existence of a novel furnishing, not otherwise mentioned, is revealed in a brief paragraph of the Session's minutes for its meeting in September, 1910, that 'the National Telephone Company has offered £3 to repair damage to the Sunday

School banner caused by acid from the batteries for the Electrophone in the pulpit'. By means of this device — an early medium of broadcast communication — aged or invalid members who possessed a telephone and the means to rent a connection for the necessary period each Sunday, could hear the whole service and maintain contact with the congregation at worship.

The ex-Prime Minister, Arthur J. Balfour — whose brother, Lady Frances Balfour's husband, Col. Eustace Balfour, was the honorary Architect, and whose successor as Prime Minister, Henry Campbell-Bannerman, was the brother of James A. Campbell — laid the commemoration-stone on May 12th, 1909, and the completed building was dedicated on Saturday, 30th October, by the Moderator of the General Assembly. The following day was all Hallows Eve, and the preacher at the evening service was Dr Donald MacLeod, come back from retirement to join in the first services in the new building on the old site.

The title *The Kirk of the Crown of Scotland*, used by Lady Frances Balfour, appears to have come into use during Mr Macrae's ministry. With it is linked the tradition mentioned in Chapter five, tracing the origin of the St Peter's Court Scots congregation to that which had worshipped in the Royal Chapel at Scotland Yard and ascribing Crown Court's name to the later presence there of the congregation with this alleged Scottish royal heritage. No trace of any such title, or of either tradition, appears in minute books or other accessible records. Crowne Court, and The Crowne Inne, in fact appear in Morgan's map of London, dated 1683; and Mr Macrae's successor discovered that the original 1719 lease describes the site of the church as being 'All that piece and parcell of ground lying and being in the parish of St Martin' in the ffields aforesaid abutting upon a Court then commonly called Crown Court'[23]. But it must have been a fine romantic moment when Lady Frances inserted a golden key in the lock of the new building on that day before Halloween, 1909, and, turning it to unlock the door, declared 'The door of the Kirk of the Crown of Scotland is now opened!'

It is evident that Mr Macrae was, as the minister of St Columba's at that time wrote, the right man for Crown Court in this critical period. 'By his magnetic gifts and pulpit power', Dr Fleming went on, 'he has made Crown Court such a centre

of interest, especially amongst the young Scotsmen and Scotswomen of London, that it was felt . . . that a work so successful
and so fruitful of good must not be left to perish under a heap
of crumbling walls. Had Mr Macrae been other than he is or
his ministry less attractive than it has proved, the decision
would undoubtedly have been different'[24].

The name of the Lady Frances Balfour has been prominent
in this chapter; indeed had she not been who and what she was
the decision to rebuild would not have been so energetically
and successfully carried out. When the congregation moved to
Pont Street she and her elder sister, Lady Victoria Campbell —
daughters of the Duke of Argyll — retained a warm interest in
the old building where not only they but their uncles had been
baptised. Their grandfather, the 7th Duke, had presented to
Dr Cumming in 1850 a handsome brass-bound Bible, to mark
the baptisms of his sons, Archibald and Walter, in 1847 and
1848. In 1911 Dr Cumming's granddaughters gave it to Crown
Court where it has its appropriate place on the Lectern. Nearby
are memorials to the two sisters — Lady Victoria, who was
Honorary President of the Crown Court Woman's Guild for
many years, and Lady Frances, who succeeded her in that
position and whose attachment to Crown Court grew with the
years. 'My Lines may lie elsewhere, but my heart lies in the
Kirk of the Crown of Scotland', she wrote in her autiography[25],
and one suspects that her 'love for it which grew into an obses-
sion', as her own minister said, produced that title and persuaded others to accept it. After her death in 1931 Dr Fleming
wrote of her courage and her flaming passion for justice (she
was a prominent suffragette and a doughty advocate for the
Travellers' Aid Society), and recalled the occasion when, despite bodily fraility, she 'went on a lonely pilgrimage to Iona
over stormy seas, and had herself lashed to the woodwork on
the deck of the creaking craft. All others were huddled below;
she, a Sea-king's daughter, faced the blast alone with the dead
duchess she was convoying. Indeed had she loved blasts a little
less her passage through life would have been less chequered and
probably more fruitful; but she revelled in dispute and co-
veted strife'[26]. 'There could, in description, be no more vivid
or pungent pen than hers, and much secret history, political

173

and personal, is hidden away in those bundles of letters from her which I have stored away over the years, many of them written from the gallery of the House of Commons. . . She was one of the great personalities of our time, and for better or worse she influenced the course of events both in Church and State to a greater extent than . . . was known'[27].

Lady Victoria's was a more unobtrusive but not less effective contribution to St Columba's, to Crown Court, and to Scotland herself. One day as a young girl she had looked through the broken window of the south transept of the ruined Abbey Church of Iona, and seen a vision which led her to dedicate her life to the welfare of the people of the Highlands and Islands of Scotland[28]. Thereafter she spent the winter months in Tiree, Iona and Bunessan, leaving a fragrant memory particularly amongst the women-folk of those parts. She was quick, for example, to note the weakly children of those cottars who could not afford the luxury of milk for them; and with quiet persistence, as effective as the more vehement adjurations of her younger sister, she persuaded local landowners to subsidise the purchase of a cow for such tenants[29]. Perhaps it was as a by-product of her adolescent vision that her father, the Duke of Argyle, entrusted the Abbey and its precincts to the Church of Scotland in 1900, and that their minister in London, Dr Donald MacLeod, more than once pleaded in the General Assembly for their restoration, and himself solicited interest and enlisted support in the project through which the Abbey Church itself was eventually restored in 1911. Another ministerial MacLeod has since seen that project completed with the restoration of the Abbey buildings, as part of the spiritually imaginative and socially creative programme of the Iona Community. Lady Victoria, we can believe, would have approved of George MacLeod's vision as an extension of her own, to serve also the needs of the industrialised Lowlands.

NOTES

1. A probationer of the Church of Scotland is generally ordained to the Ministry of Word and Sacrament by the Presbytery of the bounds within which lies the parish to which he has been called. After the Moderator has declared him to be ordained — or, in later parishes, to be inducted — both he and his congregation are charged, usually

by a senior minister of the Presbytery, to be faithful in their calling and to their Lord. These are the 'charges'. The word 'charge' in the singular refers to the congregation entrusted to their minister's care and to the parish for whose spiritual welfare they are jointly responsible. For an account of Mr Philip's ordination and induction see *Life and Work; Scotch National Churches in England Supplement,* Dec. 1885.

2.   *Minutes* of first meeting *of Crown Court Kirk Session,* Dec. 3, 1885, and of second meeting, Jan. 2, 1886. Also, *Minutes of Scots Presbytery of London,* 13th Nov., 1885.

3.   *Crown Court Session Minutes,* 5th & 11th Feb., 1896. For many years, also, the two congregations shared the same hon. auditor, Mr (later Sir) Gordon Nairne. Gordon Nairne was a founder-member of the Crown Court-St Columba's Young Men's Guild, became an elder in St Columba's in 1893, and was the first Comptroller of the Bank of England, on whose banknotes his signature became familiar throughout the land. On his appointment to that office in 1918 his minister, Dr Fleming, wrote: 'The Scottish lad who gave the willing service of his prentice hand to the modest balance sheets of a tiny Church Guild more than twenty years ago is today, while still an officebearer in the same church, the Comptroller of the untold thousands of millions that are passing through the coffers of the greatest financial reservoir in the world'. (St Columba's Magazine, June, 1918).

4.   See Chapter eight.

5.   *St Columba's Session Minutes,* 27th Feb. 1890. Dr Cumming, in soliciting support for Crown Court's Ragged School, and for other services to the impoverished_people of Covent Garden, used to write letters of appeal to The Times, signing them *Needy Neuk.* (Lady Frances Balfour, *Ne Obliviscaris,* i, 176).

6.   *St Columba's Session Minutes,* 3rd Dec., 1885 and 28th Jan., 1886. *Crown Court Session Minutes,* 1st April, 1886.

7.   *Crown Court Session Minutes,* 7th Jan., 1888. *St Columba's Session Minutes,* 19th Dec., 1890.

8.   Avoch, pronounced Auch, a fishing village on the Black Isle of Ross and Cromarty, has an interesting history. While there Mr Philip wrote *The Cathedral Kirk of Ross,* a history of Cromarty Kirk.

9.   *Crown Court Session Minutes,* 26th May and 3rd June, 1892. *St Columba's Session Minutes,* 19th May, 1892.

10. The cholera outbreak of 1849, noted in Chapter ten, led to the establishment of the Metropolitan Commission of Sewers, and the Duke of Bedford took urgent measures not only to make full use of the improved sanitary measures which followed but to improve the

state of repair of the buildings on his Covent Garden Estate. It is disappointing to read (*Survey of London*, xxxvi, 44) that in 1884 he was 'waiting for the expiry of leases in the case of bad tenants, amongst whom were Drury Lane Theatre and the Scotch Church, where the lessees displayed complete indifference to the state of their property and tolerable conditions could be maintained only by the active interference of the Bedford Office'. It was in the following year that the church was closed for a month to allow of extensive repairs. But by 1907 the whole aged structure had become dangerous and was condemned.

11. *Bedford Estate/Crown Court Leases, E/BER/CG/L 55*, G.L.C. Record Office.
12. *Crown Court Session Minutes*, 11th & 21st May, 28th Oct., and 6th Nov., 1903
13. *Bedford Estate & c.*, E/BER/CG/L55.
14. *St Columba's Magazine*, Oct., 1809 — article by Lady Frances Balfour.
15. See Chapter three.
16. *St Columba's Magazine*, Mar., 1907.
17. *Ibid*, June, 1910.
18. See Chapter six.
19. Lady Frances Balfour, *op. cit.*, ii, 443.
20. *St Columba's Magazine, Crown Court Supplement*, April 1910. Explaining that the old pulpit, of mahogany, had to give place to one of oak, conforming with the furnishings of the new church, the writer adds: 'The old pulpit, when its day is done, will still find a place in the church and be reverently cared for by willing hands'. No-one can now say what eventually did become of it.
21. *Tiree Parish Church Session Minutes* record these gifts, 20th Sept., 1923 and 18th April, 1925.
22. At least one other such chair had been made, but its whereabouts is now unknown.
23. *St Columba's Magazine*, Oct., 1921, quoted from *Crown Court Magazine*.
24. *Ibid.*, Feb., 1911.
25. Lady Frances Balfour, *op. cit.*, ii,445. 'Lines' is a misleading Scottish colloquialism for the Disjunction Certificate which the communicant member receives on leaving one congregation for another. It certifies that he or she is in good standing as a communicant, having been baptised, received into full communion by a Kirk Session upon profession of faith, and having remained faithful in the use of the means of grace and in the life and work of the Church. It is a purely temporary instrument of transference from one Communion Roll to another, bears the date of issue, and may be regarded as invalid if not presented

within a reasonable period.
26. *St Columba's Magazine*, March 1931.
27. A. Gammie, *Dr Fleming of St Columba's*, pp. 166f.
28. *St Columba's Magazine*, Aug., 1910. Lady Frances Balfour, *Lady Victoria Campbell*, p. 131.
29. *St Columba's Magazine*, Aug., 1910.

CHAPTER 13

Into the Twentieth Century

The latter years of Dr MacLeod's ministry were affected by failing health, and rather than imperil the work of twenty years through physical inability to maintain it he resigned in October, 1901. Within three months his successor had been found; and if the congregation was fortunate in so speedy a settlement it was even more so in the quality of the man to whom it was led as its new minister. Perhaps its members had not forgotten the services conducted by Mr Fleming of Newton some six years earlier when Dr MacLeod had been on sick leave.

Archibald Fleming, still in his thirties, had experience and gifts peculiarly fitting him for the special circumstances of the London ministry. He was a son of the manse, his father being minister of St Paul's, Perth. His uncle also was a minister, and his grandfather, the Rev James Fleming, had succeeded Edward Irving as Dr Chalmers' assistant at St John's Glasgow, before becoming minister at Troon; while his great-grandfather, Andrew Hamilton, had been the first minister of the High Kirk, Kilmarnock. He himself, after a distinguished University career and a probationary year as assistant at St Cuthbert's, Edinburgh, had been ordained in 1888 as minister of Newton, and thereafter had ministered at the Tron Church, Edinburgh. He had been still in his twenties when he first visited Balmoral as preacher in Crathie Kirk with Queen Victoria in the royal pew; and almost yearly thereafter the visit was repeated[1].

In his student days he had edited the Students' Column in the *Edinburgh Evening News,* and contributed occasional articles to *The Scotsman.* Shortly after graduating he took part in founding *The National Observer,* soon to become famous under the editorship of W.E. Henley. A year after becoming minister of the Tron Kirk he had been appointed editor of the Church of Scotland Magazine, *Life and Work,* and although his removal to London meant that his tenure of that office was brief he left his distinctive mark on the periodical and increased its circulation from 104 to 204 thousand copies a month.

His power as a preacher had been evidenced by filled pews in both his churches, and his concern as pastor effectively expressed in organising Tron Kirk members into groups, to work under the direction of his elders in the visitation of homes in the parish. 'Dear people', he had said to them at the beginning of his Tron ministry, 'you are all the ministers — the servants of God — of the Tron. . . And when first one and then another of our parishioners recognises in the church the home and refuge of the soul, and comes to it and waits in it humbly on God and His message, we shall be thankful, knowing that God is helping us'. St Columba's offered ample scope for the exercise of the varied gifts of such a man, and the next forty years were to prove how fully he matched them to the needs of the Scots Kirk in London in the twentieth century.

In his first sermon Mr Fleming shared with his new congregation his conception of the task and opportunity they were to share together. 'Here in London there is a Scottish population equal to that of a great city. And our chief business is with them. We are not a Presbyterian Mission to Englishmen. We are at peace and in sympathy with the great National Church of this southern kingdom, and we desire to live in charity and brotherliness with all who name the Name of Christ and depart from iniquity. We are neither Nonconformists nor Dissenters. . . We are exiled Scots, desiring to worship still under the banner of that grand old Church of our fathers, whose form of worship we love and whose traditions we are proud to inherit. . . Here, then, we are waiting to receive into open and brotherly arms the regiments of our fellow-countrymen who are poured into this capital year by year; we are saying to them that if they wish to worship God as their fathers worshipped, if they wish the friendship and warmth of a Scottish welcome, here they will find what they look for. We cannot estimate what comfort and relief it can give to many an anxious parent's heart at home to know that we are here, to receive their sons and daughters — those who will offer them friendships that are honest and kind, so that the love and care of the old Church of Scotland will still be over them and the familiar services will recall the tender and sacred associations of the home and the religion of their youth'[2].

With such a lead from its minister St Columba's became even more a centre of Scottish life in London. The numerous Scottish societies came to look to Mr Fleming for encouragement, and in 1904 they encouraged him to organise the Scottish Festival Service, which is still held on the Sunday nearest to St Andrew's Day and at which the Moderator of the General Assembly of the Church of Scotland is the warmly-welcomed preacher. In the same year he inaugurated the *St Columba's Magazine,* and his literary skills and editorial competence made it a periodical soon recognised as being far above the level of the ordinary parish magazine. Before long, in a special feature entitled 'Notes in Passing' which sometimes extended to fifteen or twenty columns, he was sharing with over 1500 subscribers (at one penny per issue) the fruits of his wide reading and of his shrewd observation of the contemporary scene in church and state. These 'Notes', reflecting the events, attitudes and personalities of the first third of the twentieth century, are of continuing interest, written as they were in an easy style which holds the attention and unfolds the scene convincingly. Even his obituary notices of famous people of his day — some of them, such as the Hon. James A. Campbell, M.P., Sir James Fergusson of Kilkerran, Lady Frances Balfour, Earl Haig, and Lord Balfour of Burleigh being members of St Columba's, and others, such as Sir William Robertson Nicoll, Sir Henry Campbell-Bannerman, Lord Rosebery, Lord Oxford and Asquith, Arthur J. Balfour and Lord Haldane of Cloan being personal friends — all shed interesting and sometimes revealing light on the character and religious convictions of their subjects.

In 1904 the University of Edinburgh honoured him with a Doctorate of Divinity. In the years 1903 to 1912 he and his congregation were much concerned in furthering plans for the continuing future of the Crown Court congregation, and considerable space in the Columba's Magazine was devoted to publicity for the proposal to rebuild the old church and for raising the necessary money.[3] A 'Note in Passing' about one particular engagement of his reminds one of earlier instances relating to a sister-church, as for example 'when the meeting was held about the French Meeting-house' in 1711, or when Mr Hubert and Mr Tubar, both ministers of French congregations, were helped on their ways in the 1720s,[4] or when the Crown Court congregation worshipped in 'the French Chappell in Castle Street' while their own place of worship was being restored in 1777[5]. Dr Fleming was the special preacher in 1911 at an anniversary service of the Huguenot congregation worshipping in the crypt of Canterbury Cathedral, and he took the opportunity of telling in his own magazine something of the story of that 350-year-old congregation[6].

Lloyd George's National Health Insurance Act became law at the end of 1911. Domestic servants had been particularly suspicious of the Bill. It is a token of St Columba's care for the interests of a large part of its membership that early in 1912 a simple explanatory article, headed 'Advice to Domestic Servants and others on the new Insurance Act' appeared in the congregational magazine. It must have been of the greatest help in clarifying the conditions and advantages, in relation to unemployment and sickness benefit, offered under this first, elementary, three-pence-per-week insurance scheme.

In 1914 the congregation celebrated their minister's semi-jubilee in the ministry with a handsome presentation at a crowded public meeting. Two other celebrations of the kind were yet to come — those of his semi-jubilee as minister of St Columba's and of the jubilee of his ordination as a minister of the Gospel. But other things were to intrude upon the even tenor of life's way before those dates.

The Great War broke into the settled pattern of British ways, and left a permanent mark on its institutions and its social structure. St Columba's felt the full force of that upheaval and played its part in the national effort and sacrifice. It may in truth be said to have made a more-than-average contribution, by its work for Scottish soldiers passing through London while on leave from the various fronts. Train time-tables to Scotland at the week-ends meant a long wait in London. St Columba's members met incoming leave trains and convoyed bus-loads of Jocks — over 20,000 each year — to Pont Street, where they were entertained and cared for in the hall, Gaelic speakers being welcomed in their own language. There, also, they were provided

181

with all that was needed for making uniforms and persons presentable for the final stage of their journey home. Mistresses and maids worked side by side as hostesses in the hall, fathers and sons as guides to and from the railway stations, brothers and sisters as scribes and messengers for the dispatch of telegrams to the folk at home. Minister and members together devoted many an hour on Saturdays and Sundays to this service, the memory of which remains warm in the minds of some now aged survivors of those four-and-half years of warfare. Neighbouring households co-operated by putting their cooking facilities at the disposal of the organisers. Now and again a Jock would go adrift and land up in some nearby public-house, with the danger not only of missing his train but of being found drunk by the M.P.s and paying the penalty by spending his whole leave in custody. St Columba's answer to that possible danger consisted of a certain housekeeper of character and eloquence, who went the round of the pubs and by cajolery or, if necessary, intimidation, saved many a soldier from being caught by the Red-caps. Best known of all to the Tommies was 'The High Heid Yin', Miss Mary Blackwood, to whose general management and control the 'Soldiers on Furlough' enterprise owed much of its success. Apart from running a girls' sewing class in St Columba's and another in Crown Court, she gave much help to the Caledonian Church in Holloway, being particularly interested in the Scout Troop there. From that Troop, whose Scoutmaster was an elder in Crown Court, came a Scout or two every week. These, with a piper, guided the Jocks from Pont Street to Knightsbridge tube station, where more than once the whole company would break into sets of the eightsome reel to the piper's music while waiting on the platform for the next train to the main-line stations for Scotland. Later the Scout Hall in Holloway was named The Blackwood Hall in honour of this redoubtable lady.

Nothing could be quite the same after the war as before, and England felt the first impact of a process of change which revolutionised class-relationships within a generation, just as racial relationships have been revolutionised since the Second World War. The Scots Kirk in London, despite the loss of many of the Scots gentry to the Church of England which the Presbytery of

Not only at the New Year, but every week-end during the 1914-19 war, Scots troops on leave – over 20,000 each year – were entertained at St Columba's.

National Library of Scotland. Illustration from *The Graphic.*

London had deplored in 1827 as encouraging the alienation of class from class, was little disturbed by this social revolution. This was not because it was a one-class congregation. By some it might have been labelled 'aristocratic'; by others, considering that more than a quarter of its membership consisted of domestic staff and artisans, it could with equal truth have been labelled as 'plebeian'. In fact such differences were largely forgotten. Class-consciousness played little part within the walls of the Scots Kirk in London.

In every Scottish Sunday School Mrs Alexander's hymn, 'All things bright and beautiful' had been a favourite since the beginning of the century, but the editors of no Church of Scotland would have thought of including the verse which reads:

> The rich man in his castle,
> The poor man at his gate,
> God made them high or lowly
> And order'd their estate.

Such a feudal — not to say predestinarian — idea was foreign to the Scottish mind, nurtured as it was on the doctrine of the priesthood of believers and familiar as it was with the operation of presbyterian government in the Church. The transition from an era when everyone 'knew his place' to the more egalitarian post-war society may have been a little self-consciously achieved but it was no revolutionary achievement in St Columba's or Crown Court. All were equal at the Table around which, symbolically, they gathered; and as the elements of the sacred feast were distributed they were received and passed on from believer to believer in the name of the One Who alone is Master and in Whom all are brothers and sisters. There was an English chauffeur who had emerged from the war, a cynic and unbeliever, but in whom the barrier broke down when at a Communion service his Scots wife was handed the Cup by an elder whom he recognised as Earl Haig. There was a judge who many years later confided to a minister how moved he had been to receive the Bread from the hand of a man with whom some years before he had had to deal privately over a matter of embezzlement but who was now, by grace, come to the Table 'with clean hands and a pure heart'. The Head Porter of the Bank of England served as an elder beside Sir Gordon Nairne, Comptroller of the Bank. And when William Jardine Dalgleish, coachman to Mr Justice and Lady Chitty, was ordained to the Elder-ship along with Earl Haig, 'it was never determined whether the Field Marshal was more proud of standing next to the coach-man or the coachman of standing beside the earl on the chancel steps'[7].

Speaking of coachmen, the oldest living member of St Columba's in 1923 was Henry Austen. He had been Lord Aber-deen's coachman in 1883 and drove him then to the ceremony of laying the foundation-stone in Pont Street. On May 2nd, 1923, he was there again. Lord Aberdeen, standing on the spot where he had laid the stone forty years before to the day, was there again. Professor George Milligan, Moderator-designate of the General Assembly, was there again, standing on the spot where his father, then Moderator, had stood in dedicating the stone. Both gave short addresses after the opening prayers had been led by the minister of Belhaven, Glasgow. He had been there, as a child; his father was Dr Donald MacLeod, the mini-ster under whom the move from Crown Court was then being made[9].

It was in the spirit of Paul's words in I Corinthians 10:16, 17, then, that St Columba's moved into the post-war years, to face its difficulties and accept its opportunities. Some of the latter were greater than could have been imagined.

In 1920, through the munificence of the Hon. Elsie Cameron Corbett, daughter of Lord Rowallan, the congregation was able to open a Hostel for Scotswomen coming to professional and business posts in London — a dream long cherished by Miss Catherine Lumsden who had become St Columba's first Deacon-ess in 1903. As 'St Columba's House for Scotswomen' it served that purpose for over fifty years, and the buildings now serve a not dissimilar purpose under other auspices[9]. It is of interest to note that Miss Frances Davidson, Miss Lumsden's successor as Deaconess, was joined in 1923 by Miss Rosamund Clark, a Church Sister of the U.F. Church, and in those two colleagues St Columba's had an anticipation of the union of the two churches six years later.

In 1922 the newly developed technique of radio-telephony was refined and brought unto public service as a means of com-munication, with the formation of the British Broadcasting

185

Company. On the last day, and during the last quarter-hour, of
that year, from the Marconi Company's office in the Strand,
Dr Fleming spoke, into a primitive microphone dangling at the
end of a cable hung from the ceiling, a ten-minute message
followed by a prayer for the whole nation. Then came the
chimes, and the midnight strokes of Big Ben ushering in the new
year. In following years Dr Fleming's voice became well-known
on the 'wireless', not only through a long succession of New
Year's Eve broadcasts, but on other occasions of Scottish
significance such as St Andrew's Day, or of national importance such as the 1926 General Strike, or the death of Queen
Alexandra.

The twenties of the century were years of great import for
the future of the Scottish Kirk, and between 1921 and 1925
legislation was steered through both Houses of Parliament,
recognising her claims in terms which finally removed the
barriers to the re-union of her national family. Dr Fleming, as
her man in London, played an important part at that end of
the negotiations. This was peculiarly appropriate, for twenty
years earlier he had foreseen the possibility of re-union in an
event which caused a furore at the time and seemed to most
people to push that possibility into the remotest future. This
was the fateful 'Church Case' of 1904 in the House of Lords.
The Free and the United Presbyterian Churches in Scotland
had united in 1900 as the United Free Church[10]. But some two
dozen ministers of the Free Church, with a body of its members, mainly in the Highlands, had refused to enter the Union.
Declaring that they were the only true heirs of the Disruption
Church and that the uniting majority had departed from its
fundamental principles, they claimed that they and they alone
were entitled to the churches, manses, schools, funds, colleges
and other property of the Free Church. Their claim, and a
further appeal, were both dismissed by the Court of Session,
where the issues, both legal and ecclesiastical, were fully understood. But their appeal to the House of Lords in 1904, heard by
one Scottish and six English judges, was allowed by a majority
of five to two. Utter confusion followed, for the successful
appellants could not possibly use, man, or maintain the properties now refted from the congregations, courts and missions of

the United Free Church. The government had to intervene, and the situation was remedied by an Act of Parliament in the following year[11].

Archibald Fleming had been present to hear the Lords' decision, and to Mr John Cowan, W.S., the Agent of the U.F. Church, who was dumfounded by the blow, he offered the encouragement of a prophecy. Out of the apparent evil, he said, good might yet come — not only the cementing of the new Union under the pressure of shared adversity, but also a fresh approach to the question of the ultimate re-union of the whole church in Scotland. He wrote to *The Scotsman* to the same effect, provoking a leading article by the editor questioning his good sense. And he used his influence with his friend, A.J. Balfour, then Prime Minister, and quietly encouraged him to retain, despite his cabinet's doubts, the appended but highly important Clause 5, in the Bill which was to remedy the preposterous situation created by the Lords' decision[12].

Now, in the decade after the war, Dr Fleming was taking part in the fulfilling of his earlier hope. As one of the Established Church's 'Hundred' he was involved in the conversations with the 'Hundred' of the United Free Church, producing a Plan and Basis of Union which would be acceptable to both Assemblies. As the Church of Scotland's man in London he was not only host to Dr John White and other official spokesmen when they visited Westminster to promote the legislation which would remove old hindrances to union: he was also himself an influential worker behind the scenes, able to explain on the spot to uninformed parliamentary officials the complex but indispensable conditions which had to be secured to satisfy both parties to the projected union. In this he could count on support from a number of his members and elders, such as Lady Frances Balfour, Sir Arthur Steel-Maitland, M.P., Sir John Milne-Home, the Earl of Stair, John Buchan, M.P., and Lord Balfour of Burleigh[13]. In July 1921 the Church of Scotland Bill was passed. It was Lord Balfour of Burleigh's son, the 7th Baron, who three years later sponsored the even more complicated and controversial Church of Scotland (Property and Endowments) Bill of 1925 on its second reading in the House of Lords; and it was with Sir John Milne-Home, another elder of St Columba's, that Dr John White had secured that Bill's provision concerning the compulsory redemption of teinds, without which the Union proposals would have been unacceptable to the United Free Church. 'I am grateful to God that it was Milne-Home I had to deal with', said John White to the General Assembly; 'He was as loyal and generous to the Church as I would have wished'[14]. It would be difficult to assess how much the Re-union which took place in 1929 owed to the help given behind the scenes by members of St Columba's and its minister.

Appreciation was not withheld. Dr Fleming's name was held in such honour throughout the Church that the congregation's celebration in 1921 of his semi-jubilee as their own minister was duplicated in an equally impressive ceremony during the meetings of the General Assembly in Edinburgh later that year, when a distinguished company gathered to make a presentation symbolising the Church's gratitude for all that was owed to him for his work on her behalf and in the care of her sons and daughters, 'the Scots of the Dispersion', during his twenty-five years in London.

Half as many years again were yet to come, and they saw no diminution in the extent of St Columba's ministry to Scots in need or trouble, in the numbers who gathered Sunday by Sunday to worship in the beautiful church in Pont Street, or in the liveliness of the thriving organisations through which all ages and interests were cared for. Emigrated Scots on their way back to visit the home country would visit Pont Street to share in the worship which they had sampled through H.M.V.s widely distributed album of recordings of two St Columba's services. Scots on holiday or business in London would drop in to say thank-you for what Dr Fleming or his deaconess or assistant had done for their sons or daughters come to study or work in the metropolis. Hospital Sunday Fund contributions from St Columba's continued to top the London list. And the burdens falling upon its minister grew no less, although in 1929 the Rev. Ian R. Gillan, B.A. was inducted as his colleague and absorbed a good part of the increasing load. The Church's greatest honour, the Moderatorship of the General Assembly, might have been his, but he felt bound to refuse for the sake of the work in London which he felt he could not forsake with a good conscience during the necessary year of that office. Not until 1938, when he had completed fifty years in the ministry and when his colleague, Mr Gillan, accepted a call to Fairmilehead in Edinburgh, did he apply to the Presbytery for a colleague and successor. The congregation marked the attainment of his jubilee as an ordained minister by making a handsome presentation, which with characteristic generosity he requested should be used to form a Trust, the income of which to be devoted to assisting necessitous cases which might come to his notice. The Archibald Fleming Jubilee Fund continues that generous purpose.

It was during Dr Fleming's ministry that there died one whose name will always be associated with the Scots Kirk in London. John Macvicar Anderson, F.R.I.B.A. (and later President of that body), was ordained an Elder of Crown Court in 1869 and became Session Clerk in 1879, an office in which he served the congregation until 1913, two years before his death. He played a leading part in the vigorous measures necessary after Dr Cumming retired in 1879. It was he who secured the site in Pont Street, became Honorary Architect for the new church there, and was one of the five generous subscribers who set the Building Fund going. Later, at his own expense, he readjusted, and added to, the church furnishings and memorials so that they might enhance the architectural unity of the whole. The new congregation at Dulwich found in him a skilled adviser and good friend. Even more, the congregation being built up by Mr Philip and his successor in the old Crown Court buildings, and by Mr Macrae in the new, owed much to him, and he remained a trustee for that congregation until his death. In the words of one who more than once crossed swords with him, he was 'one of the best Scots and Elders that ever served a Church'[15]. His portrait hangs in the St Columba's Library.

One interesting example of his work as an architect stands at the west end of that thoroughfare so closely associated with the influence of Scots settlers in the seventeenth century, the Strand. It is the head office of Thomas Coutts & Co., whose founder was a member of Crown Court. The building, recently reconstructed, faces Charing Cross Station, and retains its original frontage.

The church in Pont Street, for which he cared so lovingly and which his son continued to watch over after his death in 1918, became the victim of an air raid in 1941.

Dr Fleming himself was lying ill at that time, unaware of the destruction of his beloved church building, and died shortly afterwards. His distinguished ministry in London had covered thirty-nine years, and his contribution to the welfare and unity of the Church was acknowledged by leaders of all dominations. What he meant to his members and officebearers was in part a natural pride in his distinction as what Lord Balfour of Burleigh had called 'the leading London Scot' and his world-fame as 'Fleming of St Columba's', but much more a deep gratitude for 'the breadth of sympathy and the real and intellectual force' of his preaching, and 'his great love for his fellowmen which gives greater value to his work than any of his other marked attributes'[16].

NOTES

1. Alexander Gammie, *Dr Archibald Fleming of St Columba's*, pp. 79ff. Dr Fleming's immediate predecessors, Dr Cumming and Dr MacLeod, had also frequently preached at Crathie, as have his successors.
2. *St Columba's Magazine*, Nov., 1909, where the sermon was reprinted.
3. *St Columba's Magazine*, Dec. 1904, June 1907, June, Oct. & Nov., 1909, Feb. 1911, &c.
4. See Chapter five.
5. The receipt mentioned in Chapter seven names it 'The Helvetique Chapel'; the Session's minutes of August 1877 name it 'The French Chappell in Castle Street'. It was one of three in London which followed the founding in 1550 of the original 'peculiar church' of the French Colony.
6. The first Huguenot refugees were arriving in Britain after the Tumult of Amboise in 1560, and in 1561 Queen Elizabeth sanctioned the founding of a French congregation for the Walloons, to meet in the crypt of Canterbury Cathedral, Dr Fleming's visit was for that 305th anniversary, but over the years several London Scots ministers had preached there. It is appropriate to quote here part of the General Assembly's message of 1885 to the Scottish Synod in England: 'We will rejoice in your embracing every opportunity of cultivating friendly relations with all sister Evangelical Churches — with the great and noble Church of England — with the churches which have sprung from the devoted labours of Wesley and Whitfield — with the Presbyterian Church which has a kindred origin with yourselves — with the old Dutch

Church in Austin Friars, with whose Superintendent in the days of Edward VI our own Reformer was so closely associated — and with the members of the Huguenot churches, for whom the Church of Scotland has ever cherished a very warm regard'. *Minutes of Scottish Synod in England,* 4th May, 1886.

7. Cecil Fleming, *Paper read to St Columba's Literary Society,* Feb., 1963.
8. *Ibid.*
9. See Chapter three.
10. See Appendix C.
11. Burleigh, *A Church History of Scotland,* p. 385.
12. See Chapter four, note 12.
13. The sixth Baron (see Chapter eleven), who was joint-convener with John White of the Church of Scotland 'Hundred', died suddenly a few days after the House of Commons passed the second reading of the Church of Scotland Bill in July 1921, and from the memorial service in St Columba's later that month Scottish M.P.s hurried back to St Stephen's to record their votes on the third reading. His son, the 7th Baron, was a great-great-great-grandson, through his mother, of George Baillie of Jerviswood (see Chapter five), who was a great-great-grandson of John Knox. When in 1925 the 7th Baron sponsored the other Church of Scotland Bill in the House of Lords and saw it through its second reading there, the imaginative observer might pardonably have claimed to see the old Reformer himself playing his part in that removal of the last legal obstacle to Re-union.
14. Augustus Muir, *John White,* p. 229.
15. Lady Frances Balfour, *Lord Balfour of Burleigh,* p. 167.
16. Sir Arthur Steel-Maitland, at Dr Fleming's semi-jubilee.

CHAPTER 14

Daughter at Dulwich

On East Dulwich Road, facing the quaintly-named Goose Green, there still stands a house named 'Norlands'. It was a not inappropriate name for the meeting-place of a group of men, with unmistakable northern names and accents, who gathered there in August, 1881. They represented a colony of Scots who had settled in and around that pleasant suburb south of the Thames[1], and they were meeting to discuss the possibility of making arrangements for a place where they and their compatriots could worship God in the manner and tradition of their forefathers.

They were men of some reputation and capacity. Mr Archibald K. Murray, the travellers' friend, whose compact pocket-sized railway time-tables were affectionately known as *Murray's Diaries,* was present. So were two future Mayors of Camberwell, Mr John Somerville, and Mr William (later Sir William) Lane Mitchell, who became M.P. for Streatham and played a helpful part in supporting legislation paving the way to Church re-union forty years afterwards[2]. Other names, such as McGlashan, MacCallum, Galbraith and Moncrieff, betrayed the Scottish character of the meeting, as did its final decision. Crown Court in Covent Garden and St Andrew's in Stepney were both at too great a distance for the Dulwich colony to attend regularly, but perhaps Crown Court could advise and help. They would ask for a deputation to be received, and request that Crown Court would adopt them as a Mission and guide them in their further plans.

Crown Court, as we have seen[3], accepted that responsibility, although their own plans to move to Pont Street were well afoot. Letters of encouragement towards building a Presbyterian church in Dulwich, signed by James A. Campbell, M.P., D. Marshal Lang Esq., and G.B. Bruce supported the application[4]. The name of another member of the famous Lang family appears later in the Dulwich story. James Campbell, together with his fellow associated-elder of Crown Court, Sir Robert Jardine of Castlemilk, M.A., helped the Dulwich pioneers in the securing of a suitable site near Norlands, and with their financial encouragement and the professional help of J. Macvicar Anderson and David G. Laing, Session Clerk and Treasurer respectively of Crown Court church, a temporary meeting-place of corrugated iron, seated for 243 and locally dubbed 'The Tin Church', was erected in 1882. In response to a further request in 1883 the Crown Court Session resolved that 'an immediate effort be made to raise £1000 to enable the Committee to proceed at once with the erection of a Hall, and that Mr Campbell's offer to consult with Mr Jardine and others with a view if possible of carrying out this arrangement be accepted'[5]. Campbell and Jardine each contributed £500, and the foundation-stone of an all-purpose Hall, as the inscription on it records, 'was laid on 14th June 1882 by James Campbell, Esq., M.P., LL.D.' The substantially-built and commodious hall was soon crowded, and memories of many happy occasions within its walls were to accumulate during the next ninety years. But the enthusiasm of the quickly-growing congregation might easily have been damped by some early difficulties.

Dr MacLeod may have been relieved when the Rev. A.A. Mackenzie was inducted as minister at East Dulwich in March 1884, just before his own congregation's new church in Pont Street was opened. But Dulwich was soon to be under his care again. Dissension arose under Mr Mackenzie's ministry, a section of the congregation pressing for the deletion from its constitution of the clause which provided that the property be vested in trust for behoof of the Church of Scotland inalienably. They wished to secede to the English Presbyterian Church and to take the property with them. Mr Campbell and Sir Robert Jardine had in fact paid for the Hall on the understanding expressed in that clause, and its retention was insisted upon by Trustees and by Presbytery and Synod. Mr Mackenzie eventually resigned[6]. The charge was preached vacant on August 1885, and Dr MacLeod was again interim-moderator until the Rev. J. Niblock-Stuart, an Irishman who had ministered in Newry and Comber between 1869 and 1877, and in Port Glasgow and

Yester thereafter, was inducted to the Dulwich charge in February 1886.

Once again, however, Dr MacLeod had to shoulder the burden, for Mr Niblock-Stuart resigned about eighteen months later. It is not clear why he did so, for although it is evident that the congregation was finding difficulty in paying his stipend, his ministry, judging by the increasing numbers, was successful, and the fact that he was immediately invited to become assistant to Dr MacLeod indicates that he was *persona grata* in that quarter. He went on to become minister of Stirling North in 1889 (when Dulwich sent him a letter of appreciation and good wishes), and of Montrose in 1894; and his other abilities were expressed in three competent books which came from his pen. The Dulwich vacancy was filled by the ordination of the Rev. P. Henderson Aitken in November 1888, and Dr MacLeod was finally relieved of the care of the congregation. His interest, and that of his congregation in St Columba's, however, was by no means withdrawn. The brevity of the first two ministries in Dulwich had not damped the congregation's enthusiasm, but it had seriously held up their plans for a church building. In May 1889 the St Columba's Kirk Session heard a deputation asking help towards the building of that church, and the following year James A. Campbell was appointed Convener of Trustees for the Building Fund[7]. The total cost of the Church, which was dedicated under the name of St James' Scotch Church, Goose Green, in 1896, was not cleared until 1901, when a bazaar held in St Columba's raised the final £800.

'After this', wrote Dr Macmillan, senior elder from St James', in 1973, 'we see a church life with increasing numbers and a host of varying activities, spiritual and social'. Outstanding amongst the members who led in that work was Mr John Somerville, of whom it was recorded on a bronze memorial tablet, set into the rear wall of the church after his death in 1910: 'His courage inspired the building of the church. He served with constant and universal fidelity in every office. His faith in its purpose never faltered, and his life was an example to all to the end'. Mr Somerville was Session Clerk (also for a time Treasurer), and superintendent of the flourishing Sunday School for many years. He died while in office as Mayor of Camberwell, having been preceded in that office by a fellow- elder, William Lane Mitchell, who as M.P. for Streatham in the next decade strengthened support for Scottish interests in parliament[8]. Amongst others with whom such men and their families worked to make St James' a power for good in Dulwich, London and regions beyond were the King-Smiths, Galbraiths, Murrays, Scotts, Macmillans, Hannahs, and Moncrieffs. Robert R. Moncrieff, one of the original Trustees, for example, was for 25 years the Secretary of the Royal Scottish Corporation[9]. In more recent years another member, Miss Mildred Thomson, whose fiancé, Harry Lauder's son, had been killed in action in the first world war, bequeathed the residue of her estate to endow a special ward in the Erskine Hospital near Glasgow.

Mr Aitken had literary gifts, and it was in his time that the St James' Magazine came into being. For some time 2000 copies were printed, and distributed amongst Scots known to be in the neighbourhood. It was in his time, too, that the Dulwich column in the 'Scotch National Churches in England Supplement' to *Life and Work* took on a livelier aspect. In the July issue of 1890 it reported: 'A fine organ has through the generous enthusiasm of a few friends been obtained for the church and was inaugurated on 20th December last by special services by the Rev. Thos. Somerville of Glasgow' — who was the uncle of St James' Session Clerk. An interesting recollection concerning that organ — which is now in the hall of St Columba's — was reported in the St Columba's Magzine in January 1906: 'The oldest member in Dulwich remembered a Sunday in 1893 when Dr Marshall Lang (then Moderator of the General Assembly) occupied the pulpit, and his young son, Cosmo Gordon, begged for 'a play on the organ'. This was accorded to the boy', who later became Archbishop of Canterbury. A D. Marshall Lang, as we have noticed, had been one of the congregation's earliest supporters.

Mr Aitken, who had had several disagreements with his Session and with the Presbytery, resigned in 1898 and accepted an appointment as chaplain at Gartnavel Hospital in Glasgow and to do bibliographical work in the University there, where he catalogued the Hunterian Museum[10] and published two books. He was honoured with the University's LL.D. in 1907.

The Rev. G. Gordon Stott, who had been assistant at St Columba's, was ordained to St James' in 1898, and saw the congregation into the first six years of the new century. He was translated to Northesk in 1906 and to Cramond in 1910, and in 1920 he became a D.D. of St Andrew's. His son, Gordon, is a Scottish Law Lord.

The Rev. Ernest G. Brechin, a native of Dundee and graduate of St Andrew's, came from the Scots Kirk in Paris in 1907 and brought his own gifts to the ministry in St James'. 'Continuous progress was made', says Dr Macmillan[11], who, himself the son of a minister in Scotland, became a member of the congregation in 1918. Dr Macmillan undoubtedly played his part in that progress, which continued over the next 30 years. His fatherly interest in his patients was not confined to their physical welfare, and his recommendation to any new Scots patient to 'come along to St James' ' was not often rejected!

For a quarter of a century St James had had the use of old Crown Court Communion vessels until in 1912 it was enabled to return them, for an interesting reason. The Scottish congregation in Manchester had been in difficulties during most of that period; Presbytery, Synod and the General Assembly itself had been involved in attempts to resolve its difficulties; and in 1909 it was at last disbanded. It fell to the Presbytery of Edinburgh to dispose of its property, most of which was gifted to congregations in the north of England. The Communion Plate, however, was alloted to St James', East Dulwich[12], and consists of four chalices, two patens and a flagon. They date from 1832, and bear a heraldic shield incorporating the device later displayed in Manchester's coat-of-arms when the town was created a city in 1853. These vessels are now in weekly use for the Communion services in the London Scottish Memorial Chapel in St Columba's.

The Great War brought changes, and these included a change of minister, for in March 1914 Mr Brechin accepted a call to Avoch, where he succeeded Mr Philip, formerly of Crown Court. The Rev. Percival Mackenzie was ordained and inducted as his successor in April of the following year. Mr Mackenzie was a native of Stornoway, an M.A. of Edinburgh University, and had been an assistant minister at Rubislaw Aberdeen, Buenos Aires, and Inverness before being called to Dulwich. There St James lost his services for a time during the war when, having extensive engineering experience, he was appointed Inspector of Ordnance Machinery, his place in Dulwich being taken for the duration by the Rev. Edward Miller. After the war his congregation benefitted from his versatility when, in addition to his pastoral and preaching ministrations, he proved capable of installing a new blowing system for the organ and central heating for the church, in addition to reconstituting in expert fashion a stone pulpit and a font, both dismantled from a church in Peebles. It was a lively ministry, not least because it was marked by achievements not ordinarily thought of as within the capacity of a minister of the Gospel.

His ministerial responsibilities were added to in 1929, when the congregation at Gillingham, formerly a garrison charge and dating back to 1866[13], and latterly under the care of the Rev. the Presbytery of London, was linked with St James', East Dulwich, as a Mission. It can have been no easy addition to the burden, for the two places are over thirty miles apart; but it was carried for twenty years. Full status was granted to St Margaret's, Gillingham, in 1949.

Mr Mackenzie saw St James' through another war, during which the church was more than once damaged in air raids. On one occasion an oil-bomb came through the roof, and but for prompt and efficient action by Mr Calver the beadle the story of St James would have ended then in the flames. Despite damage the church continued to be a meeting-place where in worship and the fellowship of weekday agencies its members and their neighbours found heart to meet the daily strains, and comfort to carry the burdens of anxiety and sorrow, of those six years.

Mr Mackenzie resigned in 1949, and the Rev. David W. Norwood was called from Keig, Aberdeenshire, to follow him. He had been born in Hounslow, and spent some time in business and industry before studying in Glasgow and working as student assistant in Govan and Anderston. That varied background and maturity of experience must have been useful in

Dulwich, where St James' was facing a changing situation. 'Fewer Scottish people were coming to East Dulwich', wrote Dr Macmillan: 'The motor car encouraged members to live further out; and the general church attendance was declining. This meant greater effort by fewer people, but in spite of these difficulties St James' was very much alive and a happy congregation. The Rev. David Norwood concentrated on building up the congregation, and was remarkably rewarded as members increased'[14].

Mr Norwood accepted a call to a Church Extension parish in Giffnock in 1959, and the Rev. John Beattie, who had been ordained to the Orkney parish of Rousay in 1954, was inducted in 1960. The difficulties of ten years earlier had now much increased with a radical change in the composition of the local population. This brought about closer co-operation between the Scottish and English congregations on either side of Goose Green, but when Mr Beattie left for Plantation Church Glasgow in 1966 the membership of St James' had fallen to 170 and the Presbytery and the General Assembly's Committee on Unions and Readjustments were unable to approve of an unrestricted ministry for the charge. The congregation, small though it was, kept things going for four years, and in 1970 entered into a linking arrangement with St Columba's. Two years later that happy engagement was consummated in an equally happy union; so the daughter came back, with her 90 years of honourable service, willingly accepting her mother's name, and bequeathing her own to the buildings which were to rise on the site of her former trials and triumphs. It is no exaggeration to say that one main reason why the union was so willingly and happily entered upon was the wise and benign influence of Dr Macmillan. He died in 1977.

The site was sold to the Presbyterian Housing Association, which has erected a fine block of flats of 'sheltered housing' for aged couples, naming it 'St James' Cloister', and incorporating in the fabric three commemoration stones from hall and church and the fine carved representation of The Burning Bush — the emblem of the Church of Scotland — which had formed a feature of the stonework above the memorial window of the church. With themselves the St James' congregation brought also the proceeds of the sale of building and site, a small part of which was reserved to provide bus transport every Sunday between Dulwich and Pont Street, and the rest of which was given to the Maintenance of the Ministry and the Church Extension Committees of the General Assembly. The arrival of the 'Dulwich bus' adds a special interest to the forgathering of Scots 'frae a' the airts' every Sunday morning. They also brought the panels from the fine memorial window which bore the names of members lost in the first world war; two handsome oak chairs fashioned from the original 13th century timbers of the Old Tolbooth, Ayr, which had been given by Dr McGregor; and the fine Hunter organ, dismantled, transported, and rebuilt in St Columba's Hall by members of both congregations with professional help from a young organbuilder, a chorister in Canterbury Cathedral.

This chapter should not close without a special reference to Dulwich's greatest friend and patron, the Right Hon. James A. Campbell, M.P., of Stracathro. His name has already been mentioned in connection with the removal from Crown Court to Pont Street, and later at the time when the old Crown Court building was condemned. The Scots Kirk in London has owed much to many such men and not all can be mentioned, but something would be lacking in this story without a brief sketch of the man from whom at least three congregations received such timely help.

James Campbell, son of Sir James Campbell, Lord Provost of Glasgow at the time of Queen Victoria's visit, succeeded on his father's death to the family business and also to the family estate of Stracathro[15]; while his younger brother, Henry, succeeding to his maternal uncle's esate and conforming with the condition that he hyphenate the two names, became the equally famous Sir Henry Campbell-Bannerman of Belmont Castle, the Liberal Prime Minister. James was Conservative MP for the Universities of Glasgow and Aberdeen, being returned unopposed for 25 years and becoming a Privy Councillor in 1898. Like his brother he was an accomplished linguist, and we have already seen how greatly his judgment was respected and how expectantly his counsel sought on any matter affecting the welfare of the Church. His generosity could be counted upon without being sought, provided he could satisfy himself that the cause was worthy; but his reproof was not lightly to be incurred, as the first minister of the East Dulwich congregation found. His encouragement in word and action was sometimes given so surreptitiously as to be discovered later only by accident. His daughter, Miss Elsie Campbell, continued the family interest in St Columba's, Crown Court, and Dulwich. But the Church of Scotland was aware of other services than those rendered in London alone, and in gratitude for these his portrait, painted by Sir George Reid, was presented in 1904 to be hung in the Church offices — where it is still to be seen — with a replica for Stracathro.

There is a story, which bears the marks of probability, that his father's friend, Charles Hutcheson, a Glasgow merchant and a member of St George's parish church where the Campbells worshipped when at their Glasgow home, was visiting that home one evening and played a common-metre tune which he had just composed. It was immediately and enthusiastically approved, which so encouraged the composer that he declared that he would name it after his host's house in August. *Stracathro* has retained its popularity, nowhere more so than in London, where the Scots Kirk has special reason for thanking God for the man who succeeded to the estate of that name.

NOTES

1. It has been said that the presence of so many Scots thereabouts was due to the setting up in Catford of a factory of the Paisley jam-making firm of Robertson.
2. *Vide* Muir, *John White*, p. 223.
3. *Crown Court Session Minutes*, 13th Sept. & 11th. Dec., 1881; *Presbytery of London Minutes*, 13th Oct., 1881; *Minutes of Founding Committee of East Dulwich Presbyterian Church*, 3rd Nov., 1881.
4. *Minutes of Founding Committee &c.*, 13th Sept, 1881.
5. *Crown Court Session Minutes*, 26th June, 1882; *Scotch National Churches in England, Supplement to Life and Work*, July 1882.
6. *Dulwich Session Minutes*, 5th Feb., 26th & 31st March, 30th April, 28th & 30th June, & 6th Oct., 1885. *Presbytery of London Minutes*, 13th April, 13th & 22nd July, 1885. *Scottish Synod in England Minutes*, 5th May, 1885.
7. *St James' E. Dulwich Session Minutes*, 19th June, 1889 & 14th May, 1890. *St Columba's Session Minutes*, 3rd July & 24th Oct., 1889, &

14th May, 1890.
8. See Chapter thirteen.
9. See Chapter three. John Somerville was a governor of the Corporation for as many years.
10. See Chapter six.
11. This, and subsequent quotations from Dr Macmillan, are from a summary of St James' history prepared by him after the union with St Columba's in 1972.
12. St James' Session Minutes, 3rd Dec. 1911 and 5th Jan., 1912.
13. See Chapter eight.
14. Dr Macmillan, *ut supra.*
15. It was in Stracathro kirkyard, on the banks of the North Esk near Edzell, that John Baliol did homage to Edward I in 1296 and abdicated the throne of Scotland. This humiliation, together with Edward's theft of the Holy Rood and the Stone of Destiny, roused Scotland, under Wallace and Bruce, to that noble assertion of the right to liberty, the Arbroath Declaration (see Chapter 1), and that spirited resistance which broke the power of the Edwards at Bannockburn. Mytton and Biland and culminated in the recognition of Scotland's independence with Robert Bruce as her king, by the Treaty of Northampton.

The Campbell mansion and estate now house the well-known Stracathro Hospital.

CHAPTER 15

'A New Air of Confidence'

In September 1913 a young Irishman, who had been Dr Fleming's assistant in St Columba's for two years, was inducted as minister of Gilmerton parish in Edinburgh, leaving behind him many in St Columba's and beyond it who lamented his departure. Four years later, however, he was in London again, to be Dr Fleming's neighbour as minister of Crown Court and to lead that congregation through forty-five years of radical change into a position where it would stand on its own feet and fulfill its distinctive role as an important unit of the Scots Kirk in London.

The Rev. Joseph Moffett was born in Letterkenny, Donegal, educated in Dublin, Londonderry and Edinburgh, and in 1911 was licensed by the Presbytery of Edinburgh. War broke out within a year of his induction to Gilmerton, and he saw active service with the 9th (Scottish) Division, of which Ian Hay wrote in *The First Hundred Thousand* and whose Memorial is to be seen in Crown Court church. The Session minutes contain no note of his call and induction, but he was its minister before the end of 1917, and after a nine months' vacancy Crown Court had a leader fit for the hour and its needs.

Those were difficult days. Apart from the trials and losses common to all congregations in wartime, Crown Court lost some of its oldest friends and officebearers within a period of four years. Amongst these were Mr J. Macvicar Anderson, Lord Balfour of Burleigh, the Earl of Stair and the Hon. A.M. Kinnaird, a recently ordained elder, killed in action. By 1921 only two of the congregation's original Trustees survived, neither of whom was a member of Crown Court. But that fact did not escape the vigilant eye of the new minister, and it is indicative of his purpose and confidence that Trustees were now for the first time appointed from the membership of the congregation itself. Crown Court was not to remain forever dependent on the benevolent support of others.

This was a long-term objective, and with a congregation of only 250 members outside financial help was still necessary for many years, as by a regular annual contribution of around £150 from St Columba's and by its payment of more than half the cost of a new manse in 1922. It was not until the 1930s that membership reached the 400, but thereafter the rise was steady, until by 1936 it was over 500 and two years later had topped the 600 mark. In 1939, when the Holloway congregation[1] was linked with it, there were 691 members on the Roll, and by that time it had become possible to reduce the annual contribution from St Columba's to less than £100.

Undoubtedly the eloquent preaching of their minister, his attractive personality, his business-like methods, and his warm and kindly interest in people, had much to do with this steady advance in strength. He gave a new air of confidence to Crown Court. For a time during his predecessor's ministry a Crown Court page in the St Columba's Magazine had recorded the activities of the congregation. Now, with Mr Moffett as editor, there appeared in 1921 for the people of Crown Court a magazine of their own, which Dr Fleming, an experienced judge, characterised as admirable. It included each month a table of daily morning and evening Bible readings — 'an excellent and carefully made compilation which we have more than once been tempted to plagiarise', remarked Dr Fleming[2]. Another feature of the Crown Court Magazine for a number of years was Mr Moffett's serialised summary of *The Book of the Congregation Meeting in Peter's Court, St Martin's Lane,* which he had unearthed among the archives in 'the strong box' at St Columba's[3]. Through these extracts his people were informed of the early period of the heritage they shared with St Columba's, and this no doubt helped the process, begun in his predecessor's time, of building up their identity and giving them a sense of belonging to the Church in its wholeness.

It was important, also, that the church should not only be there but that it should be seen to be there. People still had difficulty in locating it, despite the 'enamelled direction plates' fixed in 1896 at the Bow Street end of Martlett Court and the later ones suspended from lamps at the corners of Catherine,

Wellington and Barr Streets. So these were supplemented in 1918 by an electrically-lit sign in Russell Street, reading 'To the Scottish National Church'. With the same end in view a 'Scottish Flag' was presented by Sir John Cumming, and a flagpole erected. Some discussion also took place — as had happened in 1898, when the St Columba's Session noted information about 'a change of name to read Crown Court Church', and as was to happen again in 1934 and 1935 — concerning the name by which the church should be known. The Minutes give no indication of the nature of the proposed change, but the 1934–35 discussions may have had to do with the General Assembly's Act of 1934, VI, giving full recognition to the Scottish congregations in England as part of the Church of Scotland, thus allowing the dropping of the term 'Scottish National Church' in favour of the simple 'Church of Scotland'. The minutes record no decision on the matter.

There might, however, have been a compulsory and most unwelcome change of name had a London County Council Order under the London Building Act of 1930 been put into effect. This proposed that from July 1936 Crown Court, Russell Street, would be re-named Punch Court[4]. The Session, lodging its strong objection, pointed out that although confusion did arise because of the number of Crown Courts in London, all but two of these contained no residents; that 'Punch' was entirely inappropriate and had no connection with the neighbourhood; that Crown Court Church was known world-wide and the name was carved in stone and wrought in iron on the building; that the objections of the residents in the Court were shared by those of Martlett Court; and that the only other Crown Court which did have residents might appropriately be renamed Corona Court[5]. The objection was heeded. The one surviving Crown Court still justifies the title of the church which stands in it; and London has no Punch Court — or Corona Court — in its gazetteers.

The congregation had two other series of correspondence on matters of fabric and name. In 1923 the architects of a new theatre built next to the church asked permission to use the face of the church in its erection. In refusing permission the Session were careful to insist on adequate precautions against any damage caused by demolition and excavation preparatory

204

to the building of the theatre. Two years later we find them opposing an application by the Fortune Theatre to extend its canopy along the street and into Crown Court itself. Then in 1929 a proposal for a much-needed structural improvement — the provision of a staircase connecting hall and church — had to be abandoned because it would breach the 1909 agreement with the Duke of Bedford. The matter was raised again in 1931, when that difficulty was resolved, but another latent difficulty was brought to light. A sum paid in compensation for the leases surrendered in 1903[6] had had to be held in Chancery ever since, because the title *Crown Court Church and Schools* appeared in the leases, and there were now no schools. The money, amounting now to over £2000, would have been useful in meeting the cost of the staircase. A way was found around this difficulty too[7]. On the understanding that the church would be doing work which could be called educational the Board of Education agreed to the release of the money, subject to recall if the condition were breached. To cover such an eventuality the Session inaugurated a Sinking Fund, to be built up at the rate of £15 a year[8]. The staircase was duly completed in December, 1934.

Meanwhile, amidst all these peripheral concerns, the real work of the church went on. The nature of the environment in Covent Garden had already considerably changed by the time Mr Moffett's ministry began. Improvement in housing and in educational and recreational facilities for young people was steadily continuing. The work of the Ragged and Day Schools had long since been taken over by the State. Now even what Crown Court had been doing through its Visitors' Association, Night School for Girls, Girls' Society and Band of Hope was less necessary. The 'Needy Nook' had been closed in 1898. In 1918 the Night School for Girls finished its course, 'its original purpose more than accomplished'. The Boys' Brigade faded away. Even the Sunday School was briefly suspended in 1934, but happily resumed in the following year.

The minister's alert eye, however, saw other needs which Crown Court could be helping to meet, particularly amongst London Scots. The quarterly Gaelic Service could be encouraged, and was. He involved himself and some of his members in the welfare of the Caledonian Christian Club, of whose Committee he continued for many years to be the chairman. He persuaded his Session to sponsor a special service for the Scottish Clans Association of London, and this became an annual occasion. Crown Court's links with the Caledonian Church in Holloway were strengthened, and help was given with necessary repairs there. And when a fifth Church of Scotland congregation was admitted to the Presbytery it found in Mr Moffett an interested and helpful friend.

This was the congregation of St Andrew's, Corby. In 1935 the steel firm of Stewart and Lloyds moved, with the larger part of its work-force, from Bellshill in Lanarkshire to Corby, Northants, where rich fields of iron ore were accessible to open-cast mining. To that 'Little Scotland' the home Church followed with a place of worship and a minister for its 'exiled' children; and in the fellowship of the London Scots Presbytery the congregation of expatriates found a heartening welcome. Its strongest contact was probably with Crown Court and its minister. At the first celebration of the Sacrament of the Lord's Supper in St Andrew's, Corby, communion vessels loaned by Crown Court were used[9]; they are still in use in Corby, by the more recently-created congregation of St Ninian's.

In addition to his services as one of the chaplains to the Royal Caledonian Schools (see Chapter eight) and to the Royal Scottish Corporation (see Chapter three), Mr Moffett had, early in his London ministry, been appointed Clerk, to the London Presbytery, and to the Synod in England, of the Presbyterian Church in connection with the Church of Scotland. The Union of the Churches in 1929 — which surprisingly receives no notice in the Crown Court Session minutes — gave a recognised status to the Scots Kirk in England, and combined the three English Presbyteries into the one Presbytery of England, later giving it synodical powers. Mr Moffett's competent Clerkship greatly eased that process and the re-adjustment of function, powers and funds which it entailed. As Lord Aberdeen said, when Crown Court celebrated the semi-jubilee of its minister's ordination: 'He has a knowledge of the law of the Church so intimate that he might be described as the Dr Mair[10] of the Church of Scotland in England. He is competent to be a dictator on Church matters, always with the word "Christian" before "dictator". '

That was in 1939. In the same year the Caledonian Church in Holloway became vacant, and its future came under review. Its membership was less than a hundred, and the Presbytery, unable to approve its continuance as a full ministerial charge, resolved that it should become what would now be termed a linked charge with Crown Court. Both congregations approved a basis of association that year, and an assistant was appointed to enable Mr Moffett to cope with the additional responsibility. Within six months, however, war had broken out and the assistant had left to be a chaplain to the forces. It was a trying time for the commencement of a linking arrangement with a second congregation, and although another assistant was appointed a year later the handicaps of war were to increase with his departure, and still later in 1941 when both church buildings were damaged by enemy action on the same date. The damage in Holloway was slight, but in Crown Court it required extensive temporary repairs to the roof, the gallery had to be closed, and the heating system was out of action for a considerable time. Throughout the war-years, nevertheless, the work continued with undiminished faithfulness, despite black-out, bombings, and the casualties, both military and civilian, which affected every congregation. The membership of Crown Court at the end of the war, as at its beginning, was just short of 700.

The Holloway congregation had become so small, and its buildings so dilapidated, that after five years of uncertainty it was decided to close them; and in 1950 the two congregations were united under the name of Crown Court. The buildings were sold to the Boy Scouts Association and the money which had been held from the sale of the manse in 1939 was generously applied towards the purchase of a new manse for St James', East Dulwich.

In 1947 Mr Moffett had been Crown Court's minister for thirty years, and the fact did not remain unnoticed. In the following year further recognition of his ministry was marked by the Doctorate of Divinity conferred on him by the University of St Andrews. In 1952 his congregation commissioned a portrait of him to be painted by Sir William O. Hutchinson, and in 1958 he was awarded the O.B.E. It was in that year that he resigned the office of Presbytery Clerk; but although by then he had been 45 years in the ministry — 41 of them in Crown Court —

the life of the congregation showed no sign of flagging.

The membership was now about 900, and remarkably stable around that figure considering the coming and going of Scots in London, which Dr Moffett once said made the minister's pulpit work 'like preaching to a procession'. In 1956 a notice at the church door about reservation of seats was removed as being 'at variance with the principle of offering a Christian welcome to strangers'. In 1960 the Session Clerk was appointed to attend a meeting on Christian Unity and explain the Church of Scotland's position. This ecumenical encounter, held in the Methodist Central Hall, Westminster, was to be fruitfully furthered later in that decade. The jubilee of the dedication of the building was approaching, and the re-building of the organ at a total cost of £6,200 was adopted as a feature of the 1961 celebration of that event.

In 1962, after a brief illness, Dr Moffett died, and a brilliant ministry of forty-five years came to a close.

During his time the place of worship had been beautified by a number of memorial plaques and stained glass windows of the highest artistic merit. It was fitting that Crown Court's memorial to Dr Moffett should take the form of a fine window, depicting events in the life of St Paul, and commemorating along with him his predecessors in the Crown Court pulpit. 'A remarkable man, of noble presence, polished speech and beautiful expressive voice — a man of distinguished mind and winsome nature and essential humility — he was a great leading personality in the Church of Scotland and in London'. To this quotation from the sermon preached at his funeral service may be added three sentences from a tribute paid on the occasion of his fortieth anniversary as Crown Court's minister: 'His inspired spiritual leadership and high intellect have added much to the beauty of our worship, and he has set a standard of Christian fellowship which is remarkable in a church whose members are so scattered. . . His has been the guiding hand in the Presbytery of England for 39 years, during which his counsel has been freely at the disposal of the ministers of the various congregations. . . London has been a better place for Scots — and for others — because he has laboured here'.

NOTES

1. See Chapter eight.
2. *St Columba's Magazine*, Oct. 1921.
3. *Ibid*, quoting from *St Columba's Magazine*, Oct. 1921. Was this, one may wonder, the "tin box" mentioned in Chapter 9?
4. *Crown Court Session Minutes*, 17 Dec., 1935.
5. *Ibid*, 15 June, 1936. But *Punch*, the periodical, did have a local connection. Cartoon and contents were discussed by the staff as a whole, in the early days, the 1840s, most frequently in the Crown Tavern, where also the Punch Club met and the Punch Dinners were held. Pirie, *A History of Punch*, p. 31; Mayhew, *A Jorum of Punch*, p. 63; Spielman, *The History of Punch*, passim. This was not the Crown and Cushion, next door to the church, but was located in Vineyard Yard, opposite, off Little Russell Street. Both are shown on Morgan's map of 1683 and on Stanford's of 1863.
6. See Chapter twelve.
7. Lady Frances Balfour, *op. cit.*, ii, 444. *Crown Court Session Minutes*, 14th Jan., 1929.
8. *Crown Court Session Minutes*, 21 Oct, 1931.
9. See Chapter twelve, note 15.
10. Dr Mair's *Church of Scotland Digest*, a summary of Church law and procedure, was superseded after the Union of 1929 by Dr Cox's *Practice and Procedure in the Church of Scotland*, published in 1934 and now in its sixth edition.

CHAPTER 16

'Nec Tamen Consumebatur'

Exodus Chapter three begins with the story of Moses and the vision which came to him on Mount Horeb, where he saw a bush, on fire but not consumed. It conveyed to him the conviction of the holiness of God, and of His unconditional claim to the obedience of those who encounter Him; and it sent Moses forth to lead His people out into a larger future, in the name and the strength of the One Who is greater than Pharoah or any other human authority however powerful. That passage has a special significance for the Church of Scotland.

In 1690, just after the Revolution, the first General Assembly to meet following the restoration of the Church as Presbyterian appointed George Mossman as its printer. In 1691, on the title page of *The Principal Acts of the General Assembly*, Mossman incorporated a design of The Burning Bush, encircled by the words *Nec Tamen Consumebatur*. This he seems to have done on his own authority; but by use and wont the emblem has come to be accepted as the official badge of the Church of Scotland.[1] It had already been used by the French Reformed Church, which adopted it as its official seal in 1583, with the words *Flagror, non Consumor,* or *Comburo, non consumor* as alternatives for the text. Mossman's choice of the emblem may have been quite independent of its use elsewhere, for his version of the motto comes from the 1575 Latin translation of the Bible by Tremellius and Junius[2], where Exodus 3:2 is rendered: *ecce rubus ille ardente igne, nec tamen consumebatur.* In any case the Latin of the Reformation scholars was preferred by Mossman to that of the Roman Vulgate.

Perhaps his choice of the emblem was influenced by the fact that in Stewart times of persecution the image of the Burning Bush had been used, as for example by Samuel Rutherford and by later writers looking back upon such times, as illustrating the miraculous survival of a fire-tested Church. All 163 members of the Assembly whose *Principal Acts* Mossman printed had suffered in those fires of persecution, 'yet was not the bush consumed'. It was an apt reminder of the humble reverence with which the Church should take up the task for which she had been preserved.

The Scots Kirk in London has had its own share in that tale of struggle and survival, and, as we have seen, her congregations have been marvellously led and preserved, not only through the fear and flames of actual persecution, but in the less agonising fires of hostility, desertion and apparent failure, to emerge in greater strength and usefulness on the other side of the flames. Another such episode marks the stage at which we arrive in this chapter.

This time it was a complete material destruction by actual fire, which jeopardised the whole future of the congregation of St Columba's. On the night of Saturday, 10th May, 1941, when a second wave of incendiary bombs fell around and on the church, one pierced the roof and lodged in the beams at a point inaccessible to the fire-fighters. In the resultant conflagration only the hall below escaped complete destruction. The congregation arrived for the morning service next day, to discover a ruined church and a hall inches deep in water. They could only disperse sadly — heartened however by the minister's assurance that services would be held in a meeting-place which would be speedily found.

The minister was the Rev. Robert Forrester Victor Scott. He was the son of the minister of Logie Buchan, a graduate of the University of Edinburgh, had been ordained to the ministry by the Presbytery of Strathmiglo in 1923, transferred to St Andrew's, Dundee four years later, and was called to succeed the Very Rev. John White at Glasgow's Barony Church in 1935. When Dr Fleming's colleague, the Rev. Ian Gillan, accepted a call to Fairmilehead in 1938 and in the same year Dr Fleming applied for a colleague and successor, the unanimous choice of the congregation was Mr Scott. His ministry at St Columba's began in October of that year, and at the welcome social Miss Mary Blackwood[3] produced three cards recording the presence on three occasions of L.Cpl. Robert F.V. Scott as a guest of St Columba's 'Soldiers on Furlough' scheme during the Great

War. By his side at that Welcome Reception sat one who as Miss Phyllis Graves had more than once entertained St Columba's 'Soldiers on Furlough', and was now his wife. It was a happy beginning to a ministry which was to take the congregation through difficult times with undiminished vitality and unimpaired usefulness.

Within twelve months the second world-war had broken out, and Mr Scott was released for chaplaincy duties, later accepting an appointment as an army information officer which enabled him to resume his work as minister of St Columba's. It is a tribute to the confidence his ministry had already inspired amongst his members in so short a time that on that sad Sunday morning, while they looked on the ruins of their beautiful and well-loved place of worship, he received the first donation towards a Rebuilding Fund.

The people dispersed that day, but the elders remained to meet as a Kirk Session in the manse. Energetic action followed. On the very next Sunday the congregation were able to meet for worship in the Jehangier Hall of the nearby Imperial Institute. St Saviour's church in Walton Street was generously made available for some weekday activities[4]. The minister and his family moved to a nearby flat and the manse was altered to accommodate a small chapel, a lounge, and a hall in the basement where luncheons and teas were served after services on Sundays and in which Scouts and others held their weekly meetings. A full account of all the means by which St Columba's maintained its worship and work after the disaster is given in the pamphlet, *St Columba's Church of Scotland. The New Building and the Old,* compiled by the Session Clerk, Mr J. Murray Napier and published by The Friends of St Columba's.

Welfare work for the Services continued as in the previous war, although with a difference. No longer did Scots on leave have to spend up to eight hours on Saturdays and Sundays passing through London on their way home. But a Signals Unit which was vital to communications for the defence of London was stationed nearby, later supplemented by another, of the A.T.S. Together with members of Holy Trinity Church, Brompton, teams from St Columba's organised in the crypt of Holy Trinity a canteen called The Brompton Dug-out, and later, in

Holy Trinity's Hall, another for the A.T.S., called The Rose and Thistle. A red-letter day for the former was a visit of the Queen while the King was inspecting the hush-hush Signals operations room, far underground. Besides all this, St Columba's was able also to donate to the Church's Huts and Canteens Committee two mobile canteens, which saw much service overseas.

Life in London during the war years was very much an affair of day to day, but the future was never lost sight of in St Columba's. Mr Scott's message from week to week in the Jehangier Hall might often be interrupted by the noise of falling bombs or of 'V1s' and 'V2s'; but not only did it give heart to his people for the trials of the day; it set these in the perspective of the unseen and the eternal, and inspired a purpose for the future. The loyalty of his members was unreserved; there were times when the Hall could not contain them and they had to move into the larger Examination Hall where up to 800 could come together. There was every encouragement, also, for those other plans concerning the future, which envisaged the day when a new St Columba's would arise on the same site. Already during the war an architect, Mr Edward Maufe, A.R.I.B.A., was appointed, plans were drawn, £2,000 was raised at a gift shop run by a committee; and the main appeal for £90,000 was well on its way to success when the war at last ended. All this did not hinder the congregation from maintaining former responsibilities, or indeed from undertaking new ones. Members of St Columba's took a keen and active interest in the work of *The West London Committee for the Protection of Children,* of which Mr Scott was for many years the Chairman. One visiting minister, after reading the intimations, remarked that it was a great record of activity for a congregation without a church.

The church was to come. The Queen Mother arrived to lay its foundation stone on 4th July 1950, and despite the difficulty in obtaining building licenses which followed the war the hall was dedicated in 1953 and used for worship and work while the church was being built above it. Typical of the congregation's appreciation of their minister's preaching is the comment of one, now an elder, who became a member during this period and who was charged by her invalid aunt to report, on her return from 'the church in the hall', every Sunday. 'I found to my surprise that I had no difficulty in remembering and repeating the whole sequence and content of the sermon, and that the message we had heard together as a congregation was equally helpful to the invalid at home'. A similar tribute to Dr Scott's preaching was paid in his hearing when Lord Morton of Henryton expressed the congregation's feelings at the end of his ministry in St Columba's in 1960. 'I cannot attempt to express what your words in the pulpit have meant to us all. It seems most incredible that so much should be said each week to help us on the road through life, in so short a time'.

At last in 1955 the church was finished, and in December of that year it was opened and dedicated by the Right Reverend Professor G.D. Henderson, Moderator of the General Assembly — from whose researches the opening paragraphs of this chapter are derived. A full description of the building, by Sir Edward Maufe the architect, is incorporated, with illustrations, in Mr Napier's booklet referred to above. No more need be said about it here than that it stands as a landmark at the head of Pont Street, identified, as it was its predecessor, by taxi-drivers, and pointed out to busloads of sightseers, as 'the Scotch Church'; that its generous lines and ample accommodation testify to the close co-operation between minister and architect in its planning, and that the quiet serenity of the place of worship itself draws many a passer-by, almost every day, to sit where he may feel the touch of the eternal and respond to the mystery of his being as a child of God.

Mr Scott had been honoured by his University with the degree of Doctor of Divinity in 1944. The Church of Scotland now honoured him with a call to succeed Professor Henderson as Moderator of the General Assembly in 1956. A historic event marked his occupancy of that chair, when he welcomed back into the national Church the Synod of United Original Seceders. This represented the last remnant of the Secession of 1733[5], which had stayed out from the 1852 union with the Free Church. Dr Scott's address of welcome perfectly expressed the kindly warmth of the welcome with which the mother-Church received them.

One of the congregation's most helpful ministries began in Dr Scott's time. In 1956 Miss Mary Park Lyle gifted to St

Columba's a handsome sum to be used in setting up a home for retired Scots and others unable any longer to care for themselves. She and Mrs Scott spent much time and labour in finding the right place. The result is a home in an attractive part of Putney, named, after its benefactor, *Lyle Park,* and administered by a St Columba's Committee which keeps careful watch not only over its practical needs and amenities but over the personal welfare of its thirty residents.

In 1959 came a letter from Africa which rounded out a story in which St Columba's had played a helpful part for over half a century. Somewhere around 1888 little Harry Kambuiri Matitchita, a table-boy at the manse in Blantyre, Nyasaland, was adopted by the children of St Columba's Sunday School. With their help his education continued through boyhood and young manhood, until in 1911 he became the first ordained African minister. To St Columba's he was always Harry Kamburi, and regular letters from him were printed in the magazine. Now, in October 1959, he wrote to tell St Columba's that he was retiring, and to say that he was still using the Bible and the cassock which the Sunday School had sent him in 1905 and 1911. When he had started as a minister 'there was not a Christian, or anyone who knew the a, b, c; no government, but the Angonis fighting each other and raiding the Achavas and selling them as slaves to the Yaos which is my tribe. Bless the Lord there are now four congregations and many schools!'[6].

In 1960 Dr Scott, feeling that the time had come to hand over the heavy responsibilities of his charge to a younger man, accepted a call to Auchterhouse in Angus. He retired in 1968, and died in 1975. At the memorial service in St Columba's Mr Murray Napier, his former Session Clerk there, said: 'His leadership, his courage and his resolution never faltered. . . He lovingly nursed the flame of this Church of Scotland in those difficult years and with success. . . As a preacher the gift of the gospel he offered was thankfully received by his hearers — the hungry looked up and were fed — they were filled with good things. . . As a pastor he was a guiding light to all who were bereaved, harassed, concerned, anxious, or buffeted about by the storms and stresses of life. . . The whole Scottish Community in London benefited by his presence in its midst'. The story of those 22 years in St Columba's certainly centres around the personality of this much-loved pastor and powerful preacher; but the response of St Columba's elders and members to his courage and faith was as remarkable a part of that story. 'For that the leaders did lead', sang Deborah and Barak, 'and that the people did willingly follow, praise ye the Lord!'[7]. The church might be burned, but the Church was not consumed; and to God be the praise.

NOTES

1. Much of this and the following paragraph derives from G.D. Henderson, *The Burning Bush*, chapter one — St Andrew Press, 1957. We seem unable to avoid references to George Baillie of Jerviswood, who bought his copies of *The Acts*, as well as other books, from 'Georg Mosman'. *(Lady Grisell Baillie's Household Book*, July & Dec. 1695 and Feb. 1702, when the Acts cost £6 6s. [Scots], or 10/6 sterling.)

2. Emmanuel Tremellius, an Italian of Jewish parentage, was converted to Romanism by Cardinal Pole and then to the Reformed faith by Peter Martyr, with whom he went to England in 1547. There he enjoyed the friendship of Cranmer and Parker, and taught Hebrew in Cambridge. On Queen Mary's accession he sought refuge in Germany, where he was joined in Heidelberg by young Francisco Junius, an exiled Huguenot. Junius assisted him in translating the Bible from the Hebrew and the Greek into Latin, using better sources than had been available for Jerome's Vulgate translation of 390 A.D. Junius married Tremellius's daughter; their son settled in England and with other Huguenot scholars made great contribution to scholarship there. He died in his nephew's house in Windsor and was buried in St George's Chapel there.

3. See Chapter 13. Miss Blackwood's card-index of soldiers on furlough entertained in Pont Street during the great war contained more than 48,000 cards.

4. Compare Chapter eleven, note 12!

5. See Appendix C.

6. St Columba's Magazine, Feb., 1905, Aug. 1911, Oct. 1959.

7. *Judges 5:2.* (R.V., R.S.V., Moffatt, N.E.B.).

CHAPTER 17

Yesterday, Today and Tomorrow

The names of more than thirty congregations of the Scots Kirk in London can be traced, and reference to the names and locations of others, such as are found in Lady Grisell Baillie's *Household Book*[1], suggest that there may have been a number of which no record remains. Prior to the Union of the Established and United Free Churches in 1929 none of the Scottish congregations in England was erected as a charge of the Church of Scotland[2], although the ministers of many of them were ordained to those charges by Scottish Presbyteries. Not until 1934 could any of them be recognised as belonging to the Church of Scotland[3] by which time only four Scottish National churches remained in London. Now, as we have seen, there are two, both of them descendants of one of the earliest.

The 'ifs' of history provoke intriguing speculations, and the story of the Scots Kirk in London abounds in such instances. The element of the 'might-have-been' is all the stronger because of the very close association which sprang up between the Scottish and English Presbyterians, first after the Act of Uniformity menaced both, and then when the later and happier Toleration Act released them from their semi-underground state. This close relationship might have led to an interdenominational body of English dissent if the 'Happy Union' of 1689[4] between Presbyterians and Independents had not broken down four years thereafter.

That separation did not altogether end interdenominational co-operation. Presbyterian, Independent and Baptist interests were jointly promoted early in the 18th century through a *Committee of Deputies,* and after 1727 through *The General Body of the Three Denominations,* which acted so acceptably that in 1837 it was officially recognised by government as 'the legitimate and authorised organ of communication with His

217

Majesty the King'[5]. In this the Presbyterians, as the largest body, took the lead; and more than once the General Body appointed a Scottish minister as leader and spokesman of a delegation to Court.

The next 'might-have-been' centres upon Salters' Hall, where English and Scottish Presbyterian ministers had worked together in giving the weekly Merchants' Lectures ever since the breakdown of the Happy Union. In 1719 the Committee of the Deputies of the Three Denominations convened a Synod in Salters' Hall to discuss a doctrinal point referred to London by the Exeter Assembly of Dissenters. The 'Subscriptionist' controversy which then arose divided the London Presbyterians; and the Scots ministers, who were all Subscribers, found themselves separated from their English brethren, who were almost all Nonsubscribers[6]. It was then that the Scottish National Churches in London and elsewhere seem to have made their first attempt to link themselves in a more organised Presbyterian structure, although little appears to have come of the effort at the time[7]. By the end of the century, however, the Scots Presbytery of London was well established.

In 1843 the Disruption[8] took place in Scotland, and this time the baneful consequences of the 1712 Patronage Act were felt also in England. Most of the Scottish congregations there were in sympathy with the principles expressed in the Disruption, and came out of the Church of Scotland connection. Only eighteen, including three in London, retained that connection; and although the three increased in time to six, two alone survive in the metropolis itself. We have traced their origins and history almost up to date in the foregoing chapters. What, we may now ask, is their present condition and task, and what of their future?

Much of the narrative in the foregoing chapters has been concerned with the succession of ministers, crises concerning property, and the relation of the congregations' affairs with contemporary events. More important is its record of the part played by congregations of the Scots Kirk in the struggle for religious liberty, in efforts to care for the underprivileged and to reform social conditions, and in the upholding of the standards, theological, moral and spiritual, upon which a nation's integrity depends. In such an account of events and endeavours it is easy to lose sight of the fact that Sunday by Sunday a fellowship of worshippers is being spiritually nourished in worship and inspired by the faithful proclamation of the Gospel; but the picture would be incomplete and distorted if that vitalising background to all its form and colour were forgotten. Let it be said here that this healing and inspiring ministry of Word and Sacraments continues to be faithfully exercised – in St Columba's, where the Rev. Dr J. Fraser McLuskey, M.C. succeeded the Very Rev. Dr R.S.V. Scott in 1960; and in Crown Court, where the Rev. John Miller Scott, M.A., B.D., succeeded the Rev. Dr Joseph Moffett in 1963. The motivation and the dynamic for the continuing witness of the Scots Kirk in London are to be found in the place of worship, today as in the past.

It is sometimes argued, however, that the presence of the Church of Scotland in England offends against good sense and Christian amity, considering that the national Church south of the border is Episcopalian, and that there is, in any case, an indigenous Church, the United Reformed Church in England and Wales, which has a Presbyterian strain in its heritage going back to the time of England's Queen Elizabeth. The *tu quoque* answer to the first of these arguments is of course obvious. The Church of England herself maintains certain congregations in Scotland, although there is an indigenous Scottish Episcopal Church with which it is in full communion. Moreover it maintains Anglican churches associated with every U.K. Embassy in other lands, although these Embassies are not English but British. This is hardly a worthy answer – 'you do this; why shouldn't we?' – but the parallel which it points out contains the quite positive justification for the Scottish National Church's presence in England, which is not just so that she may minister to her expatriates but that, as part of the Church Catholic, she may participate, through her care for them and through their own witness as her members, in the testimony which is not to be confined within any frontiers and in the mission which is relevant to all environments, in every age.

To the argument that any Church, not necessarily Scottish, could make just the same witness and give just the same service in the London scene, it must be answered that none does. There is a distinctive element in the ethos of the Scottish Church which must be preserved for inclusion in the reconciliation to which we are being called. The continuous flow of overseas visitors to the Scottish churches in London is evidence that, as many of them say, they find there something which is not merely distinctively Scottish but is indispensably part of the wholeness of the Christian faith and of the worship of Christ's people. This is not to say that that something is missing elsewhere, but it does suggest that the absence of the Scottish Church's witness and work from the British capital would impoverish the active working-out of interchurch relationships, the thinking-out of which is so largely centred there. We have a very long way to go along the road to unity, but mutual understanding is surely helped by propinquity in the facing of every difference and the venturing upon every step.

But the justification for any branch of the Church Catholic must be looked for in its obedience not only to its Master's word: 'Feed My sheep', but also to the vision expressed in His prayer: 'that they may all be one', and to His Commission: 'As the Father has sent Me, so I send you!' It was in token of this threefold obedience that Calvin in 1552 and Beza in 1561 pled for the formation of some general Council in which the unity of the different Reformed Churches as part of the Church Catholic might be effectively affirmed and demonstrated. In the same spirit the Second Book of Discipline of the Scottish Church speaks of 'an Assembly representing the Universal Kirk of Christ, which may be properly called the General Assembly or General Council of the whole Kirk of God'[9]. Despite this inherited vision of Christian Unity the Scottish Church has, with some justice, been accused of sometimes exhibiting a divisive rather than a reconciling spirit. But with equal — or even greater — justice it should be pointed out that she does not bar, but welcomes to the Lord's Table, the members of any branch of His church; that she 'recognises the obligation to seek and promote union with other Churches in which it finds the Word to be purely preached, the Sacraments administered according to Christ's ordinance, and discipline rightly exercised'[10], that the divisive influences have usually taken the form of intrusions on her spiritual liberties; and that in fact the Scottish churches have been pioneers in the modern movement towards interdenominational unity. The oldest of the existing agencies for fostering inter-church relations was the *Evangelical Alliance,* founded by the Free Church of Scotland in 1845, which encouraged the unions of the second half of the nineteenth century[11]. Then, following the initiative of the Rev. W.G. Blaikie of Edinburgh and the Rev. Dr McCosh of Princeton, *The World Alliance of Presbyterian or Reformed Churches* came into being and its First General Committee met in Edinburgh in 1877. Even more important was the creation of *The World Missionary Council* at Edinburgh in 1910, for in this Council the Churches now began to meet across denominational boundaries and to approach their world-task as missionary agencies in the unity of the Spirit[12]. The Scots Kirk in London played its part in the achievement; two St Columba's elders, Dr Robert Kilgour and Lord Balfour of Burleigh, were delegates, and Lord Balfour was in fact the Chairman of 'Edinburgh 1910', while another influential member, Lady Frances Balfour, was one of its most enthusiastic supporters. Thirty-seven years later, at the First General Assembly of *The World Council of Churches* in Amsterdam — the natural sequel to 'Edinburgh, 1910' — there was a Church of Scotland delegate in the Youth Section, J. Fraser McLuskey, 'the Parachute Padre', who thirteen years later and half a century after 'Edinburgh 1910' became minister of St Columba's.

It is not surprising, then, to find that the Scots Kirk in London today has been a leader in the cause of interdenominational cooperation. St Columba's is active in the Chelsea Council of Churches, of which Dr McLuskey was a founder-member and first Chairman in 1961; and Crown Court, in the person of its minister, John Miller Scott, was a founder-member and later Chairman of the Westminster Council of Churches, formed in 1965. In other metropolitan and local interchurch activities both congregations take part. The Chelsea Youth Club is financially aided by St Columba's and staffed one night a week by volunteer helpers from its Youth Fellowship. Neither congregation is exclusively Scottish, and all varieties of accent, including transatlantic, antipodean, Asian, African, Indian and Carribean, may be heard as their members gather for worship. Naturally there is a special care for Scots in old age, ill-health, or any kind of difficulty. Few weeks pass without a phone call or letter from Scotland, asking that a visit might be paid to someone in prison, or some lost person traced, or some old relative looked up, or someone, arriving at a London hospital for an operation, visited. But even some of those ministries spill over into the lives of people with no Scottish connection. Young people arriving at Centrepoint[13], jobless, homeless and moneyless, from some English city or from abroad, may be advised and helped by a St Columba's member who is there simply because so many Scots turn up there. Crown Court may be able to offer help through its voluntary workers in St-Martin's-in-the-Fields Social Unit and through voluntary work in New Horizon in Covent Garden. Both congregations are closely involved, also, in organisations concerned with the welfare of children.

Nevertheless the distinctive function they fulfil has a primarily Scottish orientation. This is more publicly demonstrated by, for example, Crown Court's Kirking of Scottish Peers and Members of Parliament at the opening of each Parliament and by its periodical services for Scottish journalists, and by St Columba's annual Scottish Festival service and its Royal British Legion and London Scottish Parades. Less publicised but more important are the day-by-day services to and amongst Scots in London, already referred to. As the Presbytery of London has more than once declared, the Scots Kirk in London is not there to proselytise, still less to imply defect in the doctrine, worship, government or discipline of the sister Church of England or any other. It is there to care for the people of Scotland who are far from the land of their birth, to offer them the ministries of the Gospel in the dearly-loved form of their fathers, to preserve amongst them the traditions of equal human worth exemplified for instance in the corporate *episcope* of the Eldership[14], and to lead them, within the life of the community where they now live, in making a contribution to that larger life which will express something of the truth and power of those principles for which their forefathers made such sacrifices because they spring from the Gospel of Christ.

This is the leadership which is still being offered. Enough has been said about men like James Mein[15] and Alex. Wylie[16], and about decisive events at the beginning of this century[17] to show that the influence of the Scots Kirk's man-in-the-pew has been strongly felt in all parts of the world, and not least in London, where the Scottish community is well-represented in high places of influence. When such men and women, in these rapidly changing times, gather weekly with their compatriots 'within the sound of the Gospel' and in the communion of the Spirit, an influence for good, we may believe, can be communicated through them upon the making of decisions, the shaping of public opinion, the planning of the future, and the presentation of stabilising values through press and television and other media of communication. What is more, there is valuable feedback to the home Church. In the past fifteen years, for example, no fewer than ten ministers and two overseas servants of the Church of Scotland have come from the membership of St Columba's church alone.

In 1906 the Rev. Alexander Macrae, then minister of Crown Court, addressing the General Assembly as spokesman for the Scottish Synod in England, said: 'Apart from religious considerations altogether, as a mere matter of policy, the Church of Scotland *must* be represented in London', and he concluded by saying that 'It would be a good thing if in that great city, instead of four or five small congregations unequally trying to represent the great Scottish Church, they had one and only one large one, with a large staff of Scottish ministers attached and constantly recruited from Scotland'[18]. There are now the two strong Scottish churches in London, and their influence is by no means insignificant. Their Kirk Sessions meet together periodically to co-ordinate their work and strengthen their testimony to Christ their Master. They are in happy and useful fellowship with all other branches of His Church. And as, by manifold tokens, He has been with them yesterday and is with them now, so their tomorrow may be entrusted to His guidance and their obedience.

NOTES
1. See Chapter five.
2. The two Scottish charges in Corby *were* erected by the Church of Scotland, but that was after Act V of the 1934 General Assembly had made the Presbytery of England an integral part of the Church of Scotland (see Appendix D). In the 18th century, however, the Secession Presbyteries in Scotland did plant several churches in England, a response to appeals from evangelically minded Scots in

the areas concerned. Examples are Lloyd Street, Manchester, by the Edinburgh Secession Presbytery in 1718, and Mount Pleasant, Liverpool, by the Glasgow Secession Presbytery shortly thereafter.

3. See note 2 above and Appendix D.

4. See Chapter four and Appendix B.

5. A letter from *The General Body* to Lord John Russell, Home Secretary, in 1836, confirmed the unbroken continuity of that Body, despite the withdrawal of the congregations which had become Unitarian, with 'that which for more than a century has had the honour of being recognised etc.' (Drysdale, *op.cit.*, p. 616)

6. See Appendix B.

7. See Appendix D.

8. See Appendix C.

9. Pardovan's 1709 collection of Scottish Church Laws also has a section entitled 'Of a General Council of Protestants'.

10. *The Church of Scotland Act, 1921;* Schedule: Articles Declaratory of the Constitution of the Church of Scotland in Matters Spiritual, Art. VII. *The Scots Confession* of 1560 defines these as 'the notes of the trew Kirk of God' — Art. XVIII.

11. Burleigh, *op. cit.*, p. 362.

12. One of the first ventures inspired by 'Edinburgh, 1910' took place in Kenya in 1913. The Church of Scotland missionaries there invited to their church in Kikuyu their colleagues of other denominations, to consult on common problems and agree on a mission of unity. A joint Communion Service there was participated in by the Bishop of Uganda but shunned by the Bishop of Zanzibar, precipitating a controversy in the Anglican communion which made Kikuyu a world-known name amongst its members. The controversy had the effect of bringing the issue of unity more plainly before the home churches, 'and that impulse from the mission field . . . had its part in advancing the Reunion Movement which arose out of the Lambeth Conference in 1920' (R.G.M. Calderwood, *Kenya Colony — Sketches from the Fields No. 7, Church of Scotland*, p. 14). See also H. Hensley Henson, *Retrospect of an Unimportant Life*, i, 159–169, for an Anglican comment on the controversy.

13. Centrepoint, an organization briefly described in Chapter three.

14. See Appendix A.

15. See Chapter seven.

16. See Chapter ten.

17. See Chapter thirteen.

18. *Life and Work, Scottish National Churches in England Supplement,* July 1906.

APPENDIX A

The Presbyterian Structure of the Church of Scotland

The Church of Scotland, breaking with the Church of Rome in 1560, reformed its structure and restated its doctrine in *The Scots Confession* and *The Book of Discipline* during the same year. In doing so they looked to the Scripture, as interpreted by the Holy Spirit, who 'is in nathing contrarious unto himself', for the truth and the right which should replace the false and erroneous. This led them to a system of Church doctrine, worship, government and discipline, based on the New Testament, where the old Jewish office of the Elder was turned to use and the office of the Deacon created, as the leading agents of Christian ministry and mission. The apostolic commission and authority, given to the faithful and represented in those who held these offices, were to be taken up again in the reformed Church of Scotland by 'men of best knowledge in God's word, of cleanest life, faithful men and of most honest conversation that can be found in the Kirk', and they were to be chosen by vote of the congregation.

In *The Second Book of Discipline* (1578) this principle was developed into the thoroughgoing Presbyterian order which obtains today.

The prelatic order which had ruled in the Old Church was abandoned as a cause of the corruptions which had required reformation. No longer was the Church's *episcopé* (a Greek word from which the English 'bishop' is derived, and which means 'oversight', 'guardianship', 'superintendence') to be exercised by a hierarchy of bishops in a pyramid of authority headed by an *episcopus episcoporum,* a bishop of bishops, the father-bishop or Papa. In the Reformed Church *episcopé* was to be exercised not by such individuals to whom authority had been individually delegated, but by Elders, acting together in council, guided by God's word in Holy Scripture, united in their faith as Christ's servants, and inspired by the illumination of the Holy Spirit. And since the words *episcopos* (or bishop) and *presbuteros* (or elder) appear more than once in the New Testament as referring to the same person (e.g. Acts 20: 17 & 28, Titus 1:5 & 7, I Peter 5:1 & 2), it could be claimed that the Reformed Church of Scotland was One, Holy, Catholic and Apostolic in a way that the old Church had ceased to be.

This conciliar principle of Church order, further developed in the seventeenth century, worked well. But its democratic characteristics clashed with the idea of an absolute monarchy. Hence James VI at Hampton Court Conference in 1604: "Presbytery as well agreeth with a monarchy as God and the Devil" (in that order!); "No bishop, no King!". Hence also Charles II: "Presbytery . . . is no religion for a gentleman".

Its inherent strength, however, enabled it to withstand the bitter persecutions suffered by those who championed it. It enabled it, also, in the end to achieve a relationship with the state in which its national standing and responsibility are fully realised, and its freedom from state interference in matters of doctrine, worship, government and discipline are as fully recognised. Its removal of the barrier between clergy and those who are called the laity in Churches where that barrier remains, and its recognition that both are one as the people of God — the *laos theou,* the phrase in I Peter 2:10 from which the word *laity* comes — has amongst other things motivated its insistence on the right of education for all. It has probably also helped the Scottish people to maintain a healthy spirit of independence, assuring them that 'a man's a man for a' that', and preserving a mutual respect in 'class' relationships which is still one of the noticeable differences between Scotland and her southern neighbour.

In the Church of Scotland there are two kinds of Presbyter. There is the *teaching elder,* or minister, whose call to the ministry has been homologated by the Presbytery within whose bounds he has lived. After a course of approved training he is licensed to preach by Presbytery; and when called to a charge he is ordained, by the Presbytery concerned, to the ministry of Word and Sacrament. Of that Presbytery he then becomes a member, and it has the power to release him from his charge on his call to another. The procedure whereby his successor is appointed and inducted is then carried through by Presbytery, which has oversight of the congregations and parishes 'within the bounds' of its clearly defined area.

There is also the *ruling elder,* equally important in the system. He is elected from the membership of the congregation, and ordained to serve with his fellow-elders in the Kirk Session, of which the minister is Moderator, and which rules the affairs of the congregation and oversees its witness in the parish. The ruling elder may also be commissioned to serve in the higher courts of the Church — Presbytery, Synod and General Assembly. In these the important principle of 'the parity of Presbyters' is scrupulously observed, namely that there must be equal numbers of teaching and ruling elders; and as a similar safeguard against clerical domination the minister in the Kirk Session, as its Moderator, has no other than a casting vote.

Although ministers are ordained to the Ministry, and inducted to their charges, by Presbytery, the right of the congregation to call its own minister is carefully respected, and only under exceptional circumstances, as when a congregation is unable to agree upon a Call within a specified time, does the *jus devolutum* come into effect and the Presbytery then itself appoints a minister.

There is a right of appeal from lower to higher courts, as e.g., from Kirk Session to Presbytery. The final Court of Appeal is the General Assembly, which meets annually for a week in Edinburgh, coping with interim developments (but not with new business unless by its own previous resolution or suspension of standing orders) through the meetings of its members in two Commissions during the succeeding twelve months.

Each year's Assembly comprises about a quarter of the teaching Presbyters, with an equal number of ruling Presbyters, all of these being commissioned by their Presbyteries to share in the representation and rule of the Church. It hears reports of the work done, the guidance prepared for future work and action, the matters on which the voice of the Church should be heard in regard to social, national and international affairs, and the numerous other concerns of a Church with a mission and a concern for unity. Each report is presented by the appropriate committee, all of which belong to one or another of seven main departments, except for those which have been appointed *ad hoc*. On the basis of each report, after full debate, the Assembly makes decisions and takes or authorises or instructs action.

Its Moderator is elected to serve for one year, and being Moderator of the General Assembly his duties officially begin and end with the week's duration of the Assembly and of the two meetings of its Commissions. But nowadays he also acts as the Church's unofficial representative and sometimes spokesman until his successor for the following year is elected; and he may be guided as necessary on special matters or urgent occasions by the appropriate standing committee of the Assembly.

The *parish* is a geographical area, and parish boundaries are so drawn that no part of Scotland is left out. The Church thus fulfils its responsibility for the spiritual care of the nation, every member of which lives in some parish, where minister and ruling elders together as a Kirk Session lead the congregation of communicant members in the Christian care of young and old.

At the grass-roots level, then, *episcopé* is exercised by the Kirk Session. The interdependence of congregations, and the responsibility for the Church's pastoral oversight and discipline in the larger local setting, hinges upon the Presbytery, which may be regarded as the cardinal, although not the supreme, Court of the Church. The main function of the provincial Synod, of which there are thirteen, including the Synod of England, is to ensure that the Church's *episcopé* is being rightly exercised in the inferior Courts; and to scrutinise any matter which is to be referred to the General Assembly, and ensure that it is passed on in proper order.

With the exception of what relates to the parish, which is not relevant to the Scottish Church situation in England, the foregoing offers a sketch of the Presbyterian structure of the Church of Scotland and may clarify some points in the story of the Scots Kirk in London which might otherwise be confusing.

APPENDIX B

The Two Theological Disputes of the Post-Revolution Period

There is a story about the young Michael Faraday which deserves to be true. A kindly passer-by found the boy one day in what seemed to be an inextricable fix, his head between two bars of an iron railing. 'Are you stuck, boy?', he asked; 'Let me help you'. 'No sir', said young Michael; 'I'm not stuck. But perhaps you *can* help me. I've got my head on one side of this railing, and my heart on the other. Can you tell me which side *I'm* on?'

It is to this kind of question that the Church — often after suffering or persecution has been followed by a period of security and ease — has sometimes found herself giving opposing answers, some holding that faith is a matter of the head and others that it is of the heart.

The early eighteenth century was such a period in Britain, producing controversies in which allegations of heresy and accusations of Arminianism, Arianism, Antinomianism, Supralapsarianism, and even Socinianism were hotly exchanged. The dangers which were held to lurk behind the thinking identified by those impressive theological labels were real enough, but the bitterness with which the labels were employed as libels arose largely from the failure of both sides to reconcile head and heart in the unity of faith. This is shown by the strange fact that the most divisive developments in two of those controversies actually arose out of efforts to allay them.

i The Collapse of 'The Happy Union'

The first of these was the dispute which broke up the Happy Union mentioned in Chapters four and seventeen. A foreshadowing of the dispute had appeared in Cromwell's time, and produced two books, which —reprinted half a century later — were to play prominent roles in the first controversy which broke up that Union in London in 1694 and in the second similar controversy which shook the Church of Scotland and was a contributory cause of the Secession in 1733.

The first of those books was a volume of sermons by an Episcopalian Rector, Dr Thomas Crisp. The sermons presented an ultra-Calvinistic interpretation of Christ's saving work, but although the Westminster divines took note of Crisp's viws they were satisfied that his errors were sufficiently exposed by his critics and too obvious to need further attention. Crisp had distorted the sound Reformation doctrine that faith is to be seen, not in obedience to the law, whether given by Moses or laid down by the Roman Church — but as response to the grace of God freely offered in Jesus Christ. Over-stressed to the point where 'works' as obedience to the moral law came to be regarded as suspect if not intrinsically wrong, this became a dangerous aberration, implying also misleading ideas about the person and work of Christ. These implications were present in Crisp's sermons, confirming the harmful effects of the Antinomianism from which they sprang.[1]

Shortly after Crisp's book appeared, Edward Fisher, an Oxford Puritan, wrote a book with the aim of showing the true middle way between Legalism and Antinomianism, 'endeavouring', as a respected contemporary wrote, 'to reconcile and heal those unhappy differences which have lately broken out afresh amongst us'. It was entitled *The Marrow of Modern Divinity,* and appeared in 1645. Its later history provoked much more dispute than the original edition, as we shall see. The same is true of Crisp's volume.

When Crisp's son republished his father's sermons, with additions, in 1690, the book found an immediate and enthusiastic response amongst those — mainly of the Independent and Baptist bodies — who had adopted an extreme form of Calvinism. They welcomed Crisp's theology as timely and salutary. This sowed dissension amongst the dissenters, not because Crisp was an Episcopalian but because supporters of his views began to accuse, with increasing bitterness, those who criticised it, calling them legalists and enemies of the pure Gospel.

To alleviate the discord some eminent London ministers, including Bates, Howe, Alsop, and Lorimer of the First Scotch Church, encouraged the highly-respected Dr Williams of Hand Alley to write a book bringing out the real issues raised by Dr

The Two Theological Disputes of the Post-Revolution Period

Crisp's sermons. This he did, with the sole aim of offering a reconciling theology in which both legalism and Antinomianism would be seen to include truth as well as error, and which might offer a position, inclusive of the truth in each, where both sides could meet. Unfortunately his book was received by some in a sharply contentious spirit, and with their refusal of the olive branch the controversy flared up more wildly still. Dark accusations of Arminianism[2] were made against Dr Williams, and even attacks on his personal character.

The alignment of the disputants soon assumed a denominational polarity, the Independents taking the ultra-Calvinistic position and the Presbyterians opposing Crisp's Antinomianism as limiting the fulness of the divine purpose, expressed in Jesus' words: 'I am not come to destroy the law, but to fulfil it'. The resultant storm wrecked the Happy Union in 1694. It was never resumed. The dispute, however, was lessened in 1696 by *A Pacificatory Paper* produced by eight conciliatory Presbyterians, and was finally allowed to pass into oblivion after 1699 when Dr Williams published a treatise entitled *Peace with Truth, or An End to Disorder.*[3]

It is to be remembered that this was the age of the Enlightenment, and the influence in England of the philosopher John Locke, particularly through his *Essay on the Human Understanding* (1690) and *The Reasonableness of Christianity as Delivered in the Scriptures* (1696), had its helpful but unsettling effect on Christian thinking. 'Liberty' and 'Toleration' became favourite slogans in the centres of learning, and disturbing breezes wafted the heady scent of 'reasonableness' from the college quadrangle to the minister's study. No longer engaged in the conflict where head and heart were drawn together in common action, the dogmatic positiveness of the Presbyterians and the immoderate fervour of the Independents tended to separate them on either side of a fence, the scent of reason smelling sweeter on the one side than on the other. The watchdogs of orthodoxy themselves tended to be misled from the trail and to lose the scent of the Gospel.

Two cases in Scotland demonstrated their difficulty. In 1715 John Simson, a teacher of divinity in Glasgow, was charged in the General Assembly with teaching Arminianism. In 1719 he was acquitted of the charge, but 'warned not to

231

attribute too much to natural reason and the power of corrupt nature, to the disparagement of revelation and efficacious free grace'. In 1726 he was again before the Assembly, charged now with teaching Arianism[4]. This time the outcome was his suspension in 1729 from teaching; but he was allowed to keep his position and stipend. The sentence might have been more severe but for the general temper of the age, when the head, almost to the exclusion of the heart, was becoming the arbiter of truth, and 'enthusiasm' was regarded with increasing suspicion.

But the Assembly was severe enough in another case which was before it at the same time. This related to the book already mentioned — Thomas Fisher's *Marrow of Modern Divinity*, which had originally been published to point a middle way between Legalism and Antinomianism.

In 1716 the saintly Thomas Boston had noticed, in a cottage in his parish of Simprin, a worn copy of the book, brought home from England by his widowed parishioner's husband, a sailor. So impressed was he by what he read there that he bought the book and spoke highly of it to his friends. One of these, Thomas Hog of Carnock, likewise impressed, had the first part of it reprinted in 1718. It found an immediate welcome throughout Scotland, except amongst those whose inclination towards the purely rational approach was making them suspicious of the 'enthusiasm' of evangelical Christianity. In *The Marrow* these 'Moderates' found certain Antinomian tendencies, and they pointed out passages in which it departed from *The Westminster Confession*. The Assembly was persuaded to forbid ministers to use or commend the book, and bade them warn their parishioners against its teaching of 'Universal Atonement and Pardon'. Boston, Hog, and their two friends the Erskine brothers with eight other ministers, distressed by that decision, challenged the report on which it had been based because it had been unfairly selective in its quotations from *The Marrow*. They further claimed that the Assembly of 1719 by that decision, and the Assembly of 1729 by another Act, had given encouragement to the preaching of 'mere morality without religion'.

Boston died in 1731; and without his saintly moderating influence the Marrow Men tended to argue their case with increasing acrimony. Finally, when in 1733 the Erskines clashed with the majority in the Assembly over a patronage issue[5], they were suspended, and in the end deposed. By that time they had constituted themselves with four others into a Presbytery, and thereafter the Secession Church grew — although not without the formation of splinter groups — both in Scotland and in England. They met a need, not only amongst those who found the imposition of patronage intolerable, but equally amongst those who were wearying of the 'cold, moonlight preaching which ripens no crops' but which during the next eighty years tended to sound from the pulpits of the national church.

This was the characteristic of the party known as the Moderates, who were on the side of the head rather than the heart, and two generations were to pass before the Evangelicals could restore the balance. For it is, surely, a matter of balance. Faith in God through Jesus Christ is no more a matter of the head alone than it is of the heart alone. It is the response of the whole man, reason and emotion combined in action, to the truth and life which he finds in Jesus Christ. The work of the Spirit, vitalising the integration of mind, heart and will in that response, is shut out if only a one-dimensional personality, trapped on the 'head' side of the railing, is accessible to His operation.

Here, it may be suggested, is the *pragmatic* justification for the doctrine of the Trinity — that paradox in which we attempt to express our manifold experience of the One God, Who is too great for our full comprehension, and Who manifests Himself and reveals Himself in ways of which we can grasp only one aspect at any one time or from any one place.

The Moderates in Church of Scotland pulpits may have stimulated the interest of their hearers in 'The Reasonableness of Christianity', but they left an unsatisfied hunger in their heart to which a succession of evangelists could appeal, sometimes with a message so narrowly and exclusively addressed to the heart that reason and toleration were excluded.

The Seceders, for their part, despite their original evangelical persuasion, were capable of refusing to recognise as genuine the work of the Spirit in any evangel other than their own; they labelled the revival at Kilsyth, and that which was known as 'The Cambuslang Wark', as delusions of the devil, because

William Burns of Kilsyth and William McCulloch of Cambuslang belonged to the Established Church, and because George Whitefield, a priest of the Church of England, had taken part in them.

ii The Subscriptionist Controversy

We return to England, and to London, to note the second unhappy dispute, which this time divided Presbyterians and Independents, irrespective of denomination, into the two parties of Subscriptionists and Non-subscriptionists.

The theological point at issue concerned the doctrine of the Trinity. Because of the way the controversy developed it has sometimes been presented in terms of Bible versus Creed, but that is a misleading simplification.

In 1719 the Exeter Assembly — which had been set up as a Presbyterian Synod in 1655 to deal with matters of doctrine and discipline, but by this time included also Independents — had to deal with a question involving the orthodoxy of three Exeter ministers, and sought to resolve it by requiring that all ministers sign the first of the Thirty-nine Articles of the Church of England which states the doctrine of the Trinity. One third of the ministers present refused to do so, or to sign the 5th and 6th answers of the Shorter Catechism which state the same doctrine.

Some ministers in London drew up a letter designed to heal the dissension, and the Deputies of the Three Denominations[6] called together all the London dissenting ministers in Salters' Hall to approve it. This famous Salters' Hall Synod met for several sessions in what became fierce debate — not about the contents of the letter which were fully approved, but about whether the ministers present should themselves preface it with an avowal of their own belief by subscribing their names to the First Article and the 5th and 6th answers to the Catechism. Put to the vote the motion for subscribing lost by 69 votes to 73, which one Presbyterian elder summed up by saying 'The Bible carried it by four'. The debate had hinged on the non-subscribers' objection to signing any declaration of faith except in the very words of scripture, so the majority could be regarded as a verdict for the Bible against any merely human creed. But the controversy which followed, in floods of pam-

The Two Theological Disputes of the Post-Revolution Period

phlets and sermons, revealed other elements in the non-sub-scribers' position. They may not at first have been conscious of these. All would probably have declared their belief in the Trinity, and many did. But by rejecting the creedal statement and adhering to Chillingworth's famous dictum: 'The Bible, the Bible only, the religion of Protestants', they were distorting the true Protestant position, in which Bibliolatry has no place. 'The Word of God, contained in the Scriptures of the Old and New Testaments' is the supreme rule of faith and life for His Church, but always 'under the promised guidance of the Holy Spirit' — *testimonium Spiritus sancti* — on which the Reformers laid such stress. The creeds may be man-made, but they derive from the Word, both Incarnate and written; and they represent the common faith of generations of Christians in words which point the direction in which the Spirit's illumination has led.

Abandoning such landmarks, the Non-subscriptionists were insensibly led, by their vehemently expressed loyalty to Scripture, into a position where faith became a matter of assent to impersonal truths in doctrine and morals, devoid of any warm personal trust in Jesus Christ as Saviour. Almost within a generation the majority of English Presbyterians, who had been the main party of the Non-subscribers, became in effect subscribers to a Unitarian creed, conforming with the speculative spirit of the times. The term 'Presbyterian' thus came, in those parts of England where this process had run its course, to mean Unitarian. Cardinal Newman, for example, in his *Apologia pro Vita sua,* has a note on the Anglican Church in which he says: 'The Church of England has been the instrument of Providence in conferring great benefits on me. Had I been born in Dissent perhaps I should never have been baptised; had I been born an English Presbyterian, perhaps I should never have known our Lord's divinity'. (p. 340). So general was this popular identification of Presbyterianism with Unitarianism that after 1843, when the Presbyterian Church in England came into being[7], its congregations in many cases carefully called themselves 'Trinity Presbyterian Church', and the year-book of the United Reformed Church today shows how many they were.

It should be said that the Subscribers — who included all the Scottish National, some English Presbyterian, and a majority of the Independent or Congregational representatives — were not without responsibility for the sad breach. The rancour they contributed to the argument probably provoked the Non-subscribers to more extreme statements of their Arian position than was necessary, and from which they later found it difficult, with respect, to retreat.

We may agree with Zwingli that 'it is a Christian man's business not to talk grandly of dogmas but always to be doing arduous and great things with God'. Sticking in the fence is even more foolish than sitting on it. The Christian Church and her members must maintain order *and* ardour in creative tension.

NOTES

1. *Antinomianism* — meaning literally 'opposed to legalism' — arose in Germany soon after the Reformation. It represented an over-reaction against the doctrine of salvation by works (or by conformity to the law, of Moses or of the Church), which had been given such prominence by Rome. It tended to exaggerate the antithesis between works and faith, between the Law and the Gospel, to such an extent that the former came to be regarded as a hindrance to salvation if not as something intrinsically wrong. The Antinomi of Germany maintained, or were said to maintain, that the moral law is not binding on Christians, and this implication tends to remain when the term Antinomianism is used, not always in the sense of Augustine's 'Love, and do what you like'.

2. *Arminianism* is derived from the latinised name of a Dutch theologian. Jacob Harmensen, or Arminius, began in the late sixteenth century to question Calvin's teaching in regard to predestination and grace. Originally he was content to assert that God's grace was offered to all, and that the non-elect were those who had themselves elected to spurn it. John Wesley, on that definition, could be called an Arminian. But just as Calvin's sterner teaching could be caricatured — as in Burns' *Holy Willie's Prayer,* and by those whom it depicted — so was Arminius's by some of his followers, until Arminianism came to mean a liberty in both religion and morals which was hardly distinguishable from the 'free-thinking' rationalism of the Socinians.

3. Dr Williams was an outstanding figure in early 18th century English nonconformity, and although he could receive no academic help from the two English Universities, which were closed to all except Anglicans, his efforts to promote educational opportunities for English nonconformists brought him into close touch with the Scottish Universities, where English students were welcomed. Having

private means he was able to give financial help by the establishment of Williams Divinity Bursaries. *The Glasgow University Calendar*, 1974, p. 658, lists 'The Williams Divinity Bursaries for training for the Ministry among Protestant Dissenters' as being now available 'For any men or woman of South Britain (i.e. England or Wales) who for the better discharge of his or her ministry wishes to pursue a 'refresher' course for at least one year. . .' in the University of Glasgow. When the youngest Scottish University — Edinburgh, founded 1582 — first conferred Doctorates in Divinity, *honoris causa*, in 1709, the recipients were all from south of the border — Edmund Calamy, Joshua Oldfield and Daniel Williams. In such ways Scotland gave encouragement to English Presbyterianism. Others of Dr Williams' many bequests were those to St Thomas' Hospital, the Society for the Reformation of Manners, and the Society of Scotland for Propagating Christian Knowledge, which did much for religious and general education in the Scottish Highlands.

4. *Arianism* was named after Arius, a presbyter of Alexandria, who died in 336 A.D. His teaching stirred up metaphysical speculation concerning the nature of the divinity of Jesus, and necessitated the summoning of the first ecumenical council (if we except the one in Jerusalem described in Acts xv), which was held in Nicaea in 325. It condemned his views as heretical, and produced the unequivocally trinitarian *Nicene Creed*. Arianism subordinates Jesus Christ the Son, as 'a secondary God' with the indefinite article, the Father being *the* God. Athanasius, who won the day against Arius at Nicaea, stood firmly for the full divinity of Christ — 'very God of very God, begotten, not made, being of one substance with the Father. . . Who for us and all men, and for our salvation . . . was incarnate and made man. . .'

5. See Appendix C.
6. See Chapter seventeen.
7. See Appendix D.

APPENDIX C

Consequences of the Patronage Act of 1712

In Chapter six we noted the passing of the Patronage Act by the second British Parliament in 1712, restoring to 'patrons' in Scotland the right to present ministers to charges without reference to congregation or Presbytery. This Act had lamentable consequences in Scottish church life.

Patronage was an unhappy hang-over from the pre-Reformation Church. One cause of the Reformation in Scotland was the misuse of the country's natural wealth, most of which had passed into the hands of the Church and was attached as beneficies to her abbacies and bishoprics. In many cases this meant that lands and their incomes had come to be regarded as the personal property of the bishops themselves, or of the lay abbots and commendators whom they had appointed. The plan of the First Book of Discipline was that this wealth should be recovered and used for the maintenance of the ministry throughout Scotland, for the maintenance of the three universities and the provision of a fourth in Edinburgh, and for the establishment and upkeep of a school in every parish so that the sons of the poor might, equally with the rich, receive a basic education[1]. But the Book of Discipline was not given legal sanction, the lay commendators who were usually members of the nobility were powerful enough to hold what they had, and the ousted bishops were allowed a life-rent of what they had enjoyed. The reformed Church's material resources were limited to the proceeds of a tax to be levied, of a third of the benefices — a temporary expedient until 'the Kirk come to the full possession of her proper patrimony which is the teinds'[2]. In the event Knox's plan, that what had been the Church's wealth should now be used for the benefit of all the people, through Church and State, largely failed because most of that wealth remained in private and secular hands. And if in those hands its posses-

238

sion entailed the obligation to pay the Church teinds it was not difficult for the owner to persuade himself and others that that obligation gave him the right of a patron, to choose the minister of the parish to which the teinds went as stipend. In William's reign, as we have seen, this 'right' was abolished; but the 1712 Act restored it, ignoring the security guaranteed to the Church in the Treaty of Union.

Patrons were at first cautious in the way they exercised their patronal privileges, no doubt fearing the storm which ruthlessness would undoubtedly have raised. But a clash between patron and Presbytery was bound to come, and when it did it involved Ebenezer Erskine, whom a number of congregations wished to have but whom no patron would present. He was the people's choice for a vacancy in Kinross, and the Presbytery, supporting them, refused to ordain the patron's presentee and continued not to recognise him as a member of Presbytery although twice instructed to do so by the General Assembly. The Assembly, for its part, was anxious to avoid confrontation with what was now, however illegally, the law of the land; but Erskine and his friends — his brother Ralph being one — considered the timid attitude of the Assembly to be a betrayal of the right of Christian congregations to call ministers of their choice, as the Second Book of Discipline laid down. The outcome was an eventual break-away under the name of the **Secession Church** in 1733, and this was recognised *de jure* in 1740, when the Assembly deposed the Erskines and their fellow-ministers. The Marrow Controversy mentioned in Chapter four and in Appendix B had some influence in arousing the Erskines and the other Secessionists to take the stand they did in defence of the Church's freedom to control her own affairs. Unfortunately a spirit of embitterment came to pervade the Secession Church, and the narrowness of its members' views on Church and State led to numerous disagreements and divisions amongst them, and to further secessions from the original Seceder Kirk[3].

Nineteen years after the Secession the Assembly again tried to curb rising antagonism to the intrusion of ministers by patrons, who were mostly episcopalian. But the not very straightforward means which it agreed to employ — on the motion of William Robertson, son of the Founders' Hall assistant mentioned in Chapter two — brought an unjustifiable penalty on one member of the Presbytery concerned. This was Thomas Gillespie, a friend of Philip Doddridge the hymnwriter, and the minister of Carnock. Deposed by the Assembly in 1761 as an example to warn others against opposing patronage, he himself proved an example of Christian forbearance, showing no bitterness in accepting the sentence, and encouraging those who followed him — and there were many — to continue to act as allies rather than enemies of the national Church. The body they formed was known as *The Presbytery of Relief for Christians oppressed in their Church privileges,* or popularly as **The Relief Church.** Crown Court's fourth minister had a Relief connection, as we have seen, and his advice to his — the first — Relief congregation in Glasgow when he left for London typifies the spirit of this denomination and its desire to work with rather than against the mother-Church for the removal of injustice. The Relief Church was the first body to open its pulpits to all Christian ministers and the Table to all believers; the first officially to sponsor overseas mission work; the first to introduce a hymn-book; and the first to oppose the slave-traffic[4]. Its unofficial motto was a variant of Melancthon's principle: *'In necessariis, unitas; In dubiis, libertas; In omnibus, caritas'.*

The Moderate party, complaisant about patronage, and more interested in the Enlightenment than in the Reformation, in the Cambridge Platonists than in the Westminster Divines, and even in the Establishment than in the Gospel, had by the middle of the 18th century come to dominate the Church's parishes and courts, and remained in control until the following century.[5] Then, as the Evangelical party gained strength, the issue of patronage again emerged. A 'Ten Years' Conflict' over intrusions of ministers upon unwilling congregations followed; and Court of Session and Parliament alike proving intransigent, the majority of the 1843 Assembly came out, relinquishing all the stipends, properties and privileges of the Establishment and constituting the **Free Church of Scotland.** This was the Disruption. The issue involved was patronage, but behind it was the principle of the Church's spiritual independence of the State — a principle at last conceded in 1921 and embodied in the articles declaratory of the constitution of the Church of Scotland.

If it were to be asked why three separate bodies had to stand in protest for the Church's freedom from the State in matters spiritual, and why the later secessions did not simply join with the earlier, it would have to be allowed that other factors, both theological and non-theological, shaped the pattern of those protests so that their supporters were slow to find common ground. It was the Free Church's foundation of the *Evangelical Alliance*[6] immediately after the Disruption which provided the ground on which they, or some of them, found they could meet. The United Secession joined with the Relief Church in 1847 to form the **United Presbyterian Church.** In 1852 the Original Secession united with the Free Church, as did the **Reformed Presbyterians**[7] in 1876, although minorities of both bodies stayed out of those unions. Then, after long co-operation, the Free and United Presbyterian bodies came together in union as the **United Free Church** in 1900. Finally in 1929 the United Free and the Established Church joined to form the re-united **Church of Scotland,** the barriers of patronage and state control of the Kirk having been removed by earlier legislation — a removal in which the Scots Kirk in London played a not insignificant part.

As we have seen in Chapters four and eight, a number of congregations of the Secession and one or two of the Relief Church appeared in England, and those in London worked closely with the Scots Presbytery until about 1840, soon after which, following their parent Churches in Scotland, they united as the **United Presbyterian Church in England.** At the Disruption, as we have seen in Chapter ten, only three Scottish National churches remained in the Presbytery, and it seems that, to begin with, the six who went out considered themselves as belonging to the Free Church. But they soon realised their position as an independent body, allying themselves with those English Presbyterian congregations which had adhered to the Westminster Confession, dropping the phrase 'in connection with the Church of Scotland', and styling themselves **The Presbyterian Church in England.** Soon thereafter, in 1863, the first proposals for union were being made between the U.P. and Free Churches in Scotland. It was more than a quarter of a century before that union took place, but in England the Presbyterian Church in England and the United Presbyterian Church of England had achieved such a union by 1876, under the title **The Presbyterian Church of England**. This, in turn, united with the Congregational Union of England and Wales to form the **United Reformed Church in England and Wales**, in 1972.

NOTES

1. The 1560 *Book of Discipline*, V, (8). Knox's *History*, ed. Dickinson, ii, 295-302. The Scottish emphasis on education, which at one stage made her one of the best-educated nations in Europe, may be said to date from that time. See Macky, *Familiar Letters from a Gentleman to his Friend Abroad*, (1723), vol. iii, passim. See also Drummond and Bulloch, *The Church in Victorian Scotland*, chapter 8, *re* Scotland's hospitality to the ideas of Lyell, Darwin and Huxley; and Gordon Donaldson, *The Shaping of a Nation*, pp. 246—7 on Scottish literacy and the high ratio of University students to the whole population in Scotland.
2. Burleigh, *op. cit.*, p. 191.
3. These further divisions amongst Seceders had to do with such matters as whether it was right to take the Burgess Oath, and in one case with the question of whether the Cup should or should not be lifted at the Great Prayer in the Sacrament. Hence the nicknames which became attached to the various groups — the Burghers and the Antiburghers, the Auld Lichts and the New Lichts, the Lifters and the Antilifters.
4. *Life and Work*, Feb., 1931. Article by Dr D.P. Thomson, then minister of Gillespie Church, Dunfermline.
5. The evil effects of patronage had by this time also been plainly seen in the timid part played during the notorious Highland Clearances by some of the ministers in that region. Being dependent on the favour of their patrons they had obsequiously justified them in the haste and ruthlessness of their 'improvements', instead of courageously championing the flocks they had been charged to shepherd. Sir Walter Scott, himself a Tory, had frankly ascribed the passing of Queen Anne's Act to absentee landlord influence, and those later events proved the wisdom of his judgement that 'the Act which restored to patrons the right of presenting clergymen to vacant churches was designed to render the churchmen more dependent on the aristocracy, and to separate them from their congregations, who could not

be equally influenced by, or attached to, a minister who held his living by the gift of a rich man as by one who was chosen by their own free voice'.

6. The bicentenary of the Westminster Assembly fell to be celebrated two months after the Disruption. It was ignored by the Established Church, but at the celebration the Free Church leader, Dr Chalmers, made a speech on Church Union which questioned the value of mere co-operation, unless it were 'with the view, as soon as may be, to incorporation afterwards'. 'The immediate outcome was a movement which led to the formation in 1845 of the Evangelical Alliance, which brought together Evangelical churchmen from many Churches in Europe and America as well as from Britain' (Burleigh, *op. cit.*, *p. 362.*)

7. The Reformed Presbyterian Church, successor to the Cameronians, Macmillanities, or Societies, is briefly noted in Chapter two, note 6.

APPENDIX D

The Scots Presbytery of London — 1760-1843

References could be cited which suggest that there existed a Scots Presbytery in London early in the second half of the seventeenth century. Alexander Shields was licensed to preach 'by Scots Presbyterian divines' somewhere between 1661 and 1685[1]. The First Scotch Church in Founders' Hall was recognised as such in 1663[2]. The English Presbyterian congregation known as Mr Muir's Meeting House 'became a Scotch congregation' in the 1740's[3]. And the Session Minutes of such congregations as Founders' Hall and Crown Court clearly indicate that at least there was an association of Scottish churches in and around London in the early years of the 18th century. There is, however, no surviving evidence that this association took the form of a properly organised Presbytery as a Court superior to the Kirk Session. Not until the half century had passed was this achieved, as recorded in the *Fasti*[4]: 'A Presbytery in connection with the Church of Scotland was established in 1760'; and of this not only does no trace of its earliest official records survive but the later records open with a thirty-year period retrospectively reconstructed in 1804 from the year 1772. Behind those two dates there lie two circumstances which had considerable significance for the Scots Kirk in London.

The Subscriptionist Controversy which followed the Salters' Hall Synod of 1719 had the long-term effect of bringing most of the English Presbyterians into a Unitarian position[5], leaving the Scottish Presbyterians in the position of leadership as champions of the Trinitarian position and of the Westminster standards. By 1772, when Henry Hunter of London Wall became Clerk of the Presbytery, the need for strengthening the Presbytery's structure so that it might more efficiently carry out this function and 'uphold evangelical truth and reasonable discipline' had become obvious, and to Hunter must be given

244

the credit for achieving this. When he died in 1802, however, his successor as Clerk could not find the Presbytery's Minute Books. It appears, in fact, as though Dr Hunter, in his last three years of failing health, had mislaid them. Fortunately his scroll minutes were discovered. On January 4th, 1804, we find that the new Clerk was 'instructed to purchase a book for engrossing the minutes of the Presbytery as far back as the Committee can find authentic documents'. The Committee's diligence is attested by the fact that although the Moderator soon 'secured from Miss Hunter minutes from 5th August 1772 to 14th August 1799, with occasional interruptions', it was determined to cover, if it could, a wider field, and on May 7th, reporting the Moderator's success, 'the Committee, desirous of possessing as many documents of the proceedings as possible, appointed Mr Young to enquire of the late Dr Hunter's family whether any of the minutes continue in their possession'. Dr Hunter's scroll minutes must have been accurate and adequate, the omissions few, and the gap following August 1799 satisfactorily filled from members' recollections; for on August 5th, 1804, the New Minute Book, with the proceedings from the beginning of 1772 until that date inscribed in its pages, following a lengthy explanatory Preamble, was laid before the Presbytery and approved.

If 1772 had been a critical time for the Scots Kirk in London 1804 was no less so. The Preamble states, amongst other things, that 'The Scots Presbytery in London, since their first formation as an Ecclesiastical Body, have conformed strictly to the Worship and Government, inviolably maintained the Faith and Spirit, and legally exercised the Powers, of their Parent Church, in the Land where Providence hath cast their lot'. It adds 'We, the members of the Scots Presbytery in London, have carefully collected and arranged the Minutes of our Proceedings from the earliest period of our existence as an Ecclesiastical Body of which we possess original and authentic Documents. We regret exceedingly that the memorial of its First Foundation, and the Proceedings consequent thereupon, are not extant, and that many which have been preserved exist in an imperfect and mutiliated State. We are however satisfied that the Collection, even in its present State, will demonstrate our steadfast adherence to the Constitution of the Church of Scotland, and may serve as a Guide to our future Proceedings'. In view of the full details regarding dates, places of meeting, sederunts, examination of students or of applicants for license or ordination, and such events as the ordination of Dr Vanderkemp[6], the sources for the reconstruction of those thirty years of the Presbytery's proceedings must have been sufficiently detailed to be reliable.

The Preamble bears clear traces of the Presbytery's concern to demonstrate its Trinitarian orthodoxy and its connection with the Church of Scotland. So does the even lengthier Declaration which the Presbytery had published in 1793 and to which reference is made in Chapter four. This had the purpose of disavowing both the Socinianism which had become a characteristic of English Presbyterianism at that time, and the anti-monarchical sentiments which the American and French Revolutions had encouraged in some quarters. It specifically dissociated 'Scottish Presbyterians residing in South Britain . . . from notions of religion and government supposed [in England] to be in necessary connection with the name Presbyterian'. It also declared firm adherence to 'the well-known Standards of the Church of Scotland, viz., the Westminster Confession of Faith and the Larger and Shorter Catechisms'. And it affirmed 'zealous attachment to the Constitution as settled . . . at the Glorious Revolution in 1688' and 'unfeigned loyalty to his present Majesty', promising to 'use every means as Ministers of the Gospel . . . to promote Truth, Virtue and Religion as being the firmest supports of Loyalty and Freedom and the purest sources of personal and public felicity'.

Clearly the Presbytery of London in those days had a strong sense of public as well as ecclesiastical responsibility, and a due sense of its own importance in both spheres of influence. It must have been regarded as a Court of some importance by others, to judge by the number of visitors from out of London whom it welcomed to its meetings, including such as the Rev. Dr Struthers of St Andrew's Scotch Church, Demerara; Dr Lang of the Scotch Church, Sydney; the Rev. Mr Fraser, 'formerly of the Presbyterian Church, New York,' (with which the Presbytery had been in protracted correspondence, probably on doctrinal matters, some years previously); the Rev. Dr Duff, who on his way back to India addressed the Presbytery on his pioneer work for education as the Church's missionary there; the Rev. Jas.

Dinwiddie of the Presbyterian Church, Georgia; and the Rev. John Weir of Newry. The Presbytery showed its own interest in education through its periodical examination of the Caledonian Asylum scholars, and of 'the poor children being educated by the School Fund of the Scottish Hospital', and its support of the London Board of the S.S.P.C.K. Examples of the width of its concerns are its 'Pastoral Letter to the Baptised of the Scottish Church residing in London and its vicinity', issued in 1828; its addresses to Parliament on the prospect of the Repeal of the Test and Corporation Acts (1828), on the new Marriage Bill (1836), and in support of the Journeymen Bakers of the Metropolis for such alteration in the Bakers' Act as would enable them to enjoy the Lord's Day (1840); and its petition to Parliament on the Non-intrusion question (1848)[7]. These external activities did not distract the Presbytery from its own important internal affairs. We find it, in 1830, at the instance of a member, agreeing to examine *The Orthodox and Catholic Doctrine of our Lord's Human Nature,* just published by another member[8], with a view to adjudging its orthodoxy; in 1832 hearing and dealing with an accusation by the Trustees of Regent Square Scottish National Church, of 'abuses of worship and discipline' by its minister[8]; and in 1832 hearing and granting a petition from the elders of Crown Court Scottish National Church for its re-admission to the Presbytery after an absence of 19 years.

One particular concerns crops up frequently over a span of years. This relates to the Presbytery's own status as a Court of the Church. We have noted its anxiety, in 1771 and 1793, to affirm that its connection with the Church of Scotland was of long standing, and its desire that that connection should be still closer. Its *Pastoral Letter,* mentioned above, reveals the seriousness with which it took its pastoral responsibility for the thousands of unchurched Scots in and around London. This was followed in 1833 by a *Memorial* to the General Assembly, pleading for official recognition as a Court of the Church of Scotland, 'chiefly for want of which the Scottish congregations in London, having received no formal countenance from their Mother-Church, have all along been comparatively neglected by the great body of the nobility, gentry and other classes of our countrymen, who disliking the idea of being regarded as dissenters ultimately become entirely alienated from the Scottish Establishment, or, what is an infinitely worse evil and prevailing to an immense extent, they decline connecting themselves with any church whatsoever and sink into a state of most lamentable indifference to divine things'. The recognition for which they sought 'would have fortified this Presbytery in opposing heresies and delusions', and it has suffered 'much humiliation for lack of it'. Previous approaches to the Assembly had been received cordially, but with no result. The same fate seemed likely to attend this one, so at a meeting on Sept. 10th the Presbytery agreed 'that each Minister of the Presbytery should draw up as speedily as possible an account of his own church in particular, adding thereto what knowledge he may now possess or be able to obtain concerning the Scotch Churches in London in times past; that these statements be transmitted to Mr Tweedie, by him to be condensed, and submitted to a meeting of Presbytery to be specially summoned, if necessary', Kenneth Black[9] states that the whereabouts of these statements is unknown, but the Presbytery minutes for 23rd Jan. 1834 record that it met 'For ye purpose of receiving ye statements regarding ye past history and present state of ye churches . . . intended for ye information of ye General Assembly to consider whether any closer connection . . . can be formed between this Presbytery and that venerable Court'; and that it appointed a committee to revise and abridge it. Then on 26th February the Presbytery met again to hear and further amend the abridgment, entrusting the final draft to Mr Brown to be fairly written out and transmitted without delay to the Assembly's Committee. There can be little doubt that the 'Tabular View of the Scottish Presbytery of London, approved by Presbytery, May, 1834'[10] represents the outcome of this careful enquiry. 'Knowledge concerning the Scotch Churches in London in times past', however, seems to have been lacking; only the eight then extant appear in the 1834 Table.[11]

The Lancashire Presbytery had been equally determined in requesting to be recognised as a Presbytery of the Church of Scotland, and the Assembly appointed a Committee on Presbyterian Churches in England, which reported in June 1835. The Assembly adopted its advice, and 'recommended the English Presbyteries in communion with this Church to form them-

A typewritten copy of this *Tabular View of the Scottish Presbytery in London* will be found in the end-papers.

United Reformed Church History Society.

selves into one or more Synods with a view to more official discussion' on the matter of their being recognised as part of the Church of Scotland. Lancashire and North-West Presbyteries immediately did so; a deputation from Lancashire visited the London Presbytery on Nov. 28th, 1838; and the latter, meeting in Crown Court the following month, resolved to join the new *Presbyterian Synod in England in connection with the Church of Scotland*. The remaining four Presbyteries followed, and in 1842 the Synod was complete and the way thus open for the promised further communication on the matter of full recognition.

Just at that point, however, the delayed impact of the 1712 Patronage Act hit the Scots Kirk in London. In May 1843, the Disruption — the third and largest secession in Scotland — took place, when over 400 ministers and their elders walked out from the Assembly's meeting-place to meet elsewhere as the Free Church of Scotland. They and those who joined them in disruption — not of the Church but from the State — surrendered stipends, manses, church-buildings and schools: so firm was their protest for the Church's freedom from state-control and for what Chalmers called 'the Christian good of Scotland'.

It might possibly be argued that had the London Presbytery been able to act *officially* as part of the Established Church of Scotland, its 1840 Petition to Parliament in support of the Church of Scotland appeal against Intrusion might have carried enough weight to swing the balance in favour of the non-intrusion cause and thus removed the need for disruption. That may be open to question — although when in 1905, and again in the early '20s, the decisive steps towards reunion required action in London, the presence of the Scots Kirk there greatly facilitated that action, as we have seen in Chapter thirteen. It is to be noted that two members of the London Scots Presbytery did vote *against* forwarding the 1840 Petition on Non-Intrusion, and recorded their reasons in a lengthy statement. One of the two was John Cumming, minister of Crown Court church. Three years earlier he had published his *'Apology for the Church of Scotland'* referred to in Chapter Ten. Three years *after* the 1840 Petition he published a pamphlet entitled *The Present State of the Church of Scotland,* which, by misleading the Government as to the firmness of Scotland's opposition to the system of patronage and the intrusion of ministers on unwilling congregations, may have encouraged it to continue to refuse to grant what the Church's *Claim of Rights* demanded[12]. 'If the Government stays firm', he wrote, 'I venture from fairly accurate information that less than one hundred will cover the whole secession'. Later he refers to 'the few manses and pulpits likely to be vacated', and still later concludes that even "few" represents an overstatement, saying 'I am not satisfied that *any* will secede'. If the Government was indeed encouraged thus to believe that few if any would have the courage to abandon the securities of the Establishment when the moment for decision was upon them, it could possibly be also argued that the Disruption might have been avoided had not John Cumming been so vigorous — and misguided — a representative of the Scots Kirk in London. The 'might-have-beens' continue to provoke fascinating, but futile, historical speculations.

One month after the disruption the Scots Presbytery of London met on 13th June in the Woolwich Scotch church. One important item of business was to arrange for the induction of the Rev. James Ferguson to the new charge of Goodman's Fields in Whitechapel. The outcome is recorded in painful terms in two different minute-books. The Presbytery appointed 29th June for the induction, with the Rev. Peter Lorimer of River Terrace to induct; whereupon 'Mr Lorimer, before consenting to comply . . . begged to be informed by the Presbytery into connection with what Church he was expected to induct Mr Ferguson, because if it was in the mind of the Presbytery to induct him into connection with the Established Church of Scotland as now constituted he could not conscientiously do so'[13]. After lengthy — and acrimonious — discussion it was moved and seconded 'That the Presbytery do omit from its usual designation the words "in connection with the Church of Scotland" '; but the Moderator (the other of the two dissenters to the 1840 Non-Intrusion Petition) refused to put the motion; whereupon it was moved and seconded 'That in consideration of the Moderator's refusal to act, Mr Lorimer be appointed Moderator *pro tempore*'. This, being put by the Clerk, was carried, and 'the newly-elected Moderator was proceeding to the discharge of his duties'[14] when a member, 'addressing the ex-Moderator, moved that the Presbytery do adjourn, and amidst loud and urgent remonstrances from the majority he did so by pronouncing the Benediction', and with three other Ministers and four elders left the Court, while the ministers and elders of the six other congregations proceeded to complete the unfinished business. The induction of Mr Ferguson duly took place on the appointed date, 'with the omission of those expressions from the Formula . . . which seem to recognise the Church of Scotland as presently established by law in Scotland'. At the Induction Service three leading ministers of the Disruption *Free Church of Scotland* — The Revs. Henry Grey, Dr Cunningham and Dr Thomas Guthrie — were present as visitors, which might suggest that the six (now seven) considered themselves to be members of the month-old Free Church. But although that does seem to have been hinted at, it was soon abandoned. They regarded themselves as the rightful continuation of the London Presbytery, but as having broken the Scottish connection. The minutes of the Whitechapel Induction follow immediately upon those of the fateful Woolwich meeting of 13th June, the majority having retained the Presbytery's books when the minority went out. At their July meeting they heard a written demand from 'the Rev. Alex McGlashan, styling himself Clerk of the Scottish Presbytery in London in connection with the Established Church, for papers, books, money etc, belonging to the Presbytery, and threatening legal measures otherwise', but this demand seems to have been successful ignored. On the title-page of the Minute-book the phrase 'in connection with the Established Church of Scotland' is scored out, leaving, as the new style, 'The London Presbytery of the Presbyterian Church in England.' This designation was adopted by the other seceding Presbyteries and by the Synod — which Courts they were able to maintain under the circumstances that the majority of the congregations in England had followed the same course. Their cause was soon strengthened, and The Presbyterian Church in England quickly grew through the accession of a number of English Presbyterian congregations which had adhered to the Westminster Confession and Standards and some of which had in any case earlier found a welcome in at least the London Presbytery[15].

In Chancery — Atty Genl v Wilton
Shewn to John Hall, on his Examination
for Deft, Thomas Lonsdale, and six other Defendants
C. J. Villiers
Exar

Minutes

of the

Scots Presbytery in London.

~~in Connexion with~~

~~The Established Church of Scotland.~~

Vol: III.

December, MDCCCXXXIV.

Title-page of Vol. III of the Scots London Presbytery Minutes, as altered by the majority at their first meeting after the Church of Scotland connection was broken following the Disruption of 1843.

Only four ministers remained in that Presbytery after June 13th, 1843. Soon they were three. Samuel Blair of Dudley, the Moderator, returned to Dudley to find that his congregation was not of his mind, and he resigned before the end of the year. Dr Brown of Swallow Street was left with but a minority of his congregation, and Alex McGlashan of St Andrew's Stepney lost a large portion of his. Only Crown Court continued almost unaffected by the crisis. The Presbytery itself had lost its Minute Books, other records, and funds, all of which had been retained by the seceding majority; and an understandable note of acerbity can be detected in the brief minute which records the meeting immediately resumed by the minority after leaving the church in Woolwich. Under the same date, 13th June 1843, and on the opening pages of the new book, it reads: 'As in the course of the said Presbytery making certain Presbyterial arrangements for the induction of the Rev. James Ferguson into the new Scots congregation of Goodman's Fields several members of Presbytery (publicly announcing their fixed determination not only to adhere no longer to the Established Church of Scotland but to refuse inducting Mr Ferguson into any ministerial connection with that Church in terms of her authorised formula relative to the settlement of ministers), proposed a motion declaring 'that the portion of this Presbytery's immemorial designation, to wit "in connection with the Established Church of Scotland", shall henceforth be renounced, discontinued and annulled; And whereas . . . the said dissentients did upon the spot violently and illegally and by a pretended vote not participated in by the constitutional members of Presbytery, declare that the said Moderator should no longer hold his office and did appoint the Rev. Peter Lorimer to seize possession of the same; Therefore the said Rev. Samuel Blair, Moderator of this Presbytery, Revs Dr Brown, Swallow Street; John Cumming, Crown Court; Alex. McGlashan, St Andrew's Scotch Church . . . immediately withdrew from the scene of the forementioned irregularities, and at a convenient place in this town did forthwith resume procedure as the Scottish Presbytery in London in connection with the Established Church of Scotland'.

With only three congregations remaining the future of the Scots Kirk in London seemed bleak, and the few congregations elsewhere in England which still adhered to the Church of Scotland were left in a condition of virtual independence with no presbyterial structure. In London, however, the growing popularity and influence of Cumming of Crown Court provided a rallying-point around which recovery soon took place, while in the provinces the isolated congregations refused to despair of a resumption of the presbyteral structure. In 1850 the English Presbyteries were again organised, and in 1851, with the approval and in fact at the suggestion of the General Assembly, *The Scottish Synod in England in connection with the Church of Scotland* was once more set up, with thirteen congregations in three Presbyteries[16].

The Minutes of the Presbytery of the Scots Kirk in London from 1772 to 1843, in three volumes, are preserved in the Library of what is now the United Reformed Church in England and Wales, 81 Tavistock Place, London. The Minute Books from 1843 onwards are deposited in the Scottish Record Office, Register House, Edinburgh.

NOTES

1. Wilson, *op. cit.*, iii, 126.
2. *Tabular View &c.*, I, London Wall.
3. *Tabular View &c.*, II, St Andrew's.
4. *Fasti*, iv, 302; vii, 471.
5. See Appendix B, section ii.
6. See Chapter seven.
7. Following upon several cases of the intrusion by patrons of ministers upon unwilling congregations in the 1830s, the General Assembly in May 1839 appointed a Committee empowered to seek harmony between Church and State by conferring with the government of the country, always maintaining the Church's inviolable principle that no presentee should be forced upon any parish contrary to the will of the congregation. This Committee (of which Mr Bruce of Kennet, father of Lord Balfour of Burleigh — see Chapter eleven — was a member) was commonly called the Non-Intrusion Committee. In support of its efforts to obtain from the government legislation to that effect, petitions signed by over 180,000 males in Scotland were presented to Parliament in Spring, 1840. The London Presbytery's petition was a contribution to that support.
8. The author — minister of Regent Square Scotch Church — was Edward Irving. See Chapter eight.

The Scots Kirk in London

9. Black, *op. cit.*, p. 177.
10. This document is preserved in the Library of the United Reformed Church, 81 Tavistock Place, London.
11. To the six congregations extant at the end of the 18th century Dudley had been added in 1826 and Crown Court, restored in 1832.
12. Hugh Watt, *Chalmers and the Disruption*, p. 294. The Claim of Rights was a Declaration by the General Assembly of 1842 'against the unrestrained enroachments of the civil courts' on the 'liberties, jurisdiction, discipline, rights and privileges' of the Courts of the Church of Scotland 'as unalterably settled by the treaty of union and the oath required to be taken by each sovereign on accession'. The government's tardy reply to the Claim intimated, on January 4th 1843, its rejection thereof. This marked the final stage of what was called The Ten Years' Conflict, and the majority of the General Assembly four months later resolved to disrupt from the state establishment.
13. *Minutes of the Scots Presbytery in London in connection with the Church of Scotland,* (vol. 3), 13th June, 1843, from which also the subsequent quotations concerning the proceedings at that meeting are taken.
14. This euphemism is more bluntly described in a contemporary press report of the occasion, probably supplied by one of the 'adhering members': 'The Rev. Mr Lorimer immediately walked up to the chair, and addressing the Moderator in broad Scotch, said — "Come oot o' that!" '.
15. That welcome may, however reluctantly, have been qualified when the Presbytery joined the Synod in 1842, since in the conference with the Lancashire Presbytery on 28th Nov., 1838, it had had to accept that 'no Minister or Elder be admitted as a constituent member of the Synod unless the Trust Deeds or the Bond to the Minister of the church with which he is connected be sufficient and satisfactory to the Synod as calculated to secure the permanance of ordinances and subjection to discipline and government in the respective congregations' (*Scots Presbytery Minutes*, 28th Nov., 1838).
16. By the end of 1844 the Presbyterian Church in England had grown to 63 congregations in 6 Presbyteries. For the later developments of that Synod see final paragraph of Appendix C. The Scottish Synod, set up again in 1851, remained a co-operating body rather than a subordinate Court of the Church of Scotland for over eighty years, despite repeated appeals to the General Assembly for deliberative representation of the English Presbyteries on that Court and for the granting to those Presbyteries, and to the Synod, of the status belonging to

all other such Courts of the Church of Scotland. Only after the Union of 1929 were such rights fully granted. Act vi, 1934, and Act vii, 1952 had the effect of merging the three Scottish Presbyteries in England as *The Presbytery of England,* an integral and constituent Presbytery of the Church. Act xviii, 1957, gave it Synodical powers. The Presbytery of England now consists of nine congregations — one each in Newcastle, Liverpool and Gillingham, two each in Corby, London and the Channel Islands. In addition to the minister and elder from each of these, Church of Scotland chaplains and retired ministers, resident in England, together with a corresponding elder for each, constitute the membership of the Presbytery, altogether making a total of about seventy.

As a footnote to this Appendix the following episode, although unconnected with the Presbytery, is of interest.

In October, 1780, "a considerable body of His Majesty's Protestant subjects of the ancient Kirk of Scotland", assembled in the house of Mr James Millar, St Martin's Court, St Lartin's Lane, drew up a Memorial, backed by three Biblical references and Chapter III of the Westminster Confession, for presentation to the Lord Chief Justice of the Court of King's Bench. It sought the right for those concerned to take the Oath in English Courts according to the Scottish form, namely "by holding up the right hand when the Oath is administered and not by laying the hand over, and afterwards kissing, the Gospels".

The Memorial failed to achieve that end, and "the persons aggrieved, finding that their brethren in other parts of South Britain still labour under the same hardships as formerly", eventually secured leave of the House of Commons to bring in a Bill whereby "the mode of taking an Oath in the manner obtaining in North Britain may in all cases where required by the party be admitted, instead of an Oath in the usual form".

Parliament exhibited its customary need for education as to the nature and constitution of the Scottish Kirk, at one point stubbornly confusing it with the Cameronians, to the amusement of all Scots; but the House of Lords eventually discovered that there already existed in law the freedom, so far denied by the Courts, to choose a form of Oath agreeable to conscience, and ruled that any magistrate refusing that right was "liable to an action at law and severe penalties".

In resolving to publish an account of their proceedings and this outcome *The United Friends of the Ancient Kirk of Scotland,* meeting at New Slaughter's Coffee House on July 19, 1784, thanked their many distinguished supporters and expressed their pleasure that Parliament's ruling would also benefit "many of H.M.'s loyal subjects not in their communion". (*A ccount ... of the Bill, &c.,* printed for T. Becket in Pall Mall; National Scottish Library, 5,2327 (24)).

INDEX

258

The Scots Kirk in London

East India Company, 22, 42.
Easton, Rev. Alex., 49, 78.
Ebenezer Church, New South Wales, 97.
ecclesia, xi.
Ecumenical Council (1869), 133; (Nicaea), 237.
Ecumenical initiative, 208, 220.
Education, Dissenters' influence in 23; Scots interest in, 117, 242.
Education, Crown Court, 169, 205.
Education Act (England), 1871, 166.
'Edinburgh, 1910', 221.
Edinburgh Evening News, 178.
Edward I, King, 201.
Edward VI, King, 2, 191.
Edward, Prince of Wales, 162.
Edwin, King, 1.
Ejection, The, 11, 15, 18, 19.
Elders, Assessor, 163; Dulwich, 156; Crown Court, 165.
Elders, Ruling; Function, 58, 225, 227; First in Peter's Court, 58; Teaching, 226.
Elizabeth, Queen of England, 4, 190, 219.
Elizabeth, Queen, and Queen Mother, 35, 164, 213, Plate 11.
Elgin, Lord, 137.
Eliot, George, 142f., 147.
Embankment, The Thames, as site for Scots Kirk, 148.
Endowment, Stipend, Crown Court, 167f; St Columba's, 170.
England, The Bank of, 22.
England, Church of *see* Church.
England, Presbytery of *see* Presbytery.
Enlightenment, The, 25, 231, 240.
'Entry, The Great', 159, 164; 'The Little', 164.
Episcopacy in Scotland, 21, 87.
Episcopacy within Presbytery, 7.
Episcopal Church in the U.S.A., 87.
episcope of the Eldership, 222, 225.
"Equivalent", The, 22, 27.
Erastian, 12.
Erskine, Rev. Ebenezer, 232f., 239; Rev. Ralph, 239.
Erskine Hospital for Limbless Soldiers & Sailors, 195.
Evangelical Alliance, The, 220f., 24.

Evangelical Party in Scotland, 240.
Ewing, Greville, 96, 128.
Exeter Assembly, 234.
Exeter Hall, 139.

FARADAY, Michael, 229.
Ferguson, Rev. James, 113, 251, 254.
Fergusson, Sir James of Kilkerran, 180.
Festival Service, The Scottish, 180, 222.
Field, John, 5.
Finsbury Temple, 114.
Fire, Compton Street, 92.
Fire Establishment; Edinburgh, 141; London, 141, 147.
Fire of London, The Great, 31; The Tooley Street, 141.
First Presbyterian Church of New York, 102.
First Scotch Church, London, *see* Founders' Hall.
Five Mile Act, The, 16, 26, 43.
Fleet Prison, 8.
Fleet Ditch, The, 31, Plate 4a.
Fleming, Rev. Archibald, 202f., 211, chap. 13; Rev. James, 178.
Fleming, Rev. Robert the Younger, 20, 43, 68, 69.
Fletcher, Rev. Alex., 114.
Ford, Dr James, 85.
Fordyce, Rev. James, 47.
Forsyth, Rev. James S., 115, 149, 192.
Forsyth, Mrs Jean, 67.
Forsyth, Nathaniel, 78.
Founders' Hall, First Scotch Kirk, Chap. 2, xii.
Foundling Hospital, 62.
Frankfurt, Reformers in, 4.
Free Church of Scotland, 52, 221, 240f., 250, 252.
Free Presbyterian Church of Scotland, 52.
Freeland, Rev. John, 78f.
French, Daniel, R.C. lawyer, 133.
French Meeting-House, 69, 181, 190.
Friendly Benefit Society, 166.
Friends of St Columba's, xiv.

GAELIC Language xi; Bible, 38, 117; Chapel, *see* Regent Square Church, 104, 106; schools, 103f.;

262

Churches in connection with the Presbytery - and their present Ministers.	When and where the the Congregation was originally constituted.	Date of present erection.	Tenure by which the Church is held, and in whom vested.	Endowments, and for for what purpose.
1. LONDON WALL Situated in the City near the Bank of England. Present minister Rev.d W. K. Tweedie, licensed by the Presb.y of Arbroath ordained by Presb.y of London 1832.	About the year 1665 in Founders' Hall, as appears from the Royal Charter of the Scottish Corporation of the foundation of Charles II.	1764 after removing from Founders' Hall	Sub-lease under the City of London recently renewed for 21 years from 1836 and vested in the Kirk Session and their Successors.	£20 per annum for behoof of decayed members.
2. ST ANDREWS Situated in the extreme East of London, near the Commercial Road. Present minister John Crombie, D.D., licensed by Presb.y of St Andrews & ordained by the Presb.y of London 1819.	Formed in Broad Street, St George in East about 1660 by English Presbyterians - became a Scotch congregation in 1741 - removed afterwards to Shakespeare's Walk under Rev.d Dr Rutledge.	1823 after leaving Shakespeares' Walk.	A Lease held from the London Hospital for 99 years, and vested in trustees, of whom the present minister and Elders are part.	None
3. SWALLOW STREET Situated in St James parish at the west end of London. Present minister Rev.d James R. Brown licensed and ordained in Scotland by the Presb.y of Chirnside in 1824.	Date of original formation unknown but existed in Glasshouse Street same parish previous to 1709 when it removed to the Old Church in Swallow Street which was taken down in 1799.	1800 built on the old Site	A Lease held from the Crown originally granted in 1709 and renewed in 1800 for 99 years and vested in the minister and Elders their Successors and assigns "In trust for the said Scots Presbyterian congregation".	£100 interest thereof for the poor of the congregation. Other bequests to the amo.t of several hundred pounds having been left to be applied a the discretion of th Session have been us and exhausted for th general purposes of the congregation.
4. CROWN COURT Situated near Covent Garden Westm.r. Present minister Rev.d Jn.o Cumming M.A. licensed by Presby: of Aberdeen ordained by Presby: of London 1832	In 1711 in Peters Court St Martin's Lane. A Scottish Congregation under the joint ministry of Mr George Gordon and Mr Pat: Russell.	About 1784 after removing from Peter's Court.	A Lease from Duke of Bedford of which 12 years remain unexpired and vested in the Elders and their successors.	Endowment on the decease of an existi life-renter to the amo.t of about £250 p annum: There are oth endowments for the poor &c. of about £1 per annum.
5. REGENT SQUARE Situated towards the N.W. part of London near the New Road. Vacant at present.	About the year 1811 in the Caledonian Chapel, Cross Street, Hatton Garden	1827 after removing from Cross Street, Hatton Garden.	Freehold properly vested in Trustees under a regularly executed Trust Deed.	None
6. VERULAM SCOTCH CHURCH Situated in Lambeth county of Surrey. Present minister Rev.d Ja.s Millar licensed by Presbytery of Glasgow. Ordained by Presby: of London.	In 1823 then assembling in Prospect Place, Southwark.	Removed in 1831 to the present place of worship.	Held on Lease (under Mortgage) for about 99 years by the present minister concerning which a Declaration of trust made by him is in possession of the Clerk of Presby: and to be executed as soon as Trustees can be procured to undertake the existing responsibilities.	None
7. CHADWELL STREET Situated in the N.E. part of London near the top of the City Road. Present minister Rev.d Jno MacDonald, M.A. licensed by Presby: of Elgin 1830 ordained by Presby: of London 1831.	In the year 1827	Lease of the present church taken in 1827	The Congregation removes in 1834 to a new church now in progress near the present one which is to be held on Lease for 99 years. The new church when finished is intended to be placed under a Trust deed which will embody a full and satisfactory constitution.	None
8. WOOLWICH Situated in Kent on the south bank of the Thames about 9 miles below London, Vacant at present.	Previous to 1800 the congregation assembled in Meetinghouse Lane under the ministry of the Rev.d Dr Blythe.	Removed to the present Scots Church in Powis Street in 1800, which was built by subscription with the sanction and support of the Presby:	A Lease vested in the minister and Elders conjointly with the Trustees of Mrs Drake's Bequest.	£30 per annum to the minister under Mrs Drake's will with £ per annum to the sam allowed by Governmen for the Royal Artil ery being accommoda in the Church.